SEO For 2011

Search Engine Optimization Secrets

Sean Odom

From beginner to advanced.

"*SEO is the science of customizing the internal and external elements of your web site to achieve the absolute best possible search engine rankings.*" *—Sean Odom*

Learn all the secrets from the pros!

MediaWorks Publishing

SEO for 2011: Search Engine Optimization Secrets

ISBN: 978-1-4507-2797-6

This book is dedicated to:

All those who spend countless hours in the pursuit of the perfect search engine placement and are willing to share knowledge with their peers. And to those who have SEOTechMasters.com over the years.

Also,

To Crystal Harwell who will always be missed.

About the author – Sean Odom

Sean Odom (Sean@SEOTechMasters.com, in Portland Oregon.) has been in the Information Technology industry for over 20 years and in that time he has written for such publishers as Que, Sybex, Coriolis, Paraglyph Press, and Media Works Publishing.

Sean is well known in the Search Engine Optimization (SEO) industry. Some of his techniques have been learned and put in to use by many others through books and news articles he has written. He has also been credited with starting an entire industry of SEO professionals and related businesses. Sean was one of the first to introduce SEO techniques and make it well known with the very first article on the subject in 1993.

Sean also employs two strategic partners in his business. Michael Monahan and Jason McCormick who in the early 1990's created several search engines and participated in designing the algorithms in use today on many of the major search engines. Together they have created techniques designed to monitor and detect even minor changes in search engine algorithms by keyword or by industry.

Along with their major accomplishments, Mike and Jason along with other developers have designed an in-house system which allows bots, crawlers, and spiders to scan the Internet on a weekly basis for keyword changes, competition changes, mentions of customers names or domains in social media and blogs, detect optimization and design problems immediately on customer web sites and much more. The system allows every customer to receive a weekly updated report on their SEO standings.

Acknowledgements

I need to thank all those who have believed in me over the years and made this book such as success. Even though I have been the bestselling SEO author since 2009 and written over 40 books, it still amazes me to see that there are over 22,000 preordered copies of this book even while I am working on it.

It is truly you the reader that I do this for. For all those who preordered the book, I apologize for the delay in getting the book out but we decided to get Google Instant and the latest information in the book to make it the best it could be.

 I also need to thank the entire team that worked together to write, edit, and get this book on the shelves in the limited amount of time we had to do it. My name is on the cover but it took dozens of people, sleepless nights to make our deadlines.

--Sean Odom

Table Of Contents

CHAPTER 6 – LINKING UP 106

CHAPTER 7- OPTIMIZING FOR MAJOR SEARCH ENGINES 115

Chapter 1 – What is SEO?

Why do I need search engine optimization?

Most companies have a website of some kind, but only about 5% know of or use Search Engine Optimization (SEO) as part of a marketing plan. If they do use SEO, they have usually learned about it because they spent thousands of dollars on a top-of-the-line website that no one came to visit. When they realized a nice website wasn't enough, they probably Googled "promoting my website" or "how to market my website."

Why are some businesses more successful with their website than others? Is there a secret?

SEO is now a requirement for any sized business to advertise with a website and be successful at it! Especially now that every other previously effective marketing tool has become ineffective or out of reach. In the days before Internet there were a number of ways to successfully advertise. Now however:

- **Code Enforcement is cracking down on signs.**
- **Radio and TV advertising is getting too expensive and becoming less effective because of the number of stations.**
- **Newspapers are virtually useless as people turn to the web.**
- **Tradeshows are few in number and most are no longer well-marketed.**
- **Almost no one uses a telephone book anymore because of the web.**
- **Bus benches and billboards cost a huge monthly fee and again, how many people look at them nowadays?**

U**The Internet is now the telephone book**U. So as a business you have to adapt and not only adapt well, but do one better than your competitors so your name comes up at the top of the list in any keyword search. No longer can you just pay $2,000 a month for a full page ad in a telephone book to stand out. You have to do the equivalent on the Internet. Your website has to stand out in the center of 2 billion other sites and outshine all the others in your industry to be successful. It's a tough task.

I have a great looking website–that's enough, right?

Looks are one thing, but what's behind the looks is actually more important than what your visitors see when it comes to marketing your website to the search engines. It is so technically complex on how to get your website in the best standings and ranked at the top for the search terms(keywords) you want people to find you with, that it is now an <u>exact- science</u> which changes from year to year.

The novice should not even attempt it. The old easy methods for marketing your website do not work and can and will get your website domain name banned from many of the major search engines. Getting back in the search engines good graces after being banned is tough and sometimes near impossible.

A Little Search Engine History

Although the Internet had been around for quite some time, search engines in the form that we know them today didn't come around until the appearance of a site called Wandex in 1993. Wandex was the first to both index and search the index of pages on websites. In that same year, Excite started using similar technology, which we call "crawling" or indexing a website. Bing.com is the latest of the major search engines to enter the Internet realm. Here is a list of the major search engines and when they started:

- Excite, 1993
- Yahoo!, 1994
- Web Crawler, 1994
- Lycos, 1994
- Infoseek, 1995
- AltaVista, 1995
- Inktomi, 1996
- Ask, 1997
- Google, 1997
- MSN Search, 1998
- Bing, 2009

Are search engines getting more advanced?

Today's search engines are more sophisticated than ever. If you type a word or phrase into a search box and click the search button, you have to wait only a few seconds to get thousands of results. Most of the time those results take you to websites that are relevant to what you are searching for. Also, on most of the major search engines you will rarely click on a link that doesn't work.

So how does all this work?

The easy answer is search engines use algorithms to process the billions of pieces of information they have collected about web pages on the Internet. The algorithms are a list of filters and rules used to decide which websites most closely relate to the search that was made. You then see the results of what the algorithms decided were the best results for your searched words or phrases on the screen.

What you don't know is little programs called bots, crawlers, or spiders have visited virtually every website on the Internet to collect information on them. These little programs collect keywords, phrases and other coding located on every website, and then stores this information in large databases used by the search engines.

Thoroughly confused yet? Let's give an example. Let's say you go to a website URL such as www.seosecretsfor2012.comU . The funny thing is, what you see (also referred to as content) on the website that comes up accounts for only about 20 percent of what search engines use to decide what makes a site relevant for any keyword searches.

> *"I have a good-looking website, better than my competitor! Why am I at the bottom of web searches and why is my competitor at the top of the searches? I even have more Meta tags than him!"*

The answer gets a little complicated. It is probably not what you see on the website. It is what is being done on the backend that you don't see! Often, what is most relevant is the code that makes up the pages, the density of use of the keywords, as well as the relevancy of links into and out of the page.

There are other factors as well: what sites you are listed on, how long your domain has been in existence, the length of your domain's URL renewal term, as well as all the following which we will explain later in this book:

- Strategic Tagging
- Website Submissions
- Keyword Research
- Meta delivery
- Title Tag Optimization
- Robots.txt Optimization
- Site mapping
- HTML Source Code
- Frequently Changed Content
- Image & Hyperlink Optimization

- Social Media Optimization
- Social Bookmarking
- Blogs
- Press Release Writing
- Article Submissions
- Video Optimization
- RSS Feeds
- Link Development
- Manual Link Requests to Related Sites
- Local & International Search Engines & Directory Listings
- One-Way Links/Two-Way Links
- PPC
- HTML design
- ASP. and other coding such as Java and Flash
- Linked URLs

Are you saying, "Oh, my." yet? Sometimes it's worth having a professional help you out. However, I am a professional at this and I will outline this all, step by step, and try to make it easy for you.

What collects all the website information for the search engines?

The job of collecting information about web pages is performed by automation using an agent called a *crawler, spider,* or *robot(bot)* which is different depending on the search engine. These agents literally look at every URL on the Internet and collect keywords, links, relevant data and phrases on each page. But before it does, you as the network administrator must allow these agents to look at the content the website provides.

> **NOTE**: *We will discuss how to allow crawlers, spiders and robots to collect information on a website later under Meta tagging in the next chapter.*

These crawlers, spiders and bots collect information from not only what a visitor of your website sees but also from the coding behind the scenes. In fact only about 20-25% of your ranking on the major search engines comes from what the users see. The rest comes from the coding and numerous other items we will discuss later in this book.

Search engines like to keep the algorithms they use as secret as possible to make it fair to everyone. In fact it is rare to find any official explanation describing just how a search engine algorithm processes the data it collects and makes decisions on it. It is known only to a rare few who either work for the search engines, or people like me: the ones who spend their entire lives testing algorithms, putting what we learn into practice on real companies' websites, and placing those companies in the top ten of any search for their specific trophy words.

NOTE: *We will discuss trophy words in the next chapter.*

Where Searches Are Made

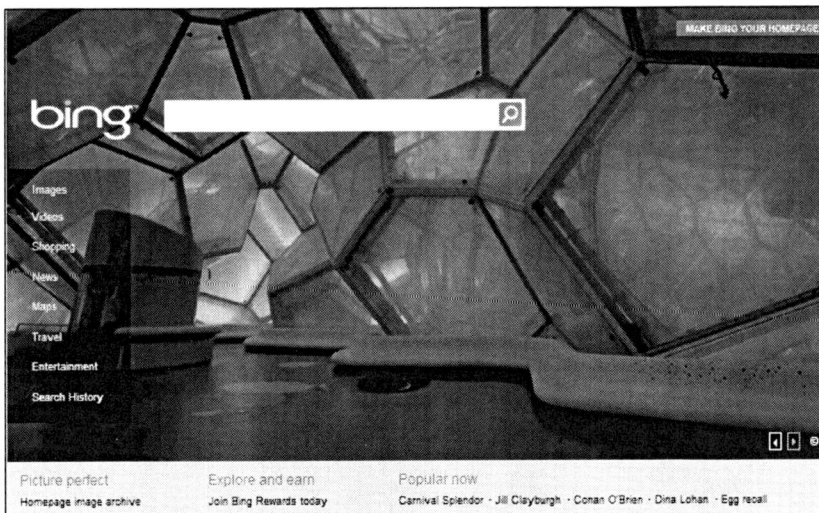

Figure 1.1

The search query interface is the most familiar part of the search engine. This is the little box where you type a few words related to what you want to find and like magic, a list of websites shows up. It is rare that you find a link to a website that isn't relevant to your search words or a website that no longer exists. You also won't find websites without updated content.

The Bing.com search interface is shown in Figure 1.1. This is Microsoft's newest search engine and its search algorithms are now being used to power Live, Yahoo, MSN, and other Microsoft sites. Bing calls itself a "Decision Engine".

It is supposed to help make decisions easier by taking into account multiple items such as location and other words you specify in your search. Thus if you type in the words, "pizza Portland" it gives you only relevant information.

What is interesting is that Bing knows if you are referring to Portland Oregon, where I happen to be, versus Portland Maine based on your IP and other information, as shown in Figure 1.2 on the next page.

Figure 1.2

Notice that I did not specify any address or whether it was for Portland, Maine, or Portland, Indiana. But the results not only gave me Portland, Oregon pizza places, the mapped local business listings at the top gave me results for pizza businesses around my office only. It is absolutely amazing how far search engines have come and how fast their advanced algorithms work.

When you type in a string of words to get relevant results and then click search, the collection of pages you see with the results are called *search engine results pages (SERPs)*. The higher your business or entity is in the search results, the more traffic you can expect to generate from searches on those key words.

It has been proven that those in the top 20 get the most clicks, as users typically do not go beyond page 2 of a search. The first three websites listed in a search, given that the description of the company or product is enticing enough, will land the most clicked visits. Your goal is to get your website in this top three. If your product or service makes a sale on an average of 1 out of every 10 visitors, the more visits you get the more sales you will make.

In trying to get information on the Bing algorithm, Microsoft spokesperson Carolyn Miller stated, We have made numerous improvements to our algorithm, focusing on spelling, freshness of results, and core ranking. Our algorithm is changing continuously to provide the best results. Although we have a six month release cycle for major updates, our algorithm is refined everyday to improve the relevance of our results and to better address our users' intent."

To learn more about Bing's search engine, you can watch a video at ***http://www.decisionengine.com.***

On July 29, 2009, Wired.com announced what I am sure Google feared. The title of the news article, "Yahoo Gives Up, Turns Search Over To Bing." This new development puts Microsoft closer to being head to head with Google, who once had over 60 percent of the search engine market before Bing entered the race. Also worthy of note is the 100 million dollars that Microsoft is rumored to have spent on advertising Bing.

Microsoft's Bing search engine essentially took over Yahoo search results and advertising using its new Decision Engine.

Search Engine Site Visitors

We've talked a little bit already about the spiders, crawlers, and robots that come visit your site to see what content you have and see what has changed since its last visit. Some search engines visit your site monthly but others (such as news websites and sites that host blogs) visit daily or even hourly. How do I know this? Well turn on your TV. The next time a major news story breaks on CNN, check the search engines to see if they have a link to the story. While I was writing this, I had CNN on my television and there was breaking news. It had just been announced 5 minutes before but Google already had links to 3 websites with the story. Incredibly fast!

Google makes it easy to see when its Googlebot has last visited a webpage. You need the Google Toolbar to view this, however. The Google toolbar is available free of charge at Uhttp://toolbar.google.comU. You download a small program, and you are ready for some easy searching. The toolbar works with Microsoft Windows NT, 2000, XP, Vista, 2003 Server, 2008 Server and Windows 7. You must also have Microsoft Internet Explorer version 5.0 or greater installed. There is also a similar version available for Firefox users. Unfortunately, Mac users are out of luck.

If you have the Google toolbar installed there is a plethora of additional tools and options you can configure including a tool called "PageRank." When you hit the check mark to place the PageRank box on the toolbar as shown in Figure 1.3a you see a small but very powerful rectangular box that is added on the Google Toolbar right next to the Bookmarks button.

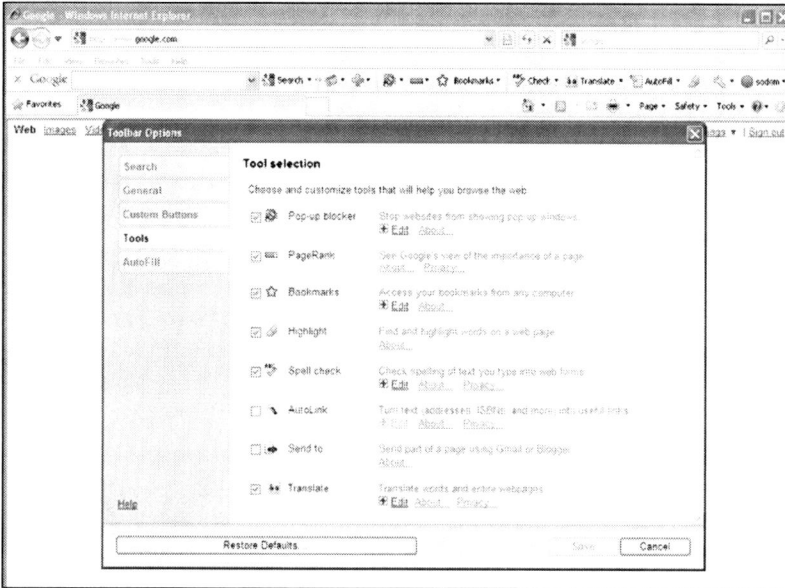

Figure 1.3a

On some versions of the Google Toolbar it can be found under tools as shown in Figure 1.3b.

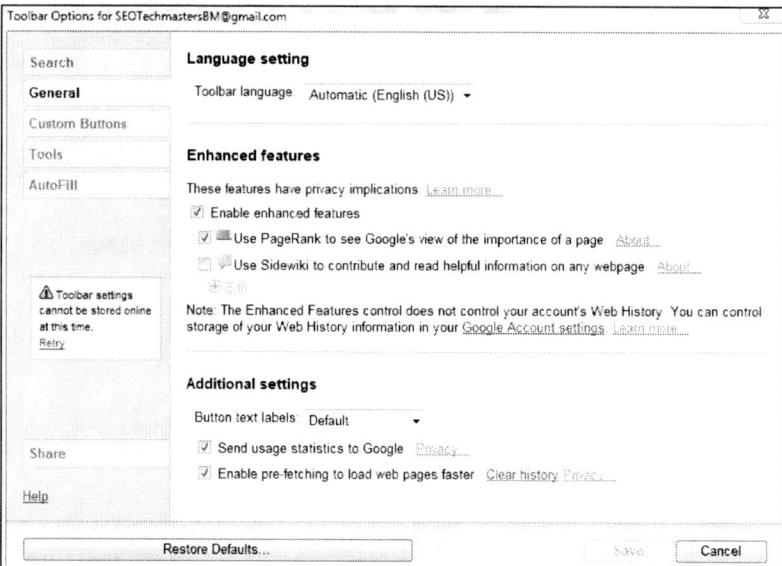

Figure 1.3b

The PageRank is in essence the term *quality scoring*. Google's PageRank is a score of a website from zero to ten (0-10). Ten is the highest and zero is the lowest. If you are competing against another website on the same keywords, the website with the higher PageRank will be higher on the SERP page when a search is performed. When you are higher on a page due to your Google page ranking, you have obtained this search. Organic listings are listings you never pay money to the search engines, but your website was at the top of the search engine results.

Google makes a ranking of a website based on the factors we have already discussed and some we will discuss later in this book. After the crawlers, spiders, and robots have gathered data from all the sites known on the web, it uses this information to determine a sites page ranking. This ranking or scoring determination is one of the most secretive parts of SEO.

The goal is to score pages based on the quality and relevance that site visitors derive from each page they visit. How good it looks visually has virtually no effect on what the crawler, spiders, and robots gather from a website, as shown on the Google PageRank tool below.

Note: *There once was a time when the keywords in the Meta tag made up the rank of a page and was the most important factor. Now they make up about one percent of the Google page ranking. Keywords are still important in web page rankings. However, they're just one of a hundred or so elements that are taken into consideration.*

I know the major influences of this score from experience and from information provided by Google and other search engines. Google as well as the other major search engines are masters of changing their algorithms and the elements that weigh in to their algorithm used to determine the PageRank of each URL. It changes so often that there will probably be a SEO Secrets Book 2012, 2013, and so on.

SIDEBAR: Value Of A Ranked Website

Every ranked website has a value and the higher the Google Ranking, the more valuable your domain name is. Let's take a look:

Domain Rank	Value
Rank of 0/10	$ 0-100
Rank of 1/10	$ 100-250
Rank of 2/10	$ 250-350
Rank of 3/10	$ 350-1,500
Rank of 4/10	$ 1,500-4,500
Rank of 5/10	$ 4,500-8,500
Rank of 6/10	$ 8,500-25,000
Rank of 7/10	$ 25,000-75,000
Rank of 8/10	$ 75,000-1 Million
Rank of 9/10	$ 1 Million +
Rank of 10/10	A LOT.

Google looks at more than the sheer volume of visits a page receives or the number of links to that page from other websites. It also looks at the pages that direct traffic or have links to your site. If you looked at it from a point system, certain types of websites (such as news sites, government sites, education sites, and sites Google has already ranked highly) give your website more points. Accumulate enough points and Google starts to rank your page highly. Accumulate more and Google increases your page ranking. Links are a heavily weighted item but it is only one part of hundreds of items that will be required to make your website rank highly.

A web page that has multiple links to it might rank lower than a page that has just a single link from a "more important" page. It is always good to create pages visitors like, but be mindful of search engines.

Want to know how your page ranks? Let's take a look at how we can view this information and much more using the PageRank Tool from the Google Tool Bar.

Google Toolbar PageRank Tool

Now let's get to the Google PageRank tool and see how useful this tool really is. It has 4 main features. Let's take a look at each one. The first really cool feature is the rectangular box. It fills like a gauge every time you visit a new website and if you hover over the PageRank box with your mouse, it shows you the site's Google PageRank, as shown on my website www.SEOTechMasters.com (Figure 1.4).

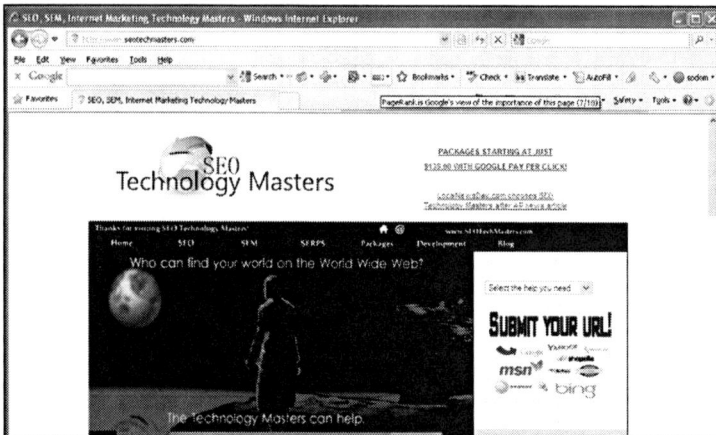

Figure 1.4

Notice in figure 1.4 that my website has a page ranking of 7/10. It takes a long time and a lot of work to do everything necessary to gain a 7/10 ranking. Without professional SEO help I find most websites which have a decent web developer and have been up a long time get a maximum Google ranking of a 2 and sometimes a 3.

The second feature actually has two parts to it. This is where you can tell on any website that Google has come to visit the site. If you click the little down arrow next the PageRank box you will see the first of three options—"Caches Snapshot of The Page." Every time the Googlebot visits, it takes a picture of the page as shown in Figure 1.5.

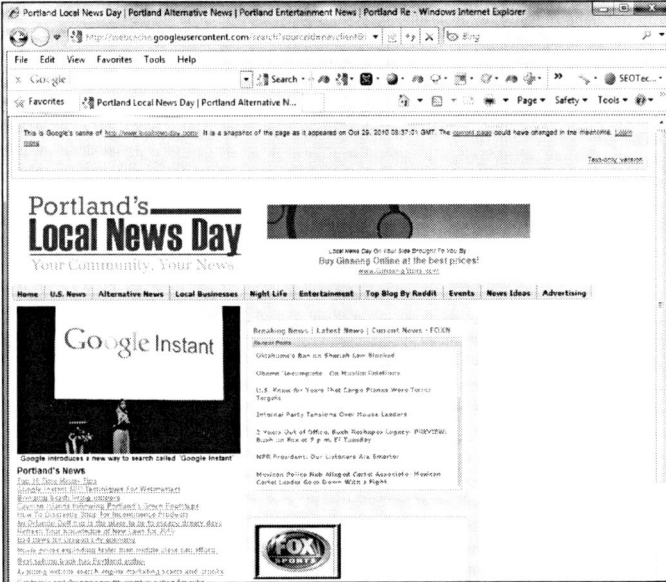

Figure 1.5

Along with a picture of the website, the time and date of the snapshot is also logged. You also have one other important tool here! Notice to the right a little link that say "Text-only version." Click this and see what the spiders, crawlers, and bots really see (Figure 1.6).

Figure 1.6

It is amazing to see how little text relating to their website is found on some web pages. All the text on the site is contained in the pictures. I have one customer who had the one of the best looking websites. It was all done in Flash. However, she had a page ranking of zero, even though she had had the website up for 8 years. Her website was better-looking and more interactive than all of her competition.

Nonetheless, her competition was at the top of the organic searches and winning all the clicks, whereas she was at the on page 23 for her best keyword.

When she became a customer, you can't even imagine how upset she was when I told her we would have to limit the Flash and include text instead to get her rankings up. It is hard for some people to understand why Flashy isn't always better.

The third feature is called, "Similar Pages" (Figure 1.7).

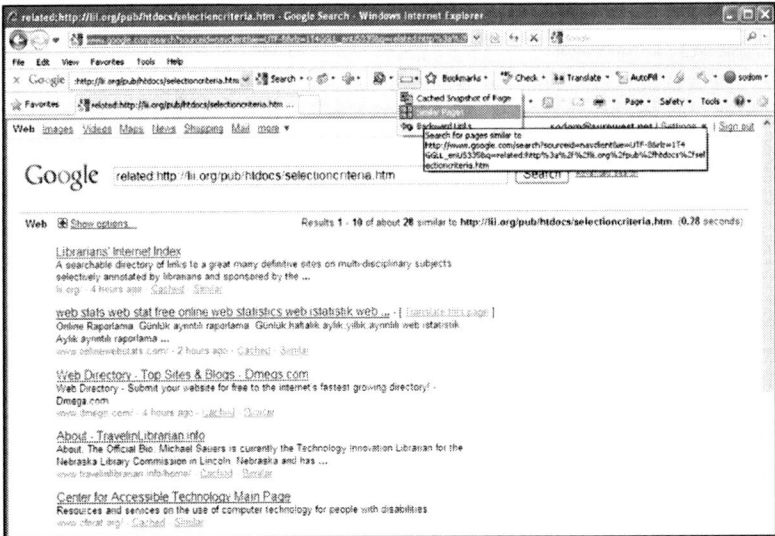

Figure 1.7

The Similar Pages option provides you with, not surprisingly, links to pages which Google deems similar; these links are prime candidates for link exchanges which we will talk about later in this book. Since Google already believes they are related to your industry. The more relevant the links to and from your website are, the higher Google will make your PageRank score.

The last feature you will find on the Google PageRank Tool is the "Backwards Link" option (Figure 1.8).

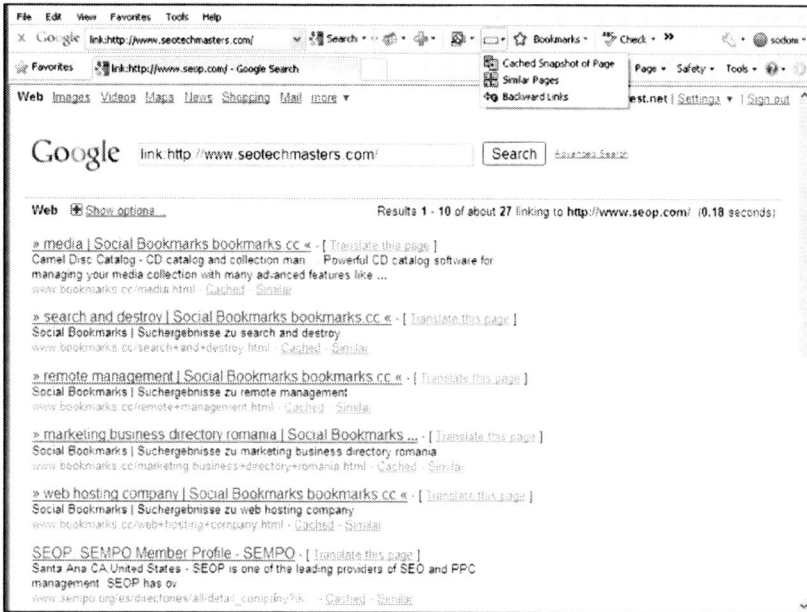

Figure 1.8

The Backwards Links option takes you to a list of links that the Googlebot has found that link directly to your website. These are very important to know. The more of these from relevant sites that Google knows about, the higher your PageRank will be.

There is a lot to cover in this book, so let's get started in the next chapter with understanding Meta tags

NOTE: *Here's a link to the Google Toolbar for Mac.*

http://www.google.com/mac

Chapter 2 – Choosing Keywords And Meta Delivery

Keywords in Meta tags are no longer a requirement for Google, but they are helpful on other search engines. Google scans the actual relevant content that is on all the pages on your website (with correct linkage that is.).

> **WARNING:** *We already touched on this a little but for websites that have their relevant content or words mainly in pictures or in Flash the search engine crawlers cannot read this. This is why the most Flashy and spectacular looking websites are on page 284 of a keyword search.*

Now I said that having Meta tags on Google was not a requirement, but, I wouldn't leave them out. If you were looking at this from points prospective, your description, keywords, and other information in your Meta tag all give you more points if they match the content on the landing pages of your website and the title bar. It all adds up to what the search engines see as relevant content.

In this section we will look at how to properly format meta tags to allow prime optimization, allow the bots, spiders and crawlers to visit more than your landing page, how to make them relevant to your keywords, add location based meta data, and much more!

Keywords

As I said earlier, keywords in your Meta tags are just one of about three dozen elements that are taken into consideration when search engines visit your website to collect information about your website. But choosing those keywords and correctly placing those keywords on your websites landing pages and matching them to the Titles and Meta tagging of your website absolutely is.

Some keywords absolutely have value; and more important, keywords can cause damage your websites reputation and make it almost invisible if not used properly.

Choosing Quality Keywords

> *Targeting your trophy keywords is absolutely important!*

It's complicated I know. As I said earlier, keywords in Meta tags are no longer a requirement. When I say it is not a requirement, I see companies with a ranking of one or two on Google all the time that don't have a single Meta tag. Not only a list of keywords but no description either.

Their domains longevity, linkage, and relevant content sped them along in the process to get ranked. But it won't get them much farther in the ranking process. Each stepping stone that you make on the list gets you a little higher in the ranking process.

I always like to explain it to customers that each item you do equals a point value to the major search engines.

- Have a website that has been online for a long period, add points.
- Have your website registration paid so it expires in 5 years, add points.
- Have it expire in less than a year, subtract points.
- Have Meta Tags, add points.
- Have relevant content, add points, have quality and relevant links, add points.
- Have an SEO company that is a Google Ambassador, add points.
- Have news articles published about your website on websites that are determined by Google to be "Official News Sites" such as LocalNewsDay.com, DailyTrib.com, FoxNews.com, etc., add a lot of points.
- Have links from .gov and .edu sites, add points.
- Have a good website quality score, add points.
- Do well on all 137 factors I outline here in this book, get higher rankings!

The higher the point values, the higher the rankings can become. The more points needed is based on a number of factor, including the industry you're in, the competition you have, competing companies with SEO vying for the top spots, local or national campaigns, traffic to your website, two way links, and much more, but obviously not based on your keywords alone. In fact, it barely has an impact on rankings.

Now this imaginary point's scale I have created to explain to clients and you how rankings work have nothing to do with the quality scoring, which I will talk about in Chapter 7. However, deciding on your keywords has a major impact on this score.

Weights Of Keyword Placement

Now, knowing that overall the keywords in the Meta tags we decide to use only has a small overall percentage in relevancy and rankings on search engines, it does have a more noticeable impact if we use those keywords in different places of our website to make our word density higher and our website seem more relevant to the search engines. In fact here is a chart we have put together to show just how much of an impact on relevancy placing our keywords on our website can be:

> **Keyword in the Title Tag(6%)**
> **Keyword as the first word(s) of the Title Tag(6%)**
> **Keyword in the Root Domain Name (e.g. keyword.com)(6%)**
> **Keyword in the H1 Headline Tag(5%)**
> **Keyword in Internal Link Anchor Text on the Page(4%)**
> **Keyword in External Link Anchor Text on the Page(4%)**
> **Keyword in the H1 Tag(3%)**
> **Keyword 3 Times in the First 100 Words in HTML on the Page(5%)**
> **Keyword in your domain name (7%)**
> **Keyword in a subdomain (seo.seotechmasters.com) (3%)**
> **Keyword in the page name URL (ww.seotechmasters.com/seo.html)(3%)**
> **Keyword in other H Tags (3%)**
> **Keyword in image ALT text(3%)**
> **Keyword repeating in the HTML Text on the Page(3%)**
> **Keyword in image names on the page (keyword.jpg)(3%)**
> **Keyword in <b> or <strong> tags(2%)**
> **Keyword in List Items <li> on the Page(3%)**
> **Keyword in <i> or <em> Tags(2%)**
> **Keyword in the Meta Description Tag(2%)**
> **Keyword in comment tags in the HTML(1%)**
> **Keyword in the Meta tagging (5%)**

This is average relational information we have gathered here at SEO Technology Masters and target Google's results from our experiments. This actually changes from month to month and industry to industry. Changes in algorithms and requirements change so much that we now are publishing this book every year with the new updates.

Long-Tail Keywords

Long tail keywords are a type of keyword phrase that have at least two, and some times as many as five words in the phrase. Long tail keywords are used to refine search terms to the web page, as well as when the searcher is looking for something rather specific. Like normal keywords, long tail keywords are used to define what is on the web page and what the publisher wants to be found under in search engines and on search engine results pages. These keywords are highly specific, and draw less traffic for the website, but tend to draw more quality traffic, which leads in more conversions than normal keywords. Long tail keywords can also be used by the website creator and visitors in different ways.

When the website creator uses long tail keywords, they are searching to corner a market that might be smaller than normal, but has just as much potential as other, larger, more exposed markets. Using long tail keywords can also be less expensive when it comes to pay per click biding, and other paid inclusion methods, as there are less people attempting to place bids on those keywords for pay per click ads on search engine results pages.

Visitors use long tail keywords to narrow down what they are searching for. When a visitor is looking for "sacramento welding supplies" it makes more sense. Especially, if you only sell welding supplies in Sacramento.

Working with long tail keywords successfully means that a website creator needs to know which long tail keywords actually get hits or are searched for on the major search engines. Research is the only way to know if long tail keywords will work or not, and that if the smaller investment will still pay off at the end of the publishing campaign.

Keyword Stuffing

I can see what you are thinking right now. As a website owner you're probably jotting down a list of every word you can think of as a keyword for someone to search with to find your website. I had a private eye who came to me for SEO services and he had more keywords in his Meta tagging than on his whole website. When we were done deciding on the eight keywords he would use, we didn't even use one of the keywords he had on his list before he came to me.

His list, I kid you not, had every city in Southern California, with every possible scenario spelled out that you might need a private investigator for. It was probably close to a thousand keywords and is an extreme example of what is known as, "keyword stuffing".

There a defined science to finding and using the right keywords on your website. When I get done with a website I have eight to twelve keywords I focus on and I call those words, "Trophy Words". I use these words to improve your site's ranking.

As a consultant I spend countless hours finding and applying the right keywords for my customers and working with those who design websites for my customers. Finding the most effective keywords is a fine science and I have to weigh using popular and effective keywords on a website but weighing those keywords against the amount of competition. Let me give an example. I do the SEO for a website that does roofing here in Portland.

The keyword, "portland family counseling", is a term that is searched on about 1,500 times per month in Portland. But, there are 2,000 counselors with websites that are competing for the same keyword. On the other hand there are 1,250 searches in Portland for, "divorce counseling" but only about 100 therapists with websites competing for that term. This is a small example but you can see I would choose the second keyword term over the first even though there are fewer searches. Only, after I took in to consideration the site rankings of the competition which we will discuss later in this chapter.

Determining Your Best Keywords

Well we have talked about the keywords and what they can do for you, but picking the right keywords is the, well, the key.

If you are a small-business owner, you will want your website to be readily visible on each and every search engine for the right keywords. In fact using the right keywords in your website's content can mean the difference between being listed as one of the first 20 sites returned from search engine results (which is good) or being buried under other web sites forty pages into the results which means hundreds of results are returned before someone sees your site.

There have been many studies showing that searchers rarely venture past the second page of searches and majorities choose websites on the first page of the results when looking for something online.

Per Page Keyword Focus

Now this is worth all the money you paid for this book because it is a major change from all the books I have every made and it is a change that happened in mid 2010. You want to pick only 1-3 keywords per page as your trophy keywords if you are optimizing for Google any more than that and Google will most likely find you relevant for none.

The smaller the keyword focus (meaning focus on one keyword) the better. Why? "Google Instant" started on September 8, 2010 and has created a lot of hype around the effects it will have on the future of search marketing and Search Engine Optimization(SEO). Not just organically but also on sponsored listings.

Google Instant turns search into a real-time stream of results which flow onto your screen as you type your query letter by letter. With each letter you type, a whole new set of results flash by. This is important for several reasons. First and foremost, you will now see many more search results than you would have by typing in your search query and just pressing enter.

This had an immediate effect on a users search pattern and causes people to shy away from doing a click through to the second page or more of the search results. Google's average user behavior and keyword usage hasn't changed much as a result of Google Instant but there are some keys to how you should optimize your pages.

At the basic level there are many things as a website owner or SEO guru you should know. Including the fact that Google Instant will only affects a portion of Google searches.

There are several limitations and Google Instant functionality is turned off in the following circumstances:

1. If you are not logged in to a Google account.
2. If a user types a search query directly into a browser or toolbar.
3. If you are located outside of the US, UK, France, Italy, Germany, Spain or Russia.
4. If your browser is outdated.
5. If you choose the deactivate Google Instant.
NOTE: *It is definitely worthy to note that not all searches are at Google.com. They are in search bars such as in Firefox or in the URL bar in the case of Google Chrome.*

So how do I modify my website's SEO practices to help me with users search pattern changes in optimizing my website? Do I just optimize pages for parts of keywords? The answer surprisingly is a 'no'. Google definitely hates websites with bad mechanics. Spelling issues are a problem with gaining relevance on Google so that is definitely not the answer.

SIDEBAR: What is the purpose of Google Instant?

For this answer you need to know a little bit about the history of Google and really understand a major driving force behind this change in their search engine results pages (SERPS). As recently as 2008, you could optimize a page and find relevance for 15 to 18 keywords. In 2009, it became smaller. For most website to find good rankings website developers needed to concentrate on less than 5 to 8 keywords in 2009. In 2010, it became 1 to 3 keywords. This new indexing method makes it really one page optimized for one keyword.

Why would Google do this? Well only around 5-7% of the websites on the Internet employ any type of purposeful SEO techniques. Out of those, only a small number of those actually use updated or good SEO techniques and of those only a small fraction get professional SEO services that keep them up on the techniques. The rest of those website owners don't know how to make multiple landing pages, get indexed correctly, stay up on the latest SEO principles, and understand site maps so they can focus on multiple keywords.

What this means is that the average website not employing the latest SEO techniques to focus on multiple keywords has to pay money to stay competitive for more than one keyword. For Google this money goes primarily to AdWords and this is going to be a cash windfall for Google. The fewer the words you can stay competitive for, the more you need AdWords to stay on the first page of Google.

So getting back to the topic of this chapter, Meta tagging and keywords. You probably have the question now of what I need to do to stay on top and be found with users new search behaviors? Through our testing of Google Instant we have determined that a majority of the time Google is looking at the first word of the characters in the domain name, Title tag, and third the words in the Meta description tag to decide the most relevant pages to display. You should modify your web pages or add pages so that your singular keyword search term on your pages contain only the individual key search term and its plural form. Here is an example:

<title>USB Converter | USB Converters</title>

You will have to create pages and optimize them for other keywords you have in secondary or later positions to remain competitive for those keywords. Don't forget you need to modify your Meta Keyword and Meta Description tags to include your keyword as well using your first keyword in the Meta Description tag as well.

For most website owners these changes will be a burden and require many new pages, but the sooner the changes are made, the sooner you will reap the rewards.

> **NOTE**: *There is a lot more to Google Instant than just Meta tags and I cover these in detail in Chapter 7.*

More to help your understanding of keywords.

Let's do a few examples to help your understanding of how to pick your keywords correctly. Let's say you have a website that reviews films and rates them. If one of your keywords is, "films", that is too broad. Do you sell films? Do you develop them? Do you make them? Do you have cleaning products to clean different films? No. You have to make your keywords more relevant. Now if one of my keywords in my Meta tagging was, "feature film critic" or "feature film reviews". That would be more relevant. Notice that a keyword is more like a key phrase than a word.

There are two ways of keyword stuffing. One is by being too broad on your Meta keywords and having way more than three and Google finds you relevant for nothing.

Let's say that you are a convenience store and you put a list of products you carry as keywords such as donuts, sodas, fountain drinks, bottled drinks, ice drinks, etc. You would be stuffing your keywords.

The other way of keyword stuffing is using the keywords you have too many times in your content. This is an extreme example of keyword spamming, but let's say you have the convenience store and to make website seem really relevant, you take the list of your keywords and you put them on your websites landing page 200 times at the end of your homepage. This will trigger a ban not just from Google but many others. Google really dislikes this practice.

Let's say you make the wording the same color as your websites background so that you are hiding it from those searching or viewing the content on your website. Well not only are the bots, crawlers and spiders smart enough to find it and penalize you for it, you might wind up on the list of websites that got banned from Google as well. Being banned from Google is like being blacklisted from the Internet. You are better off getting a new domain, domain hosting company, a company name and starting over.

Understanding How Keywords Are Used

It helps to decide on keywords if you understand how people search the Internet using search engines. When you go to a search engine and want to find a place that sells welding supplies, you open a search engine such as Google and you type in, "buy welding supplies" and click search. You get about 60,000 results but none of them are places you can go locally and get a welder. You're not likely going to order a large welder online. The shipping would cost as much as the welder.

Are you going to go searching through the 64,000 results for a local place to buy one? No. You're going to refine your search down to something less broad like, "sacramento welding supplies" which will have better results.

If I sell welding supplies in Sacramento, I would make one of my keywords as "Sacramento Welding Supplies". I would have less of a chance if my keywords in my Meta tagging are "sacramento, welding, supplies, supply" as these words individually are more broad and have less relevance to the search. Each one is treated by most search engines as an individual search term. Sacramento is a city, welding could refer to any number of items, how to weld, welding stories, training schools, metal fence welding, etc. I typed in just "welding" in to Bing and on the first page was a job listing working as a welder to build cruise ships. The point I am making is that users are now educated to refine their search. We can keep going on but I think I have made the point here. Using the exact phrase people will use as a search term in your keywords can make all the difference on whether your site will show up on a search engine search.

Keyword Research Tools

There are many tools on the Internet to help you find the exact keywords to use for your website. The trick is to understanding how keywords work, which you should use, and the best ways to use them. If you choose the most relevant keywords and properly design your site using those keywords you will have a highly visible and successful website.

At a basic level, keywords capture the essence of your website. Keywords are the words or phrases a potential visitor to your site enters into a search engine to find websites only website related to the specific subject matter they are looking for. If you went to Google and did a search and had to go through 30 pages of content to find a website the matched what you were looking for, you would stop using Google and go back to the telephone book, or choose Yahoo! instead. That is why choosing keywords that match your websites content are so important. The keywords that you choose are used throughout the optimization process applied to your website. And if it isn't well then don't expect to have anyone find your website, unless they know the exact URL to find it.

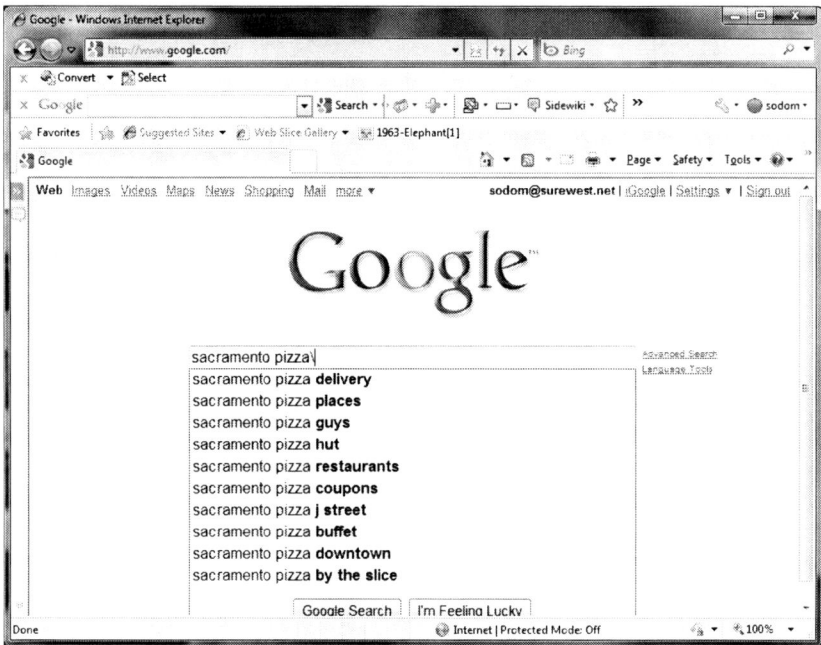

Figure 2.1

So let's ask ourselves some questions:

1. What words best describe my website content?
2. How do I know which keywords to use?
3. Where do I find help in deciding?
4. Once I know my possible keywords, where do I see how many people search on those keywords?

All of these are great questions and knowing the answers to these questions will save you a great deal of time when creating a website.

First off you can go to Google and start to type words that apply to your site. The most commonly searched terms will populate for you as shown in Figure 2.1, where I began to search for "Sacramento Pizza".

There are five hundred software packages, books, and website out there to help you determine your keywords. One of the best, if you want all the work done for you is www.WebsiteSubmiter.org.

However, if you don't want to spend the money, do what I do. Have Google do the work for you. "Say what? Google do the work for me?" you ask. Who wrote this book? He must be off his rocker!

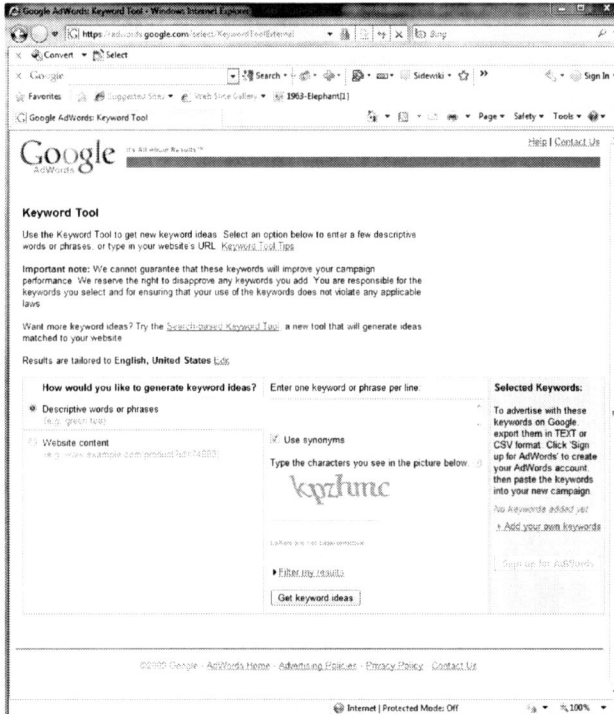

Figure 2.2

No really. Google has a little known website tool for determining keywords. They advertised its existence to Google Ambassadors but it is generally unknown to most website owners or the general public. Let's take a look at what this tool can do for you.

If you go to the URL of:

https://adwords.google.com/select/KeywordToolExternal

(You will find this tool as shown in Figure 2.2.)

Notice you have a couple of options. You can put a generalization of your keywords or, if you already have a website, you can choose to have Google crawl your website and decide the words that will work best.

The search reply that you get back will be incredibly long and many of the results will most likely apply to your website. But the ones that do, you can see how many searches there were on a average on a local level or on a global level. Not only that, but a measurement of how hard the competition is for each keyword!

Let's take a look at both options in detail.

Google's Keyword Search Tool

Now it's not called the Google General Keyword Search Tool but I had to have a descriptive name in the title. I am fortunate enough to have a very large alternative news site as a client, and so I will use the search terms "alternative news" as shown in figure 2.3a. In Figure 2.3b you will see Googles new Keyword Search Tool Beta.

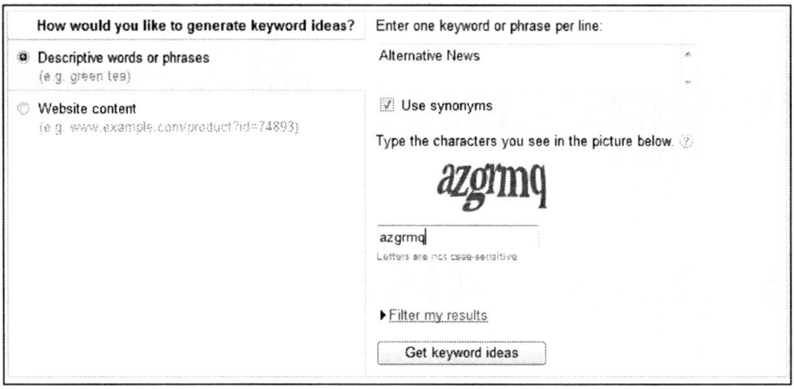

Figure 2.3a

Figure 2.3b

Here are the results in Figures 2.4 shows search results from Google's Keyword Search Tool. Figure 2.5 shows the same search results from Google's new Keyword Search Tool.

Keywords	Advertiser Competition	Local Search Volume: September	Global Monthly Search Volume	Match Type: Broad
Keywords related to term(s) entered - sorted by relevance				
brand new alternative press		Not enough data	36	Add
alternative news		18,100	27,100	Add
alternative news media		Not enough data	390	Add
alternative press news		Not enough data	58	Add
alternative news papers		Not enough data	28	Add
alternative news paper		58	58	Add
alternative daily news		Not enough data	590	Add
alternative news magazine		Not enough data	91	Add
alternative news weekly		Not enough data	320	Add
alternative news magazines		Not enough data	36	Add
alternative news headlines		Not enough data	16	Add
alternative weekly news		Not enough data	320	Add
alternative news sources		1,000	1,300	Add
alternative newspapers		Not enough data	1,900	Add
alternative newspaper		5,400	5,400	Add
alternative independent news		Not enough data	91	Add
alternative news source		210	390	Add
alternative news sites		590	590	Add
alternative news blogs		Not enough data	28	Add
alternative news links		Not enough data	36	Add
alternative news website		Not enough data	58	Add
the alternative news		Not enough data	170	Add
alternative news blog		Not enough data	46	Add
alternative news websites		Not enough data	210	Add
alternative news from		Not enough data	140	Add
alternative news online		Not enough data	720	Add
alternative news site		46	110	Add
alternative news network		Not enough data	73	Add
alternative news video		Not enough data	73	Add

Figure 2.4

Notice in Figure 2.4 and 2.5 is merely suggestive keywords. Also the list can be downloaded in either a text, .csv (for excel), or .csv formats to review later. You will notice to the right a new field that shows by month how many searches have been made for that keyword over the last year.

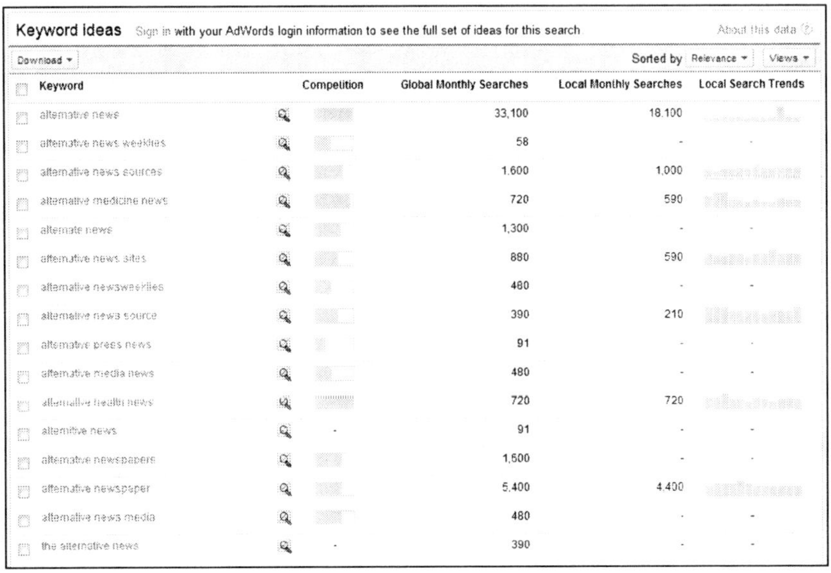

Keyword		Competition	Global Monthly Searches	Local Monthly Searches	Local Search Trends
alternative news	🔍		33,100	18,100	
alternative news weeklies	🔍		58	-	-
alternative news sources	🔍		1,600	1,000	
alternative medicine news	🔍		720	590	
alternate news	🔍		1,300	-	-
alternative news sites	🔍		880	590	
alternative newsweeklies	🔍		480	-	-
alternative news source	🔍		390	210	
alternative press news	🔍		91	-	-
alternative media news	🔍		480	-	-
alternative health news	🔍		720	720	
alternative news	🔍	-	91	-	-
alternative newspapers	🔍		1,500	-	-
alternative newspaper	🔍		5,400	4,400	
alternative news media	🔍		480	-	-
the alternative news	🔍	-	390	-	-

Figure 2.5

Now let's look at what happens if I let Google crawl the site and come up with search terms.

Google Keyword Search Tool

Again, the title of this section is not an official name for their search tool. Also, I am going to use one of my customer's websites called www.localnewsday.com. I haven't asked their permission to be in the book, but I do a good enough job that I don't think they will care, and since they are reeling over the fact that they had over 16,000 unique hits last month, my competition will have a hard time wooing them as a client.

So let's use them. In figure 2.6, I chose to have Google crawl the site to determine the best keywords to use.

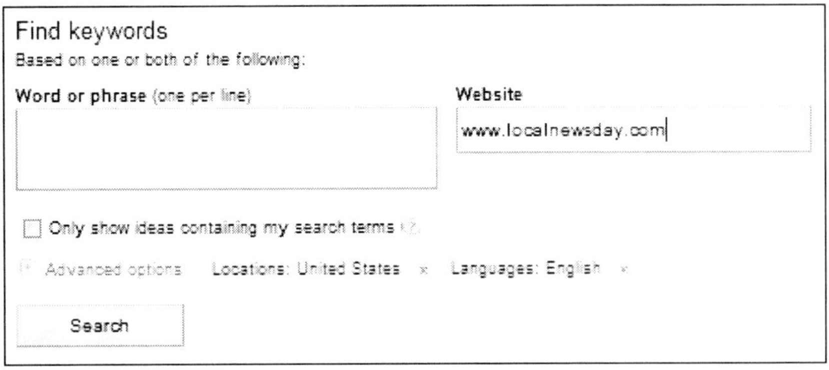

Find keywords
Based on one or both of the following:

Word or phrase (one per line)   Website

                                        www.localnewsday.com|

☐ Only show ideas containing my search terms ⑦

⊞ Advanced options   Locations: United States ×   Languages: English ×

Search

Figure 2.6

When it gets done let's take a look figures 2.7 to see what the difference are.

medical and dental insurance	9,900	8,100
health insurance portland	2,400	2,400
private medical insurance	27,100	8,100
medical health insurance	74,000	60,500
travel medical insurance	135,000	49,500
medical indemnity insurance	2,400	880
medical liability insurance	12,100	9,900
dental insurance portland	390	390
insurance broker portland oregon	480	390
insurance portland oregon	4,400	4,400
pre existing condition medical insurance	9,900	6,600
medical insurance companies	110,000	74,000
aetna insurance	90,500	90,500
get medical insurance	4,400	3,600
maternity insurance	40,500	27,100
cost of medical malpractice insurance	1,600	1,600

Figure 2.7

You will notice that some of the keywords don't fit. Like "health insurance" This caught me off guard until I went to the website and saw that there was a news story related to health insurance as shown in Figure 2.8.

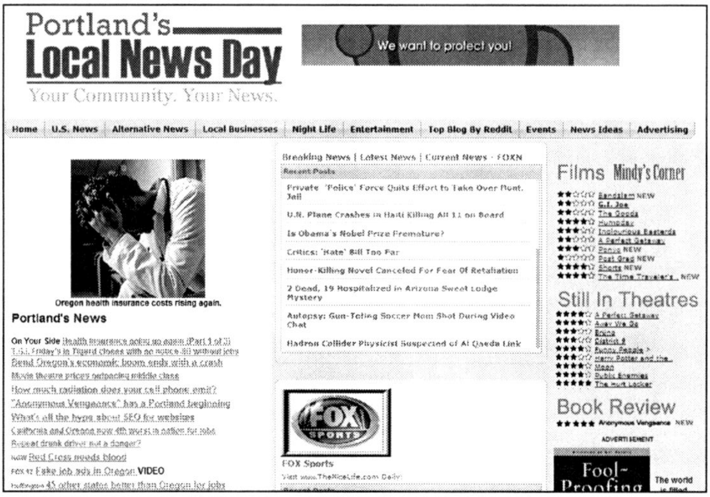

Figure 2.8

How to Decide Your Keywords

Well we have collected the information we need to decide on our trophy keywords for our website but probably not which ones to use. We know the possible keywords, the number of local and global searches, and an estimate of how much competition there are for those keywords.

As I said before, as a consultant I spend countless hours finding and applying the right keywords for my customers and working with those who design websites for my customers. Finding the most effective keywords is a fine science and sometimes it's an experimental process.

Many times I will add, subtract and reorder my Meta tagged keywords based on what is working and what is not on my customers websites. I can tell a lot about how well a keyword is working by tracking a Pay-Per-Click (PPC) campaign. But we will discuss that later in this book.

Now that I have my possible keyword list from Google in the last section, I have to weigh using heavily searched on keywords against the amount of competition I have. If I have a high Google ranking I can compete against whoever I want for the keywords, but if I am just starting out and my ranking is low on Google, I have to choose words that have less competition.

If I went right out for the search term "daily news" as shown in figure 2.7 for my customer LocalNewsDay.com it would be a big mistake. Sure, there are 2.7 million searches a month for that term but there are 600 sites ranked higher than LocalNewsDay.com's site and it would wind up on page 43 of any Google search for that term.

However, if I went for the search term "portland daily news" on the other hand, there is a good chance that even with a low ranking I will wind up on page 1 or 2 with basic optimization in a few months because there is less competition for that search term.

Meta Description

The description is what most people see on the end of a Google search, right under the link to the website page is the Meta tagging description. Now that we have decided our keywords, you now need to formulate your keywords in to your description using complete sentences. This is not as easy as it sounds.

If you use long tail keywords you must use them in the same order in your description and you need to keep you descriptions to 155 characters or less. This is the number of characters most search engines will display.

Let's give some examples:

sacramento excavating, sacramento excavation, sacramento dump truck, sacramento tight access excavating, sacramento residential landscaping, sacramento track hoe,loader.

Now the description should be:

We are Sacramento Excavating professionals who can handle any Sacramento excavation job needing a dump truck, tight access track hoe or loader. Whether you are doing landscaping or clearing a site we come with a full size dump truck, track hoe and the loader all at one great price.

Meta Title tags

The title that you see may be one of the most important parts for any website as shown at the top of figure 2.9.

Figure 2.9

Remember those keywords we decided on? We want to use as many of those and in the same order as you can. Google allows up to 66 characters (including spaces) for title tags, whereas some others look at up to 120 characters. The numbers change frequently and last year the general rule was don't put more than 70 characters.

Figure 2.10

If your title tags exceed those limits, they'll be truncated to fit into the maximum space allowed. To ensure that you're getting the most value for the character limitations of title tags, the World Wide Web Consortium (W3C) recommends that web site designers keep their titles to 64 characters or less in length. In figure 2.11 you see the title tag which appears below. In the next section we will show you how to configure the Title as well as the rest of the Meta Tags.

You notice again in the top of figure 2.10 that the title looks a lot like keywords. Why? Because it is! You should use as many of your keywords as you can in your title and in the order that they are listed in your Meta tags.

Search engine crawlers, bots and spiders use these title tags as one of the main source for determining the web-page topic. Spiders, bots, and crawlers examine the title, and the words used in it are then uses this information as a key source to determine the topic of the page. It's always best to use your keywords in your page title, and to use them as close to the beginning of the title as possible.

There should also be a unique title tags for every page of your website which creates relevancy and distinguishes the difference in content. Make the title as descriptive as possible and use the most important keywords you've decided on for the page. Words you use in your Title tag will appear in the reverse title bar, or the tab title, of your web browser, as well.

The Science of Meta Tagging

Did you know that the search engines don't usually send their creepy crawlers to index your site without your permission? This is one of the biggest mistakes website owners make.

I can see many of you reading this have your eyes wide open, asking yourself if you have done this part! It is a good question to ask because I would say 7 out of 10 people desperate for my SEO help don't have this done and anything else they do to help doesn't make a difference.

There are two ways you can allow spiders, bots and crawlers to come index your site. You can include a file called robot.txt with permissions (we will talk about this later in the book.) or you can use the Meta Robots tags to do this which is the most efficient way. If you haven't done this, well you might see your landing page on a website, but you will never see a good ranking and none of your other pages will get indexed.

Sidebar: The Meta Robots Tag

The gives you the ability to specify whether search engine bots, spiders, and crawlers should index that page or follow the links appearing on that page.

The following is the Meta Robots tag which should be on your landing page. (You will learn where to put your Meta tags in the next section.) I add it to every page of the website:

<meta name="robots" content="index, follow">

There are other syntaxes you can use instead of "index, follow" which are:

- **index:** This allows the spider to index that page.

- **noindex:** This instructs the spider not to index the page.

- **follow:** This instructs the spider to follow the links from that page and index them.

- **nofollow:** This instructs the spider not to follow links from that page for indexing.

- **all:** This is identical to "index, follow".

- **none:** This is identical to "noindex, nofollow" telling the search engines to ignore the web page.

The other acceptable tags:

```
<meta name="robots" content="noindex, follow">
<meta name="robots" content="index, nofollow">
<meta name="robots" content="noindex, nofollow">
<meta name="robots" content="all">
<mcta name="robots" content="none">
```

Keep in mind you only use one of the tags. They are not used in combination with each other.

Meta Tags Creation

We already learned earlier in the chapter that that our Meta tagging starts with determining our keywords. Also, known as our "long tail keywords" because they are not usually a single word. I could go section by section here but let's go and analyze the keywords all at once. But I think you might understand it better is I just show you what the keywords should look like and then break it down tag by tag.

So our imaginary furniture store called "Sacramento Excavating Contractors". I did a Google search to make sure it wasn't really a business. Of course, in my last book, I created an imaginary company and someone took the name, started a company and is using the exact Meta tagging I created. So I guess for this one it will be first come, first serve.

Anyway, our imaginary business provides a tight-access track hoe and loader to dig pools , create retaining walls and any other residential or commercial work which might need our loader and track hoe as shown below fin figure 10.11.

Figure 2.11

I already did the research and my long tail keywords are:

- Sacramento Excavation Contractors
- Sacramento Excavating Contractors
- Sacramento Excavating
- Sacramento Excavation

Note: *I actually came up with about 40 more keywords but these are the most basic. Also I would concentrate on the same keywords but replace the city name with every local city around Sacramento. These would be Loomis, Roseville, Citrus Heights, North Highlands, Folsom, Elk Grove, South Sacramento, and Rancho Cordova.*

So let's take a look at what I came up with for the title and Meta tagging for this website.

```
<HEAD>
<Title> Sacramento Excavating Contractor | Sacramento Excavating</Title>
<Meta http-equiv="Content-type" content="text/html; charset=ISO-8859-1">
<Meta name="keywords" content="sacramento excavating contractor, sacramento excavating">
<Meta name="description" content="We are a Sacramento Excavating Contractor with a tight access trackhoe and loader for your Sacramento excavating needs.">
<Meta name="googlebot" content="index, follow" />
<Meta name="robots" content=" index, follow ">
<Meta name="Revist-After" content="7 days">
<Meta name="city" content="Sacramento">
<Meta name="country" content="United States (USA)">
<Meta name="state" content="CA">
<Meta name="zip code" content="95838">
<Meta name="subject" content="Sacramento Excavating">
<Meta name="author" content="Sean Odom">
<Meta name="copyright" content="Sacramento Excavating Contractors">
</HEAD>

<Body>
(This is where the visible portion of your website is configured.)
</Body>
```

So let's take a look at each one of these in the next sections.

Configuring the Keyword Meta Tag

So I am going a little out of order but I need it to make sense to you and reiterate what I have been trying to explain through this entire chapter. That is, keywords are IMPORTANT. You shouldn't even think about the Title tag or the Description tag until you have decided on your keywords!

In the last section I showed you the keywords I decided. If you don't know how I determined my keywords, I taught you this a few sections back. So the tag is configured like this:

> <Meta name="keywords" content="sacramento excavating contractor, sacramento excavating">

I made keywords bold for this example. The keywords aren't bolded in the configuration. You might notice something else. All the keywords are in lower case. Why? Well Google doesn't care but we need to think about all the search engines and some are case sensitive and most people don't capitalize their word searches. They just type in their keywords to search.

Configuring the Meta Title Tag

The title tag is located somewhere in between the opening <head> tag and before the closing <\HEAD> tag. It doesn't really matter where it is, but most people put the Title above the Meta tags.

Now remember our keywords? Notice that I used the first 3 which are my main "trophy words" in the Title.

> <Title> **Sacramento Excavating Contractor | Sacramento Excavating</**Title>

Configuring the GoogleBot and the Robot Tags

Here is the Meta Robots tag that we discussed a few sections back in a sidebar. You might notice another tag though. Google really likes it when you put its own Meta tag in your website and tell him what to do. That tag is called "googlebot" and the instructions are similar to the Robots tag as shown:

> **index:** This allows the GoogleBot to index that page.

> **noindex:** This tells the GoogleBot not to index the page.

> **follow:** This allows the GoogleBot to follow the links from the landing page and other pages it finds and index them.

> **nofollow**: This instructs the spider not to follow links from that page for indexing.

> **Noodp:** Prevents the search from using the page's description.

The tags are easy and should be in any website you have. Also, you never know what users or links Googlebot or other creepy crawlers arrive from and so these should be in the Meta tags of every page in your website.

<Meta name="googlebot" content="**index, follow**" />
<Meta name="robots" content=" **index, follow** ">

Configuring the Meta Revisit Tag

Google and other major search engines typically visit your site once per month on average. But let's say your website's content changes more frequently such as a news website? How do you tell the search engines spiders, bots and crawlers to visit more frequently? The "Revisit-After" Meta tag is used just for this purpose.

<Meta name="Revist-After" content="**7 days**">

Configuring the Meta Location Tags

These tags are really important to Bing.com and other search engines to help identify the geographical locations. In a few section we will look at a new GPS type of geographic location tool and add the Meta tags as well. In the example below, we add the city, country, state, and zip code, just as if you were mailing yourself a letter as shown below:

<Meta name="city" content="**Sacramento**">
<Meta name="country" content="**United States (USA)**">
<Meta name="state" content="**CA**">
<Meta name="zip code" content="**95838**">

Configuring the Meta Subject Tag

This tag arguable has very little influence with the major search engines but it does have some with smaller ones. I typically place the first long tail keywords in my Meta Keywords tag here which should be the most important subject of our website as shown below.

<Meta name="subject" content="**Sacramento Excavating**">

Configuring the Author and Copyright Meta Tags

These two tags do very little to enhance your search engine rankings and have more to do with identifying who owns all the hard work you put in to your website. I see parts of my books in other books and on the Internet all the time. Most have the common sense to give me credit, but when they don't, I get upset. I spent blood, sweat, and tears to get this done. Not to mention the time I didn't get to spend with my family because I was writing and doing other things.

The "author" tag is the person or company name that created the content in the website. The "copyright" tag identifies who own the copyright. I will remind all the readers that Sacramento Excavating Contractors, Inc. is entirely bogus and at the time of this writing didn't really exist.

```
<Meta name="author" content="Sean Odom">
<Meta name="copyright" content="Sacramento Excavating
Contractors, Inc.">
```

Meta Redirect Tag

Have you ever wanted to redirect someone to another site when they got to a page? Say you changed your websites URL. Well you can with just one line! Let's take a look at this one liner:

```
<Meta http-equiv="refresh"
content="5;url=http://www.sacramentoexcavatingcontractors.co
m/newpage.html">
```

Now the "5" indicates the number of seconds to wait. If you don't want search engines to ding you as if it is a doorway page which we will discuss later in this book, then it needs to be set to 5 seconds or longer. The last part is the URL that you want to redirect the page to. In this example I chose the page to be the blog.html page.

> **NOTE:** *There are many other not so important Meta Tags. You can learn them all at: http://www.metatags.info*

Now let's take a look the new geographical Meta tag that is really catching on using GPS and longitude and latitude.

Adding yourself to GeoURL

Figure 2.12

Identifying your businesses location in your Meta tags is jumping up in high tech and Google and other search engines are catching on. GeoURL has started a new Meta tagging system to identify where your business is located.

This helps the search engine identify how close you are to a customer and give proper mileage. If you are a retail establishment such as a store or restaurant, doing this can actually help you show up on GPS device searches as well. Take a look at GeoURL in Figure 2.12.

First you need to identify where you are. If your website is about your business you will need the coordinates for your businesses location.

You can go to *http://geourl.org/add/helper* to not only get your coordinates for your tag but to generate your tags as well if you are in the US as shown in Figure 2.13.

Figure 2.13

Remember my fictitious company in the last section. I have made up an address and entered it in to the GeoURL Head Generator and it actually gave me the tags that I need to use with the GPS coordinates for my business.

GPS coordinates are in the form of a latitude and longitude, separated by a comma. Remember that minutes and seconds are in 60ths, so if something is X degrees, Y minutes, and Z seconds, the decimal equivalent is $X + Y/60 + Z/3600$.

So let's add our new tags to our website in the next section.

Configuring Meta GeoTags

You can go to the GEOTags.com website to get the following Meta tags to add to the <head> section of your web page:

```
<meta name="ICBM" content="XXX.XXXXX, XXX.XXXXX">
<meta name="DC.title" content="THE NAME OF YOUR SITE">

<meta name="ICBM" content="38.650959, -121.468749">
<meta name="DC.title" content="Sacramento Excavation Contractors">
```

Note: *If your site uses frames, you must add the meta tags to your* **top-level** *page which contains the <frameset> tag.*

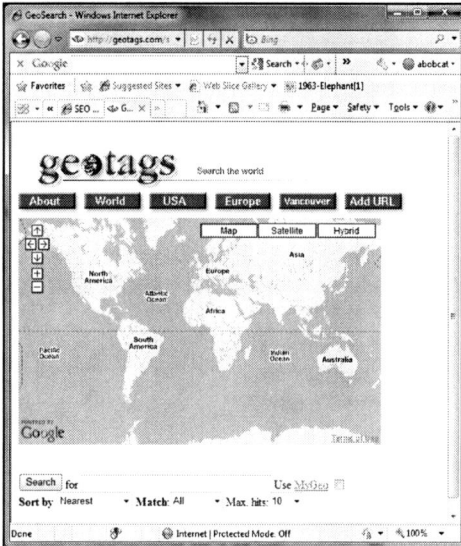

Figure 2.14

We'll also index *http://www.geotags.com* style "geo.position" meta tag as per their documentation at: *http://geotags.com/geobot/add-tags.html*

The reason it is called the x is that this was actually used for generating geographically-correct maps. This became known as one's ICBM address or missile address, and some people include it in their sig block with that name.

```html
<HEAD>
<base href="http://www.SacramentoExcavatingContractors.com/" />
<Title> Sacramento Excavating Contractor | Sacramento
Excavating</Title>
<Meta http-equiv="Content-type" content="text/html; charset=ISO-
8859-1">
<Meta name="keywords" content="sacramento excavating
contractor, sacramento excavating">
<Meta name="description" content="We are a Sacramento
Excavating Contractor with a tight access trackhoe and loader for
your Sacramento excavating needs.">
<Meta name="googlebot" content="index, follow" />
<Meta name="robots" content=" index, follow ">
<Meta name="Revist-After" content-"7 days">
<Meta name="city" content="Sacramento">
<Meta name="country" content="United States (USA)">
<Meta name="state" content="CA">
<Meta name="zip code" content="95838">
<Meta name="subject" content="Sacramento Excavating">
<Meta name="author" content="Sean Odom">
<Meta name="copyright" content="Sacramento Excavating
Contractors">
<meta name="geo.region" content="US-OR" />
<meta name="geo.placename" content="Sacramento, CA" />
<meta name="ICBM" content="38.650959, -121.468749">
<meta name="DC.title" content="Sacramento Excavation
Contractors">

</HEAD>
```

Chapter 3 - Submitting your websites URL to the search engines

Let's assume that you, as most people, had a web developer design this completely awesome site but he or she who designed the site didn't have a clue about SEO. Some of my customers have spent thirty thousand dollars on a web site and it didn't even have a single Meta tag on it!

We already talked about matching the title, Meta tags, Meta descriptions, Meta Keywords to the root pages of your web site and having all the same appear in all those areas, right? If you didn't catch that and you are about to submit your web site(s) please go back to the last chapter!

If you are done with that, then you are ready to go to the next step!

First Stop, Google.

Why Google? Well, about sixty percent of all web searches happen right on Google, which means that although there are other major search engines, you want to make Google happy first. (I will include a step later where you go to http://www.websitesubmitter.org and submit your web site to the 200+ little search engines for about $35.00. This will save you about 100 hours of your precious time, if not more.)

First off, you will want to go to Google and create a Google account for Google Webmasters.

Step 1 - Add Your Site to Google Webmaster Central

Google's Webmaster Central (as shown in Figure 3.1 below) can be used to notify Google of the existence of a web site, verify with Google that you have control of the web site (Webmaster), identify the site map location for a web site, access keyword research tools, verify the Robot.txt file, and locate any errors within a web site.

To add your web site to the Google Webmaster Central, do the following:

1. Go to http://www.google.com/services as shown in Figure 3.1. Then click on the Webmaster Central Link.

2. After you have created the account you should be able to access Google Webmaster tools. Right in the middle of the page should be an icon that says, "Add site".

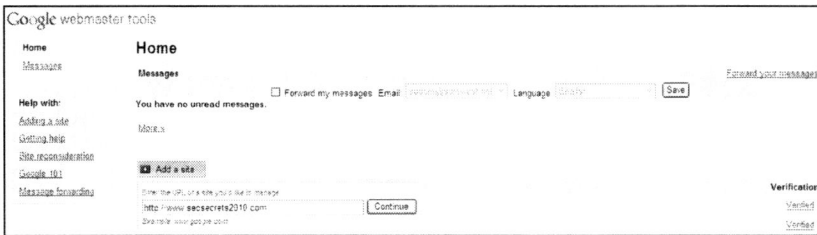

Figure 3.1

3. You can then place a Meta tag which Google gives you on your web site or upload an HTML file. This is used to verify that you truly are the webmaster. Once Google confirms it has verified your web site URL, the next stop is Google Analytics.

    NOTE: *Later we will add a Google Sitemap.xls to the web site to help Google index all of your pages.*

Step 2 - Add your site to Google Analytics

1. Go to http://www.google.com/services as shown in Figure 3.2 below. Then click on the Analytics link. You should already be logged in but if not, log in using the same account you used for the Google Webmaster Central.

2. After you have accessed Google Analytics, again right in the middle of the page should be an icon that says, "Add New Profile".

3. Then add the web site URL as shown below and click Finish:

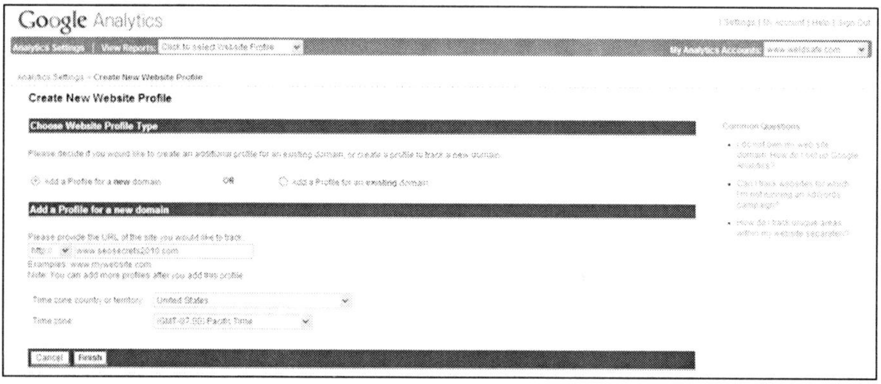

Figure 3.2

> **NOTE:** *If you want your business to be seen in the Local Business Results on Google, see Google Local Business Listings and Bing Local Business Listings in the next chapter.*

Step 3 - Submitting your site to Yahoo!

At the time of this writing, you can still submit your web site for free to Yahoo.com at: http://siteexplorer.search.yahoo.com/submit. But that is expected to change as Yahoo is now going to get its results from Bing.com.

Submitting your site for free to Yahoo! (as shown in Figure 3.3):

1. Create a Yahoo! ID at http://www.yahoo.com
2. Go to: http://siteexplorer.search.yahoo.com/submit
3. Enter the web site URL and press Submit URL as shown below.

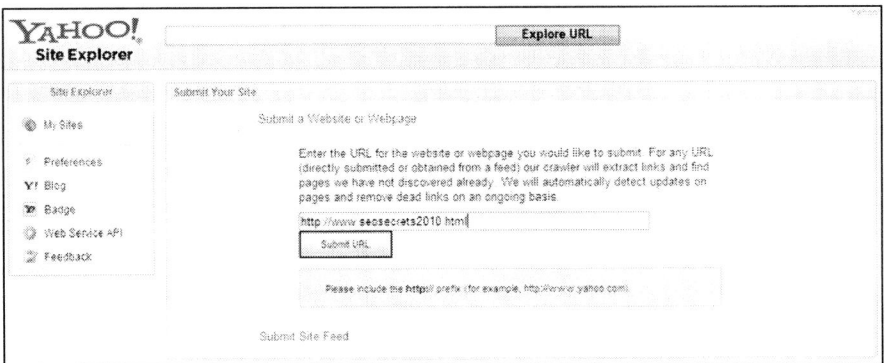

Figure 3.3

Step 4 - Submitting your site to Bing

Bing.com is gaining an incredible market share—especially since they are owned by Microsoft and the engine is used to perform searches not only on Bing, but on MSN, Live, and many other smaller sites. And guess what? Now, some Yahoo! results as well as a deal was made to allow Bing to provide the results and advertising on Yahoo! as well.

To submit your web site to Bing.com, follow these instructions:

1. Go to the URL of: http://www.bing.com/docs/submit.aspx as shown in Figure 3.4.

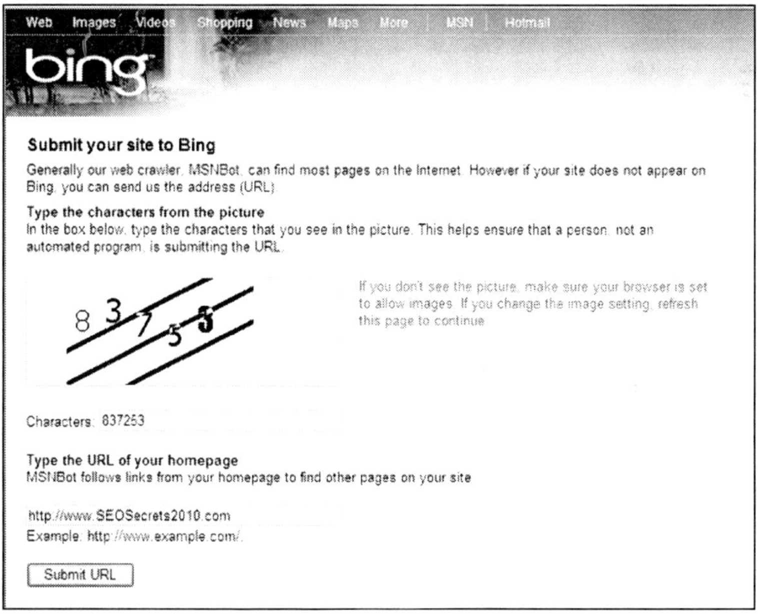

Figure 3.4

2. Enter the verification characters.

3. Enter the URL of the web site you want to submit to Bing.com and then click "Submit URL".

4. You get a message thanking you for submitting your site to Bing as shown below in Figure 3.5:

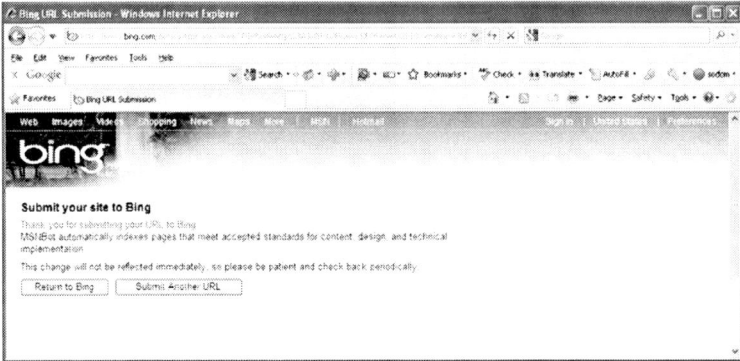

Figure 3.5

Bing's Webmaster Center

Bing's Webmaster Center, as shown below, can be used to notify Bing of the existence of a web site, verify with Bing that you have control of the web site (Webmaster), identify the site map location for a web site, access keyword research tools, verify the Robot.txt file, and locate any errors with a web site.

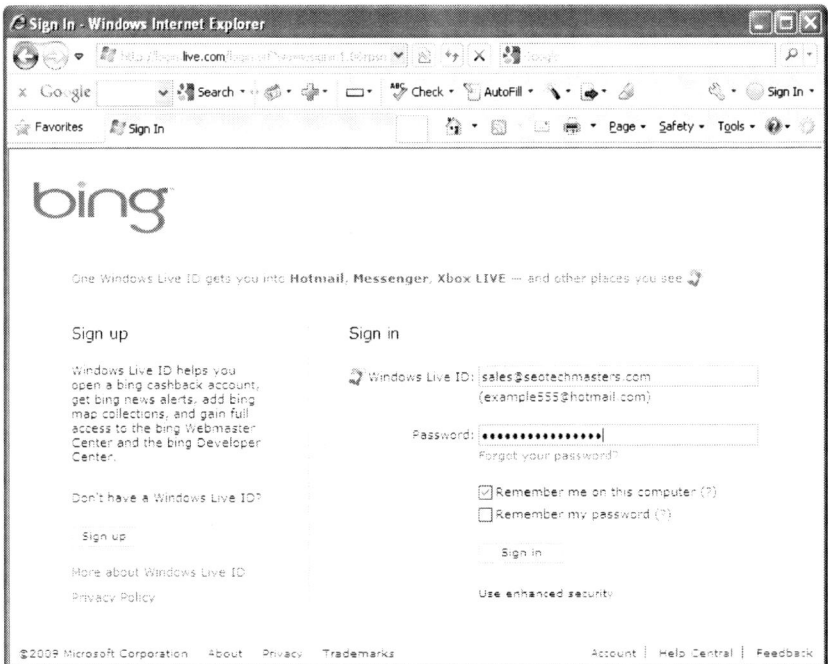

Figure 3.6

The Bing webmaster console as shown above can be found at:

http://www.bing.com/webmaster/WebmasterManageSitesPage.aspx

In Figure 3.6 above, you see that you are logging in. Since I have a new client who is an author of travel guides, let's add their newest web site to the Bing Webmaster Console.

In Figure 3.7 you will notice that I have added their web site address, the address of the site map I have created, and the email address. Since I do their SEO services, I enter my email address as the Webmaster's email.

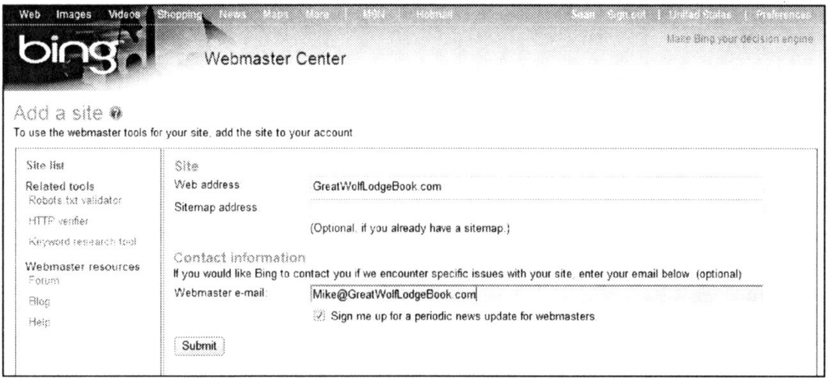

Figure 3.7

Bing then gives me a screen which makes me authenticate the web site, as shown in Figure 3.8. I can either add an additional Meta tag to the tags I have created or upload a verification file to the web site to verify that I am the owner or webmaster of the web site. I usually download the file as you never know what will happen to the landing page of the web site in the future.

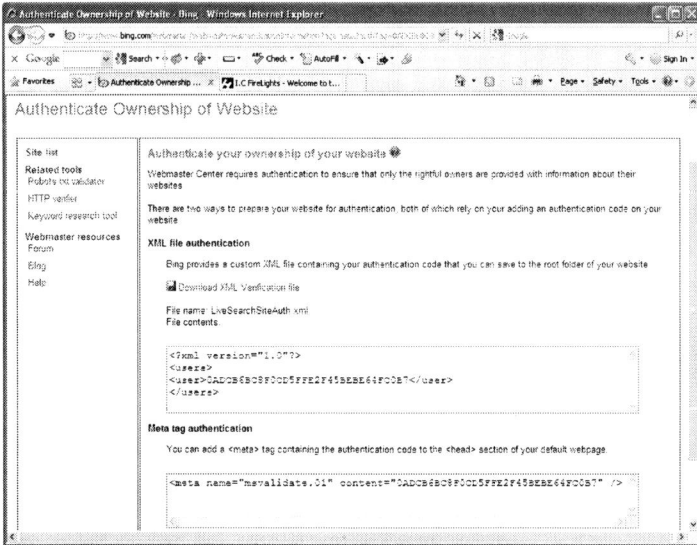

Figure 3.8

In Figure 3.9, you will see the web site amongst other web sites I have verified. It shows the web site name and on the right it shows how I authenticated the web site. The middle characters are the verification code assigned by Bing.com.

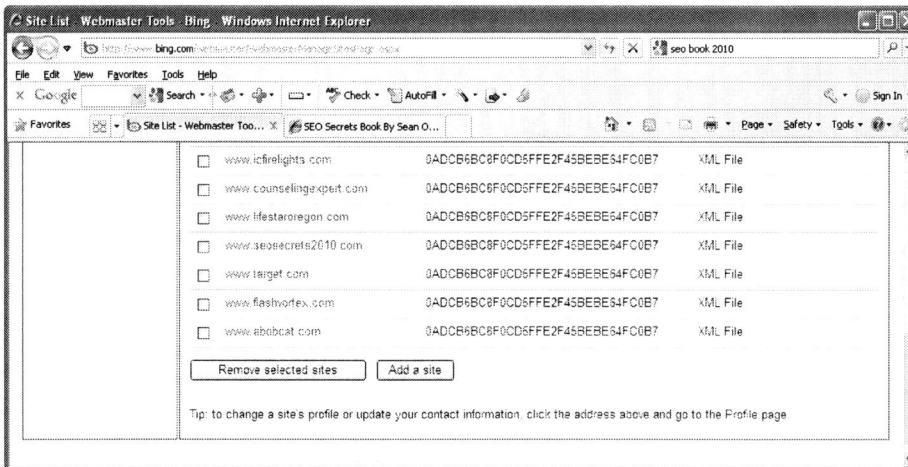

Figure 3.9

Step 5 - Submitting to DMOZ

DMOZ (also known as the Open Directory Project), as shown in Figure 3.10, is important because AOL Search, AltaVista, HotBot, Lycos, and Netscape Search all increase the ranking of your site if they are listed there. Follow these rules and instructions for submitting your site there:

1. Go to http://www.dmoz.org
2. First find the category that best fits your web site.
3. Choose "Suggest URL" in the top right corner. If it is not available it means that there are more subcategories and you need to drill down and choose the one that best fits your business.
4. Add the Site URL, title and description as shown below. Then select submit at the bottom of the page.

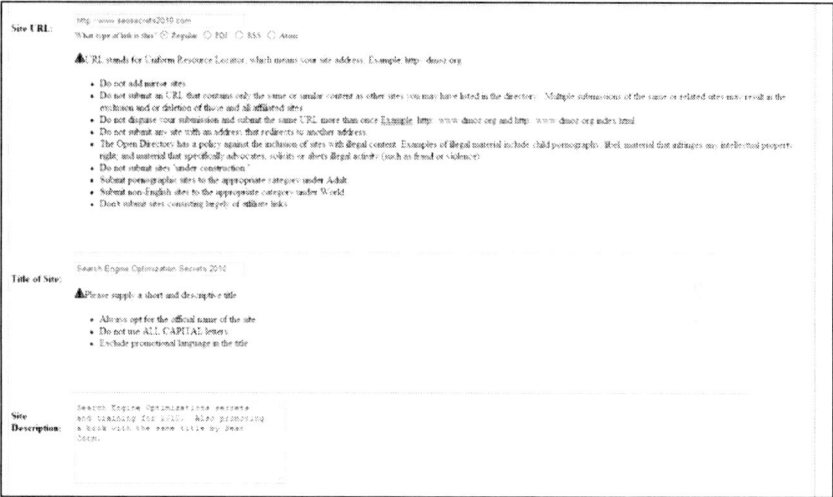

Figure 3.10

DMOZ has certain rules to follow, as seen on their web site:

- Do not add mirror sites.
- Do not submit an URL that contains only the same or similar content as other sites you may have listed in the directory. Multiple submissions of the same or related sites may result in the exclusion and/or deletion of those and all affiliated sites.
- Do not disguise your submission and submit the same URL more than once.
  > Example: http://www.dmoz.org and
  > http://www.dmoz.org/index.html.
- Do not submit any site with an address that redirects to another address.
- The Open Directory has a policy against the inclusion of sites with illegal content. Examples of illegal material include child pornography; libel; material that infringes any intellectual property right; and material that specifically advocates, solicits or abets illegal activity (such as fraud or violence).
- Do not submit sites "under construction."
- Submit pornographic sites to the appropriate category under Adult.
- Submit non-English sites to the appropriate category under World.
- Don't submit sites consisting largely of affiliate links.

Violating any of these rules can get your URL removed or not listed at all.

Step 6 - Submitting to Alexa

Submitting your web site to Alexa is important as this is another site that helps demonstrate your web site's importance to major search engines. To add your web site, do the following:

1. Submit to Alexa as shown in Figure 3.11 has a lot of weight to Google and other search engines.

2. First go to http://www.alexa.com/edit

3. Once you submit the URL it will give you the option to update the URL information as shown below.

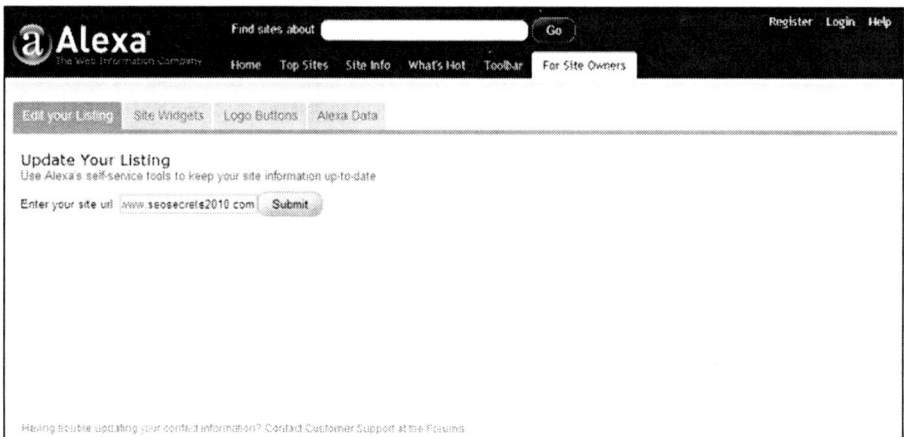

Figure 3.11

4. After you have completed the entry it will give you two options to verify the information: It can either e-mail you a confirmation or give you an info.txt file to place at the root of your web sites FTP folder.

5. Once you have entered an e-mail or uploaded the info.txt file, press one of the confirmation link buttons.

Step 7 - Submitting to AllCanSee

Adding your site to AllCanSee.com (as shown in Figure 3.12) couldn't be easier. To add your web site to AllCanSee.com, do the following:

1. First go to this URL: http://www.allcanseek.com/add

2. Enter a verifiable e-mail address.

3. Enter your sites URL and press submit as shown in the picture below:

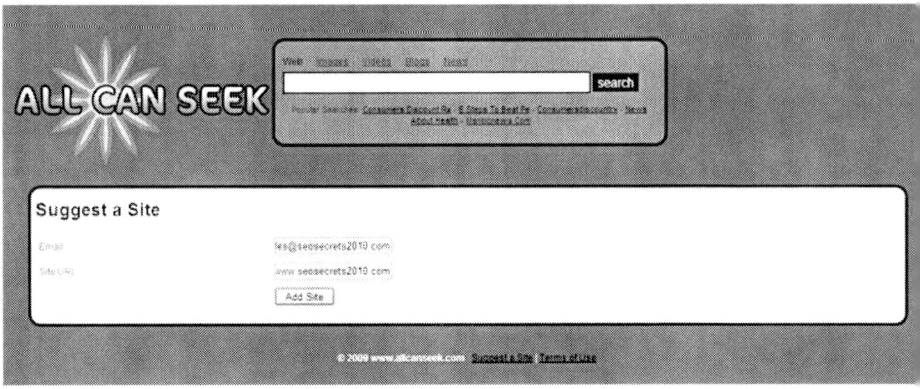

Figure 3.12

Step 8 - Submitting to CanLinks

CanLinks.com creates categorical links to your web site. Google and other web sites then crawl these links and give additional relevance to your site's rankings for your key words.

First go to the URL of: http://www.canlinks.net/addalink

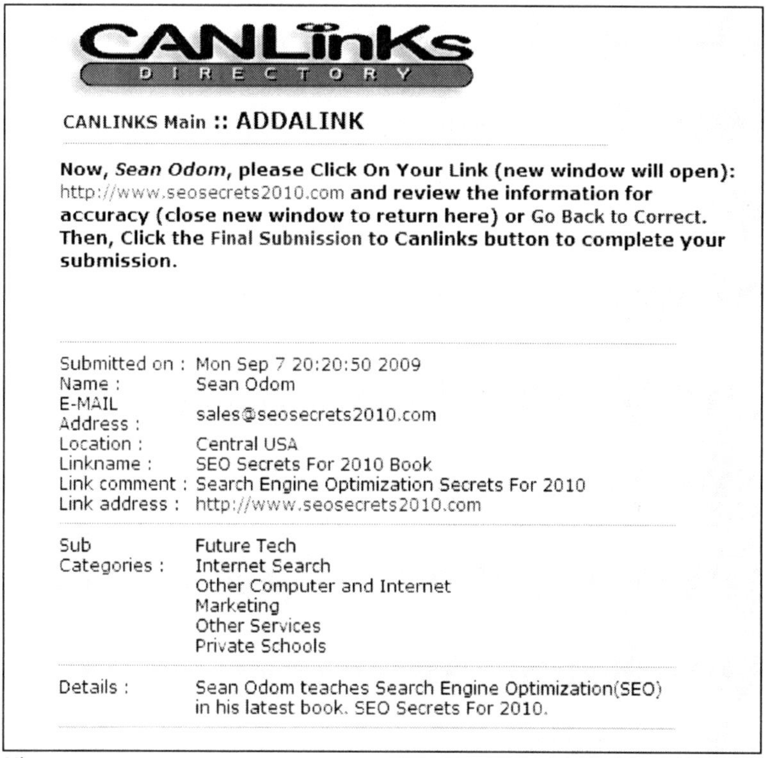

CANLINKS Main :: **ADDALINK**

Now, *Sean Odom*, please Click On Your Link (new window will open): http://www.seosecrets2010.com and review the information for accuracy (close new window to return here) or Go Back to Correct. Then, Click the Final Submission to Canlinks button to complete your submission.

Submitted on : Mon Sep 7 20:20:50 2009
Name : Sean Odom
E-MAIL Address : sales@seosecrets2010.com
Location : Central USA
Linkname : SEO Secrets For 2010 Book
Link comment : Search Engine Optimization Secrets For 2010
Link address : http://www.seosecrets2010.com

Sub Categories : Future Tech
Internet Search
Other Computer and Internet
Marketing
Other Services
Private Schools

Details : Sean Odom teaches Search Engine Optimization(SEO) in his latest book. SEO Secrets For 2010.

Figure 3.13

1. Enter your name, the name of the site, description, and choose up to six boxes which closely match your web site type. Then press continue.
2. The next page you see should allow you to do a final submission after you verify or edit the information you have provided.

Step 9 - Submitting To Jayde for Business To Business Web sites

Jayde is a specialized search engine catering to businesses only. To add your web site to Jayde, do the following:

1. Go to the URL of: http://submit2.jayde.com/

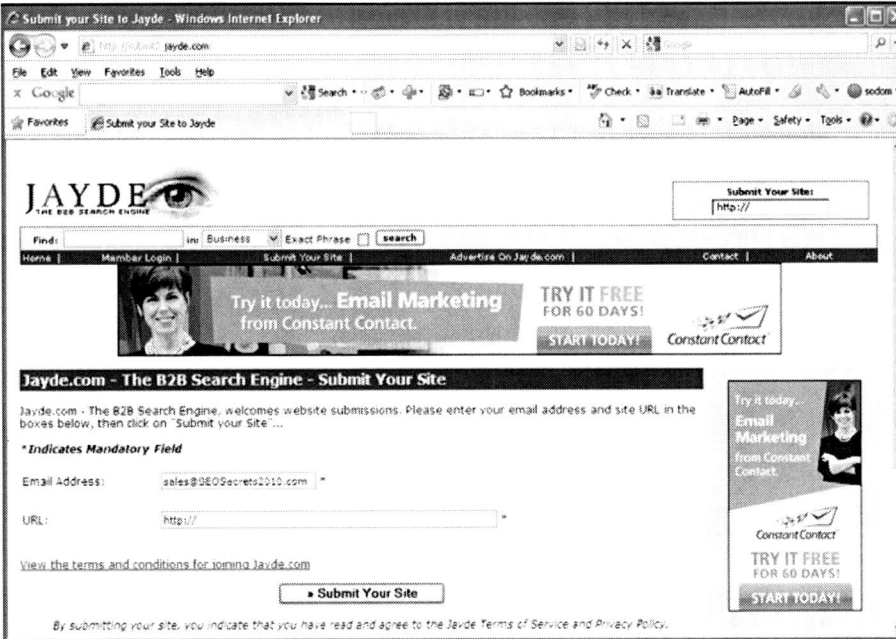

Figure 3.14

2. Enter your email address.

3. Enter the URL you are submitting and press Submit your site.

4. It should return with a message:

"Thank you for submitting to our directory"

Step 10 - Submitting To the Librarians Internet Index (LII)

The Librarians Internet Index is absolutely important to rankings on the major search engines. To add your web site to the Librarians Internet Index, do the following:

1. Go to the URL of shown in Figure 3.15:
   http://lii.org/cs/lii/create/todo

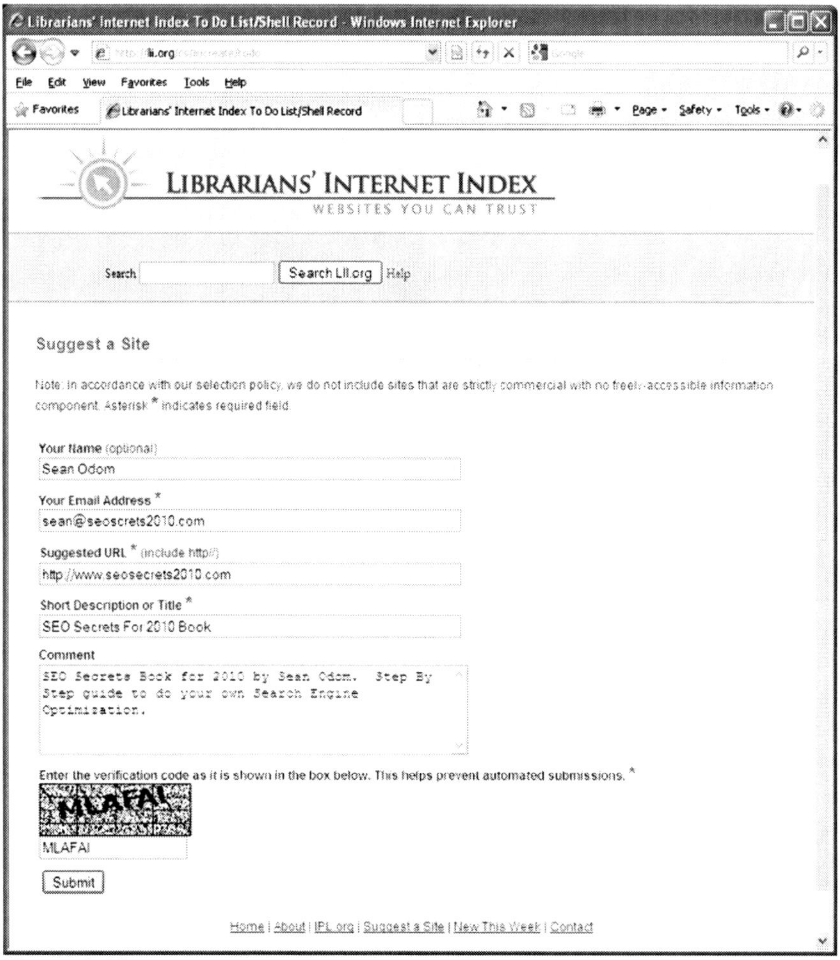

Figure 3.15

2. Enter your name.

3. Enter your email address.

4. Enter the URL you are submitting.

5. Enter a short description of your web site.

6. Enter a comment or a more in-depth description.

7. Enter the verification characters and press "Submit"

You will get a confirmation email that suggests registering your web site through their contact form as well, which I highly recommend.

They do have some criteria for what types of sites can be listed. You can find the criteria here: http://lii.org/pub/htdocs/selectioncriteria.htm

Step 11 - Enlisting your URL and company on Merchant Circle

Merchant Circle (as shown in Figure 3.16) is one of those web sites that didn't seem like much when it first started but then caught on quickly. If you have a web presence on the web you should join and list your business there. It creates a link to your web site as well as generates local and national advertising for your business.

Figure 3.16

Step 12 - Enlist your URL on WhatUSeek

WhatUSeek.com is a search engine used by businesses on the Internet. To add your web site to WhatUSeek.com, do the following:

1. Go to the URL of: http://www.whatuseek.com/addurl-secondary.shtml

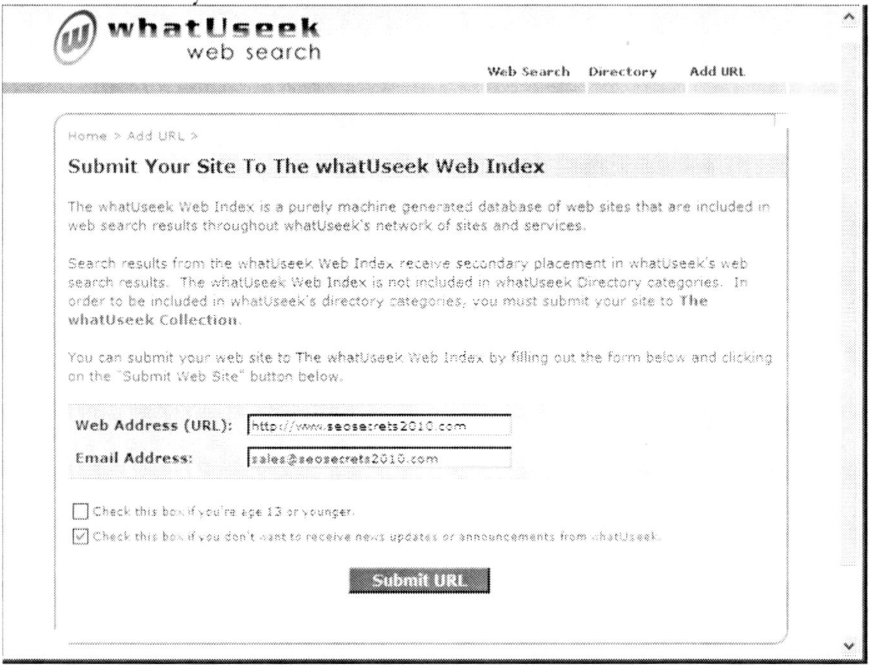

Figure 3.17

2. Enter your web sites URL.

3. Enter your email address, check the appropriate boxes, and press submit URL.

   NOTE: *Listing your company is free. However, the next screen will give you paid options which are not required.*

Step 13 - Submitting To National Directory

National Directory (as shown in Figure 3.18) is a directory, not a search engine. To add your web site, do the following:

Go to the URL of: http://www.nationaldirectory.com/submit.php

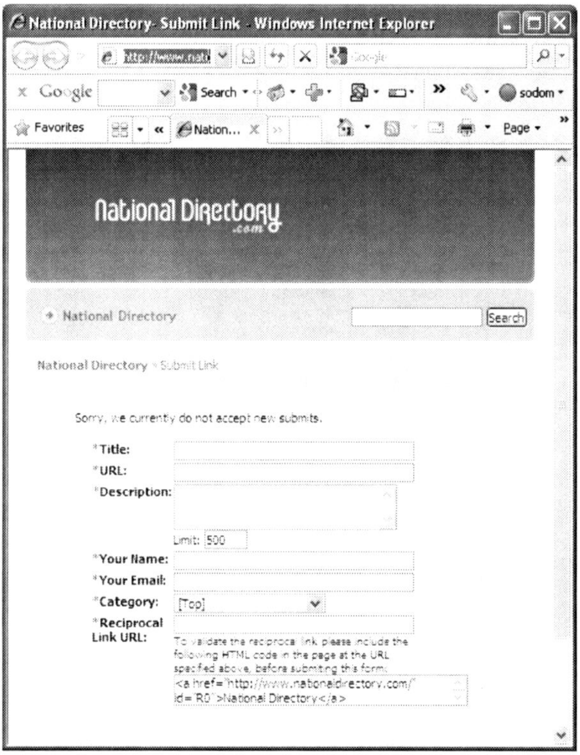

Figure 3.18

1. Add your title.

2. Add your web site's URL.

3. Add a description that includes at least the first three keywords in your keyword's Meta tag.

4. Add your name and email address.

5. Select the category of your business.

6. Add the URL of the webpage. You will enter the tag information they give you below to verify your ownership of the web site.

Step 14 – Using Web site Submission Engine to Make the Rest of the Job Easy

There are hundreds of other smaller search engines and directories, as well as major search engines for other countries. You never know when someone is going to use one of these smaller search engines; since you are competing with a lower number of sites, your chances are higher that the smaller number of users will find your web site a greater percentage of the time.

You might have Figured out that getting your site included in search engines and directories is no easy task. It takes a lot of time, research, and if you don't follow all the directions to the letter, you risk the chance of being refused for listing on web sites.

There are submission web sites which use custom tools that are automated software programs and applications that remember the repetitive information that must be provided in order to get your web site listed in hundreds of search engine and directories.

Many submission tools try to scam web site owners by promising to submit their site to thousands of search engines and directories for one low fee. The problem with that claim is that most of those search engines are either nonexistent or mostly worthless to your site.

You absolutely need help in submitting your web site to the smaller search engines and directories as there are hundreds of them. It would take you months to add your site to every one of these sites on your own. However, for about $15.95 you can have a company that specializes in submitting web sites do it instantly.

We highly recommend the Submission Complete (as shown in Figure 3.19) at http://www.submisssioncomplete. It's the engine that we at Website SEO Professional's use as well as many other SEO companies. They are reputable and always get the job done right.

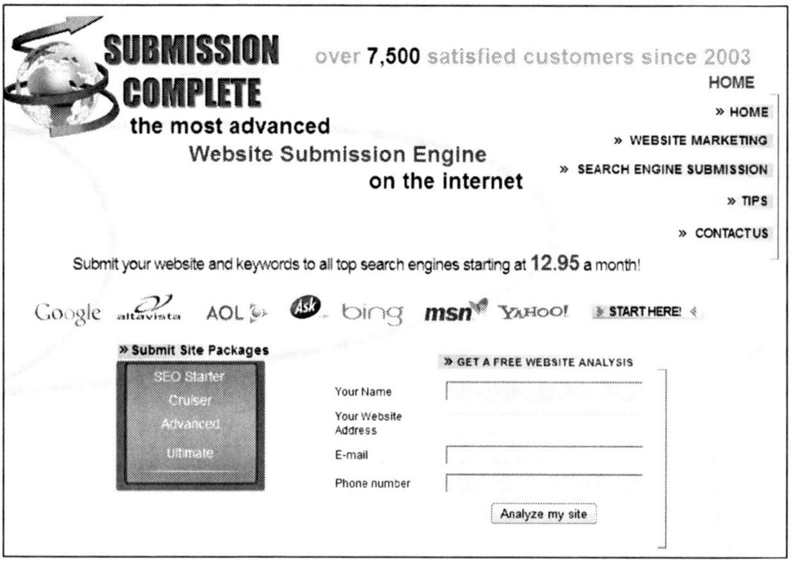

Figure 3.19

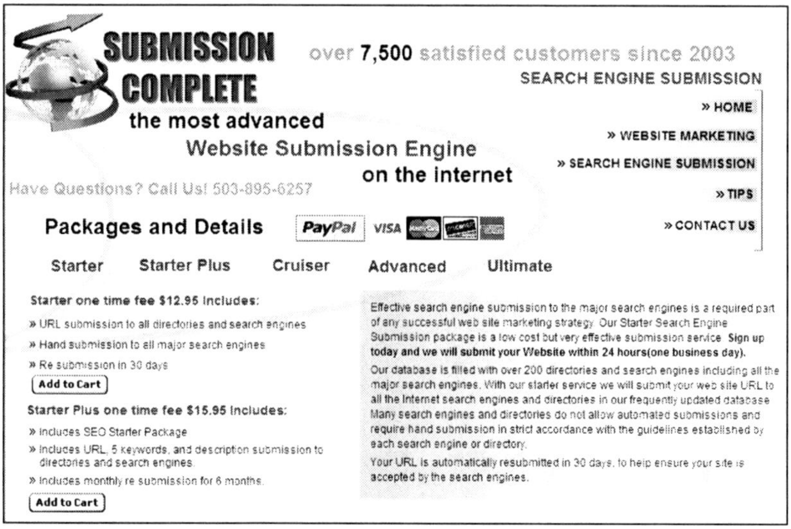

Figure 3.20

There are many packages that you can choose from in Figure 3.20. If you are doing your own *search engine optimization*, the bigger the package you get, the less you have to do on your own. In fact the high end packages actually help you decide your keywords, create your Meta tags, and scan your site of optimization problems. Most of the important work is done for you.

Chapter 4 – Local Business Listings

Local Business Listings help consumers find retail locations. If you have a local business or a business with local store locations you can list those stores in the Local Business Listings on either Google or Bing. Keep in mind that by listing the business on Bing you are listing the business on MSN, Live, and most likely Yahoo as well.

One of the great things about the local listings as shown in figures 4.1 and 4.2, is that they automatically appear at the top of the listings. And your retail location shows on the map that is provided as well.

Let's take a look at the Local Business Listing results for "portland pizza" on both Bing and Google starting with Bing in figure 4.1.

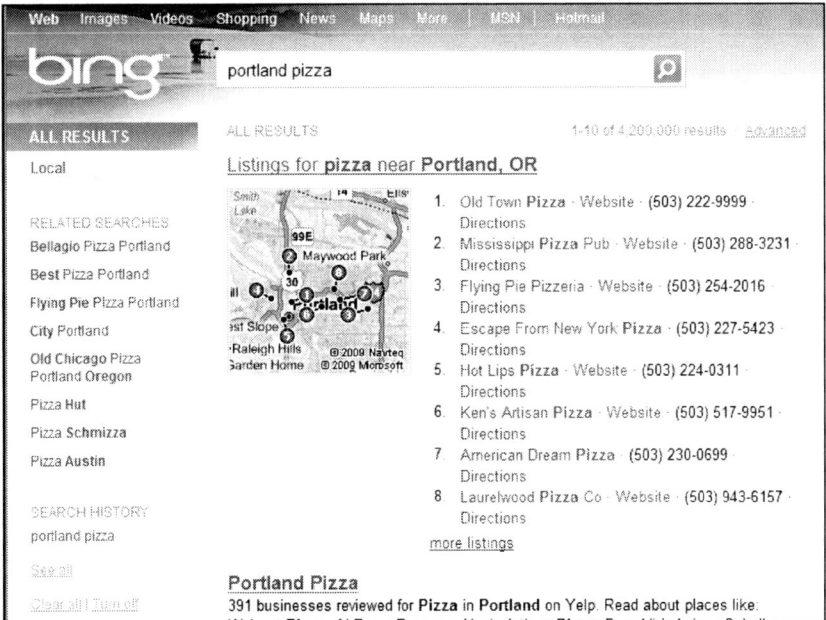

Figure 4.1

Next let's look at the same search on Google in figure 4.2.

Figure 4.2

They are very similar. Again, there are some differences. Google usually wants to see relevance to the search term such as "portland pizza". Bing not only wants to see relevance but also that your address is the closest to Portland Oregon. If your business is in Oregon City and you come up first in the organic listings for the search term, "portland pizza" you did a great job optimizing your website making it relevant to the search term.

On the other hand, your businesses physical address is not in Portland, so other companies that are in Portland or very closer to Portland will show up on Bing's Local Business listings before your company does.

There is also one other factor that helps in this situation. Each listing allows you to click on it and get more information on both Google and Bing Local Business listings. Each gives you the ability to see more information on the business and give reviews. It's these reviews that have some weight as to whom is shown on the listings.

A good recommendation is to give your customers a suggestion either by email or some other advertising form encouraging them to leave positive reviews if they like your product or services. Both Google and Bing are pretty good at identifying false reviews. Especially if you leave more than one from the same login or IP address.

So let's take a look at adding your business to the Local Business listings of both Google and Bing, starting with Bing in the next section.

Adding a Local Business Listing To Bing

First off you need to know where to go. And for Bing the Local Business listings are added at the Local Listing Center as shown in figure 4.3 at the following address:

https://ssl.bing.com/listings/ListingCenter.aspx

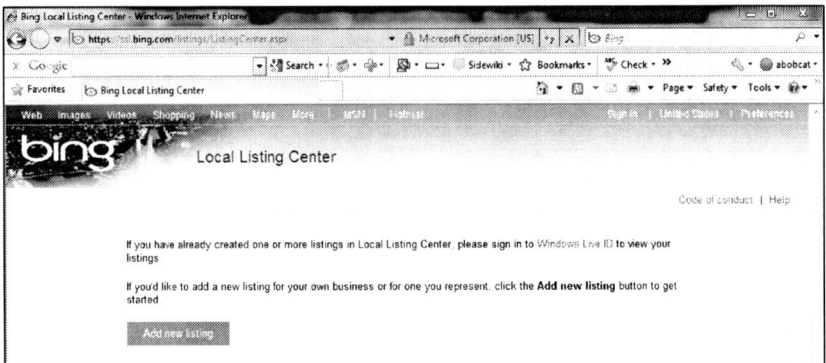

Figure 4.3

I can go ahead and add a new listing and create a login. I already have a login and so I will login and it will immediately show my current listings as shown in figure 4.4.

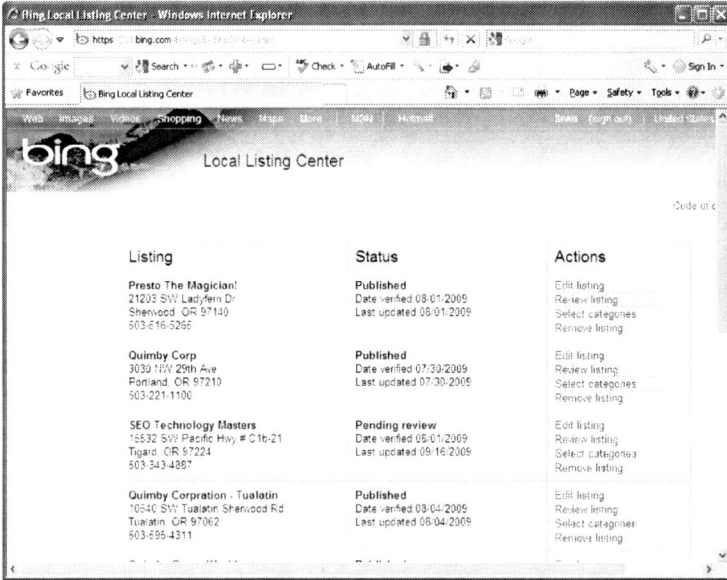

Figure 4.4

Now again, back to the website ICFireLights. I will use them as an
example and add them by clicking Add New Listing to the Bing Local
Listings Center starting in Figure 4.5. All this information is public
information so there is not any confidential information here.

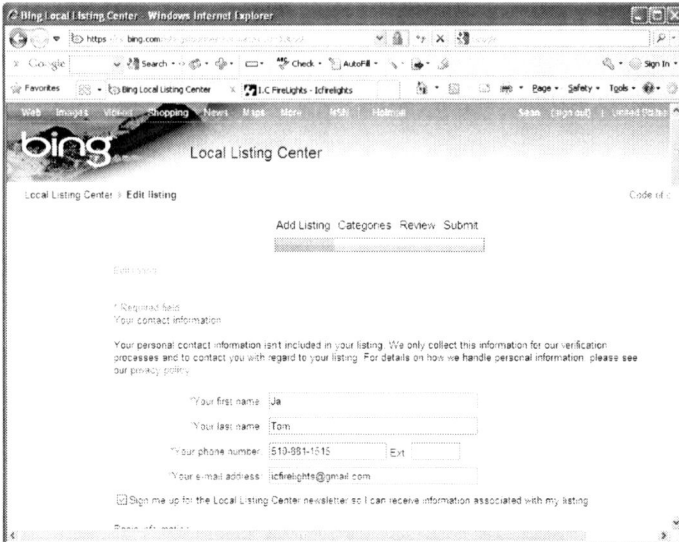

Figure 4.5

You will notice I only added the required name, and email address to get started. They don't have a public address so that was not shown on the screen. I also check the option to not display the address on the Local Listing. The next screen I get in figure 4.6 is the hours of operation. Since they sell online 24 hours a day I selected the first option stating that they are "Open 24 hours a day". I also clicked on all the forms of payment that their website is willing to take by checking each option.

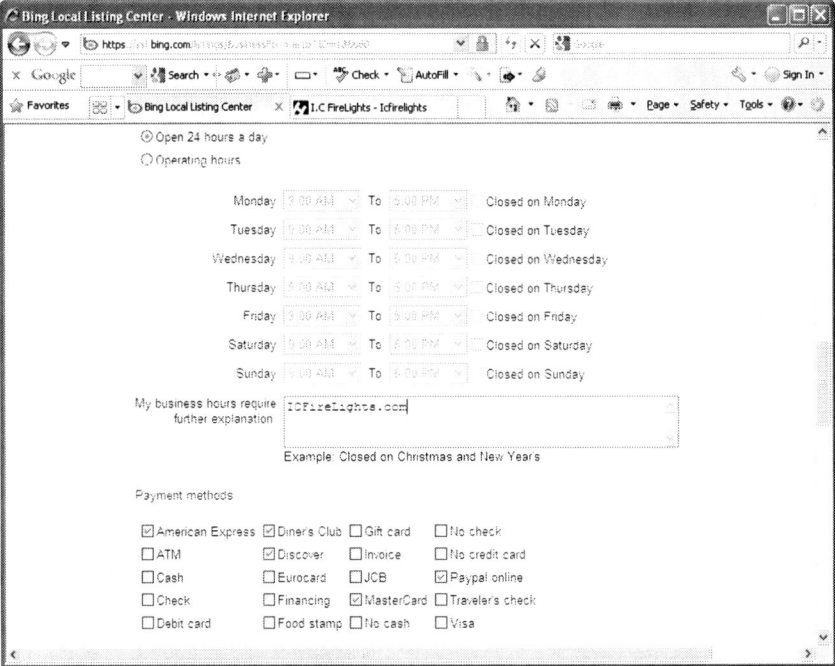

Figure 4.6

The next screen you get in figure 4.7 allows you to enter the year they were established, a tagline, business description, brands carried and any specialty items or services the business provides.

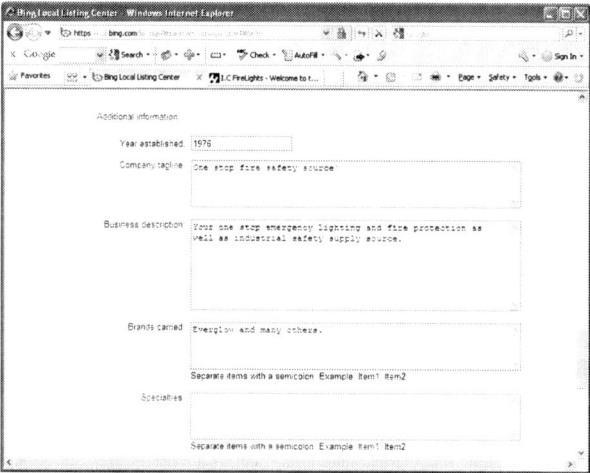

Figure 4.7

The next screen shown in figure 4.8, allows you to choose the predefined categories that your business falls under. You can choose up to 6. Choose the best that fit your company based on the keywords you came up with in Chapter 2.

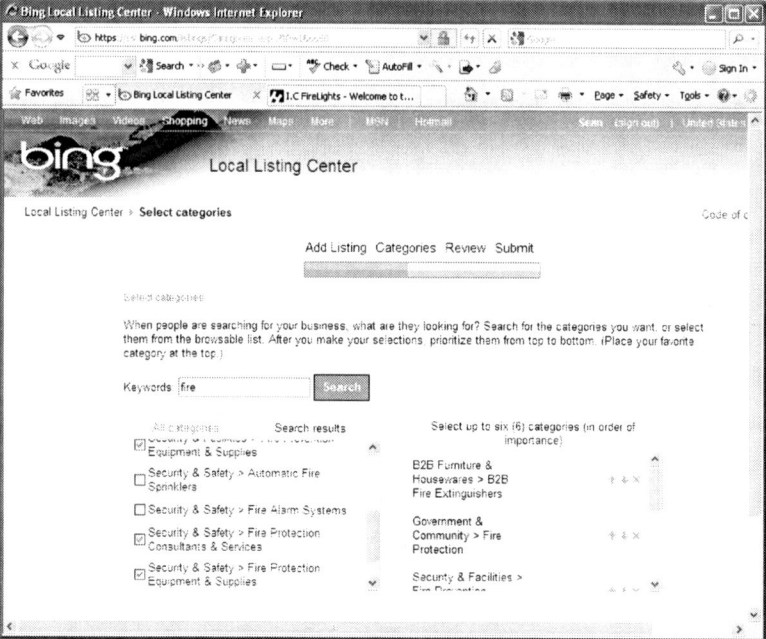

Figure 4.8

Once you have entered all the information in the previous screens, Bing outs all the information together to let you verify it as shown in Figure 4.9

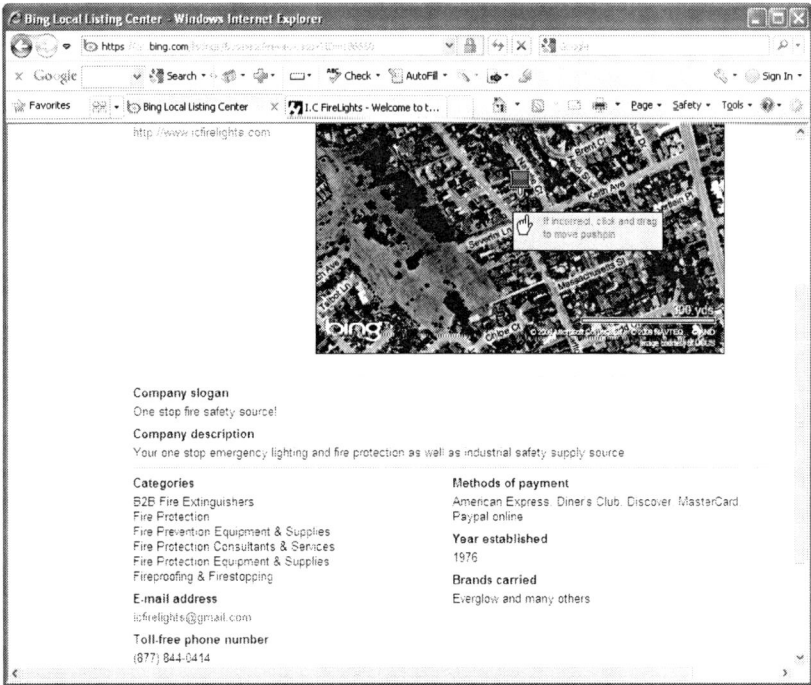

Figure 4.9

Next step is to verify that your business really is at the location you specified. Bing will send you a post card with a pin number to the address you entered. When you come back to the listings shown in Figure 4.4 a few pages back, the Status column allows you to enter the Pin number from the card when it arrives in the mail as shown in Figure 4.10 below.

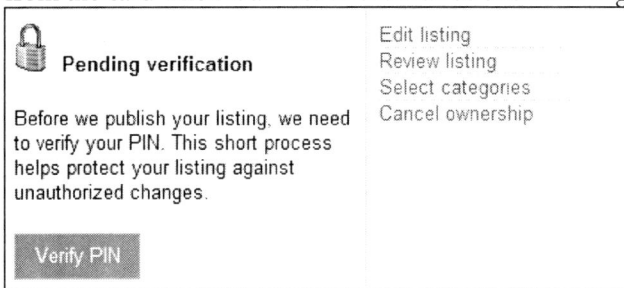

Figure 4.10

Adding a Local Business Listing To Google Places

First off you need to know where to go. For Google the local business listings are added at the Local Business Center as shown in Figure 4.11 at the following address:

http://www.google.com/local/add

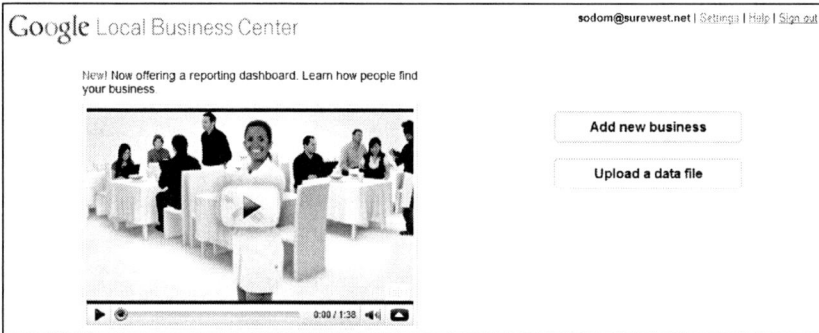

Figure 4.11

If you are already logged in to Google and you have been here before it will list all your current business listings as shown in figure 4.12.

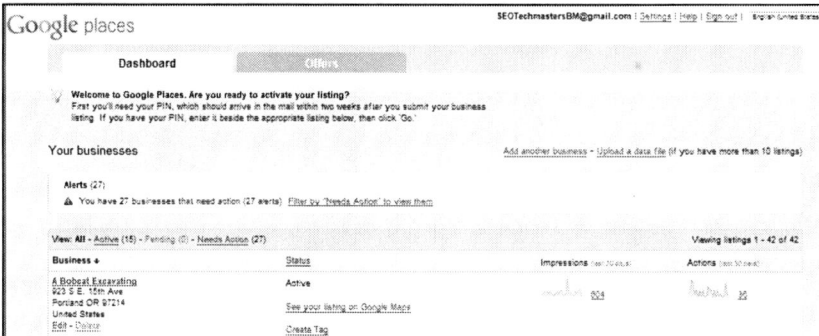

Figure 4.12

You will notice from Figure 4.13 that there are a few more options than we saw on Bing's version. Also you see how many times your business was shown on the listings and how many people clicked on it. Only recent information is shown. Notice the option to "View Report". This will show you legacy information and give you a more accurate view.

Since we are focused on adding your business lets click on the Add New Listing option and begin as shown in figure 4.13 and 4.14. I had to make it two figures because the screen was so large.

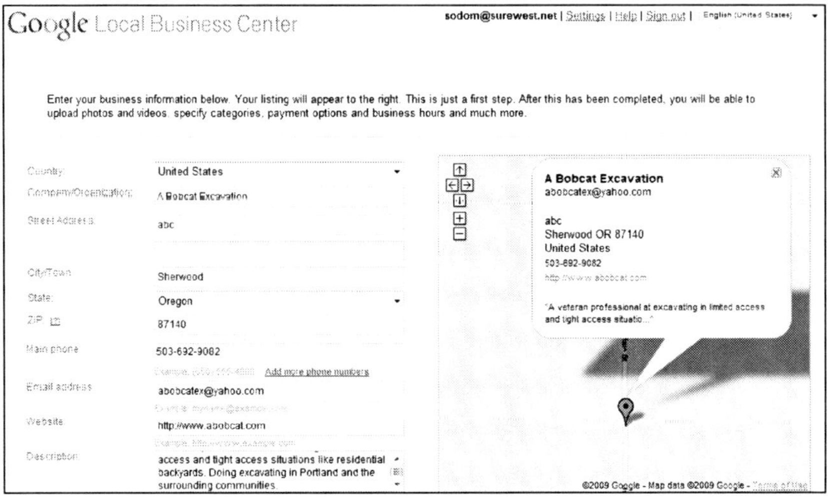

Figure 4.13

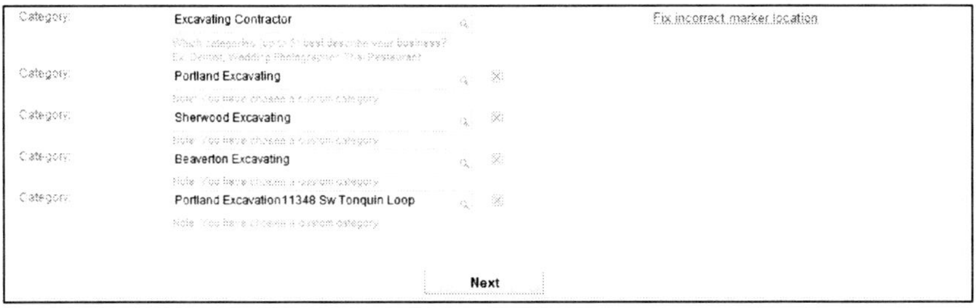

Figure 4.14

Then next screen you see appears in figure 4.15 below. This screen allows you to enter the hours of operation and the payment types that your business accepts as shown below.

NOTE: *Google has a complete guide to Google Places at: http://www.google.com/support/places/?hl=en&rd=1*

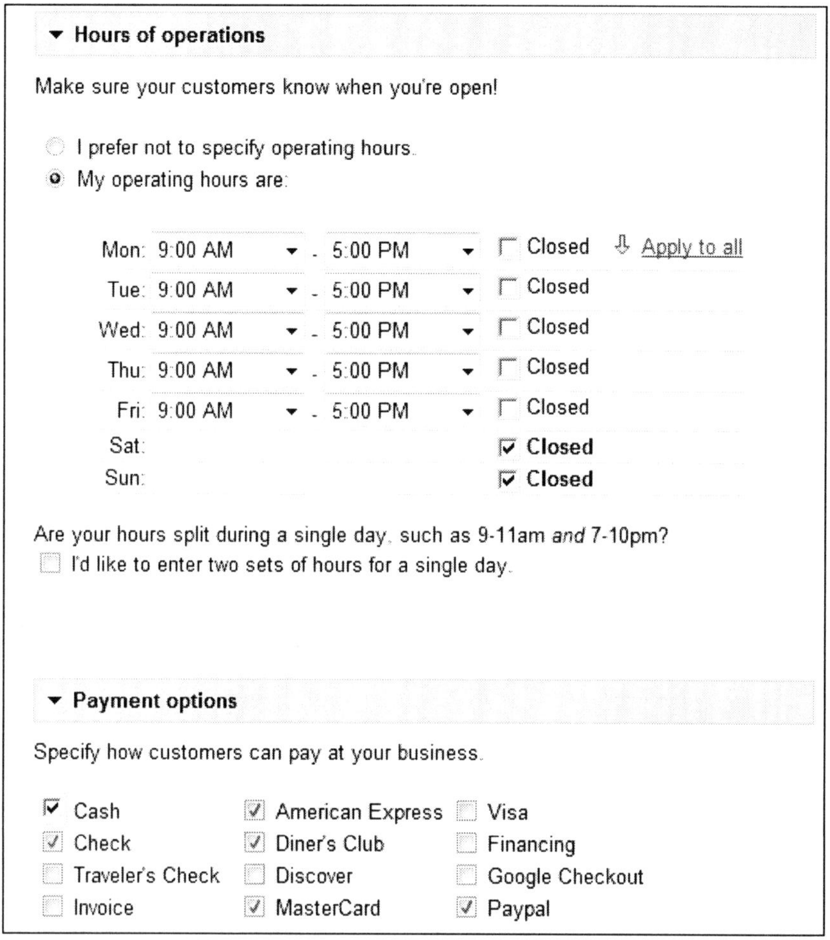

▼ **Hours of operations**

Make sure your customers know when you're open!

   ○ I prefer not to specify operating hours.
   ◉ My operating hours are:

Mon:	9:00 AM ▾	- 5:00 PM ▾	☐ Closed	⇩ Apply to all
Tue:	9:00 AM ▾	- 5:00 PM ▾	☐ Closed	
Wed:	9:00 AM ▾	- 5:00 PM ▾	☐ Closed	
Thu:	9:00 AM ▾	- 5:00 PM ▾	☐ Closed	
Fri:	9:00 AM ▾	- 5:00 PM ▾	☐ Closed	
Sat:			☑ **Closed**	
Sun:			☑ **Closed**	

Are your hours split during a single day, such as 9-11am *and* 7-10pm?
☐ I'd like to enter two sets of hours for a single day.

▼ **Payment options**

Specify how customers can pay at your business.

☑ Cash	☑ American Express	☐ Visa
☑ Check	☑ Diner's Club	☐ Financing
☐ Traveler's Check	☐ Discover	☐ Google Checkout
☐ Invoice	☑ MasterCard	☑ Paypal

Figure 4.15

The next screen allows you to add a logo, picture, and even video describing your business as shown in figure 4.16.

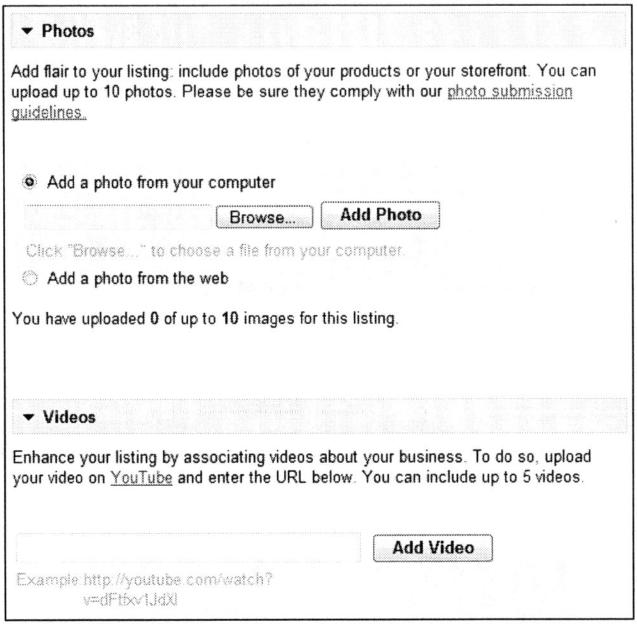

Figure 4.16

Lastly in figure 4.17 you have the option to add brands you carry and other details about your business.

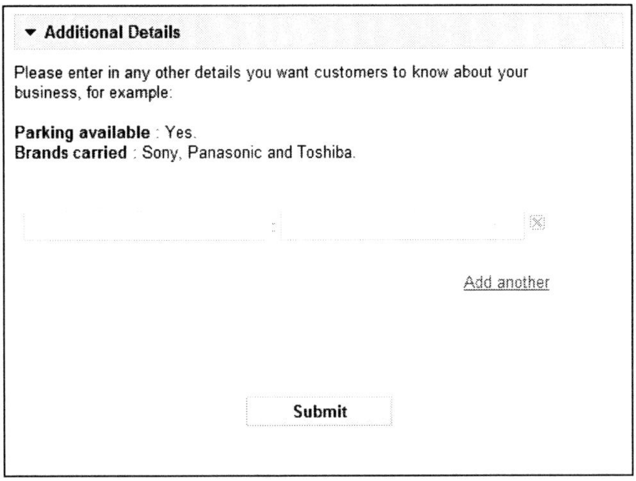

Figure 4.17

The last screen shown in figure 4.18 sums up all the information you have entered. You will see in the figure another customer of mine, Local News Day's information on Google Local Business Listings.

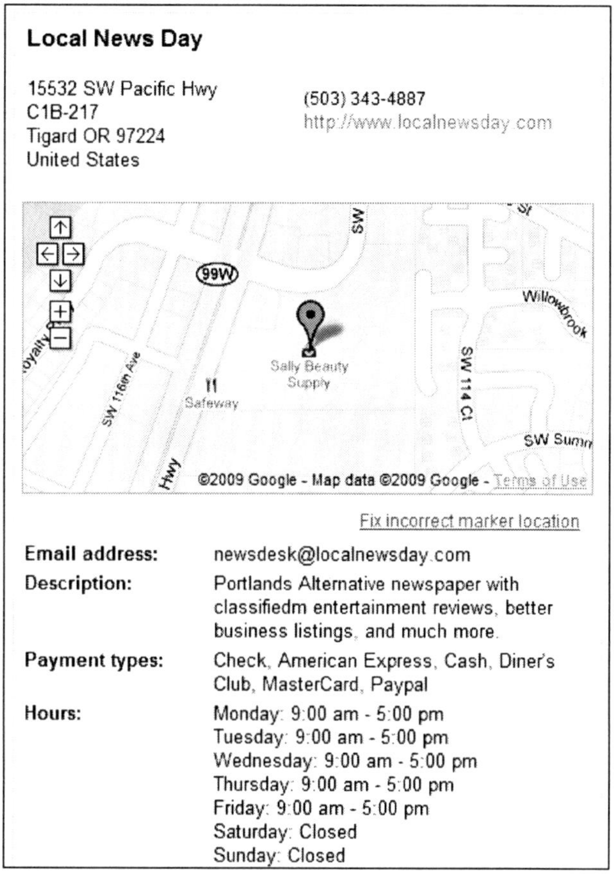
Local News Day
15532 SW Pacific Hwy
C1B-217
Tigard OR 97224
United States
(503) 343-4887
http://www.localnewsday.com
99W
Willowbrook
Sally Beauty Supply
Safeway
SW 116th Ave
SW 114 Ct
SW Summ
Hwy
©2009 Google - Map data ©2009 Google - Terms of Use
Fix incorrect marker location
Email address: newsdesk@localnewsday.com
Description: Portlands Alternative newspaper with classifiedm entertainment reviews, better business listings, and much more.
Payment types: Check, American Express, Cash, Diner's Club, MasterCard, Paypal
Hours: Monday: 9:00 am - 5:00 pm
Tuesday: 9:00 am - 5:00 pm
Wednesday: 9:00 am - 5:00 pm
Thursday: 9:00 am - 5:00 pm
Friday: 9:00 am - 5:00 pm
Saturday: Closed
Sunday: Closed

Figure 4.18

The last thing we have to do is choose how we want Google to verify our business. Google allows you to either verify the phone number by calling you and giving you a pin number over the phone. Or you can verify the address by waiting for them to send you a pin number by mail as shown below in figure 4.19.

Google Local Business Center

How would you like to validate your listing?

For your protection, we need to verify the information you've just given us. This can be done one of 2 ways:

○ **By phone**
We'll call you at this phone number (503) 692-9082

◉ **By postcard (2-3 weeks)**
We'll send you a postcard in the mail to this address

Figure 4.19

Verifying by phone is the quickest, but if you do, have the phone sitting right next to you because it is less than 10 seconds sometimes before the phone rings to give you your pin number which you enter in on the main listing screen which lists all the businesses you have listed on the Google Business Listing's as shown in Figure 4.20.

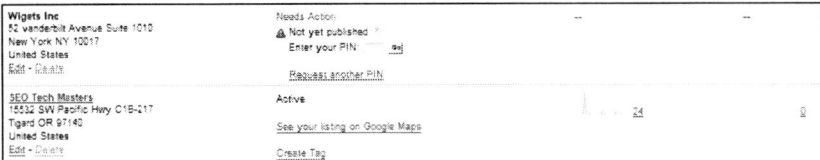

| Wigets Inc 52 vanderbilt Avenue Suite 1010 New York NY 10017 United States Edit - Delete | Needs Action ⚠ Not yet published Enter your PIN: [   ] go Request another PIN | -- | -- |
| SEO Tech Masters 15532 SW Pacific Hwy C18-217 Tigard OR 97140 United States Edit - Delete | Active See your listing on Google Maps Create Tag | 24 | 0 |

Figure 4.20

One more really interesting thing you can do in the Google Business Listing's is offer coupons. If someone clicks on your local business link next to the map on searches you can offer them a coupon. Once your business is verified go click on the Coupons Tab and choose "Add new coupon" as shown below in Figure 4.21 which shows a coupon offer I have already entered for a Free Network Analysis from one of my SEO customers.

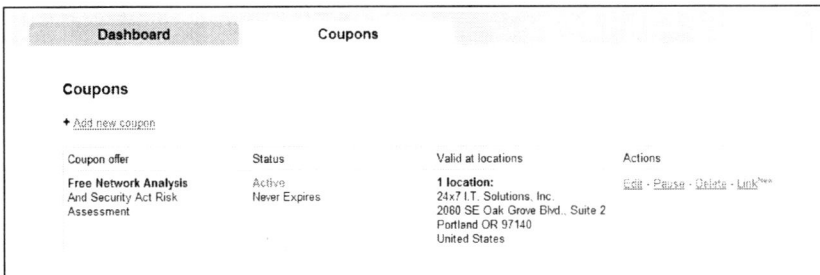

| **Dashboard** | Coupons | | |

Coupons

✦ Add new coupon

Coupon offer	Status	Valid at locations	Actions
Free Network Analysis And Security Act Risk Assessment	Active Never Expires	**1 location:** 24x7 I.T. Solutions, Inc. 2080 SE Oak Grove Blvd.. Suite 2 Portland OR 97140 United States	Edit - Pause - Delete - Link

Figure 4.21

So let's sum up this chapter. We entered our local business listings with Bing.com and with Google. Learned how to verify our company information so we can start being listed in the both search engines Local Business Listings, how to increase our relevance by having customers give good reviews of our business, and add coupons to our listings in Google.

Adding Multiple Locations For The Same Company

The store code is a unique ID that you can assign to each of your businesses. A store code must refer to the exact same store across multiple versions of a bulk upload These codes can help you identify your businesses at a glance.

Examples:

store1, store2
locationNY, locationFL, locationCA
101, 102, 103

> **Note:** *The store code must be under 60 characters in length and not contain any leading or trailing whitespace.*

Adding Your Local Listing To Yahoo!

Yahoo is still in the top 3 search engines and with their partnership with Bing.com, you can bet their share of the search engine market will only grow. Here are the instructions to add your website to the local business listings of Yahoo!.

1. Go to local listing to add your business at the following URL as shown in Figure 4.22:

    http://listings.local.yahoo.com/csubmit/index.php

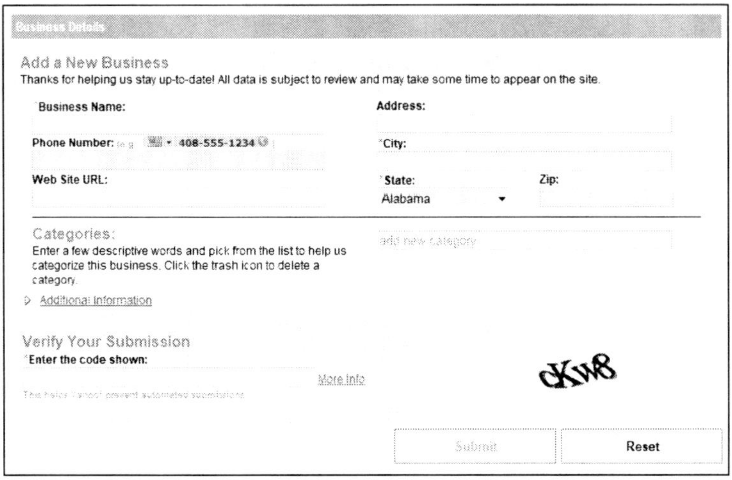

Figure 4.22

Enter in all your pertinent information for your business including your business hours, phone numbers, and the types of payments you take as shown in Figure 4.23.

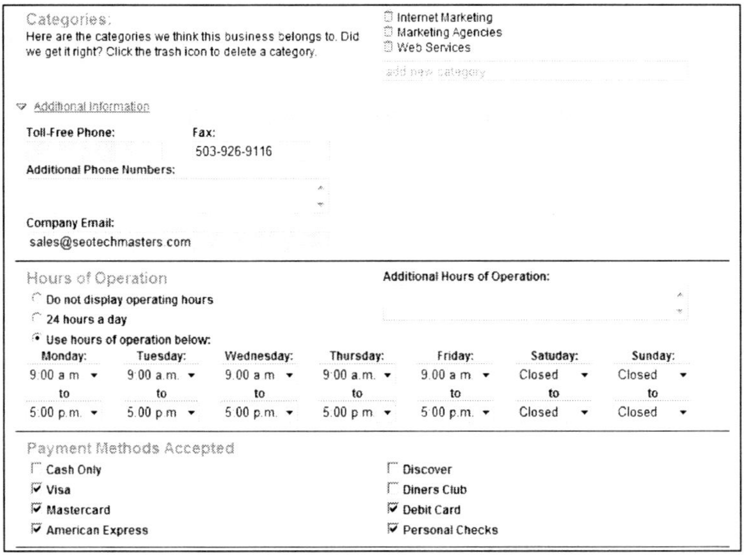

Figure 4.23

1. After you have completed entering all your information including the year and history and verification information press submit and you are done as shown in Figure 4.24.

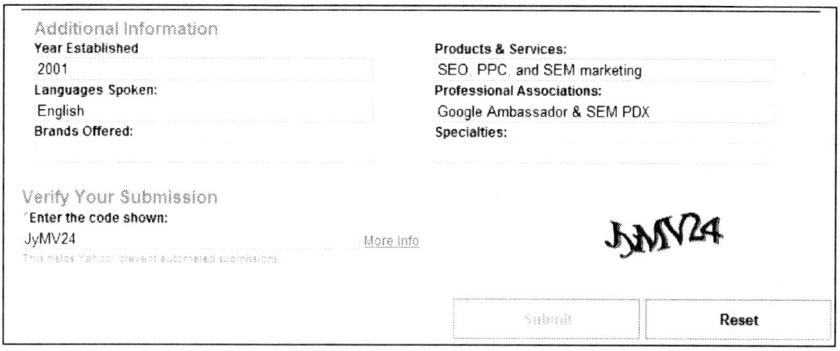

Figure 4.24

Other Local Listing Sites

ASK City http://national.citysearch.com/guide	**To Add Edit Delete listings on AskCity.** They gets editorial and user reviews from a variety of sites around the web including **CitySearch, Yelp.com and Insiderpages.**
TrueLocal http://www.truelocal.com/listabusiness.aspx	**To Add Edit Delete a listing. TrueLocal** is a **local search engine** free to hundreds of thousands of users. It is an Internet business directory with brains because you can **full text search** on it.
LocaL.com https://advertise.local.com/	**To Add Edit Delete a listing Local.com**, launched in August 2005, is a **local search engine** owned and operated by Interchange Corporation.
AOL local MAPQUEST http://www.mapquest.com	**To Add Edit Delete a listing** powered by Mapquest and core data provided by InfoUSA - AOL Local Search provides access to relevant information specific to your region. Find local businesses, breaking news and other information for your area.
YP.com http://listings.yellowpages.com/	YellowPages.com and YP.com registration is the digital version of the Yellow Pages.

Chapter 5 – SEO Needs To Be In The Design

This is the chapter that some of you will look at and want to cry. Probably because you spent tens of thousands of dollars on this all Flash-based, super cool-looking website that will do nothing to get you better rankings and make your site seem more relevant to the different search engines.

I often hear similar things from prospective customers when I tell them their old site won't work: "What do you mean? My site looks awesome! It's all flashy and things move here and there. It's awesome!"

Well, this is a true story. Last night before I started working on this chapter I met with a new client who is starting his own business doing psychological counseling. He paid an out-of-state guy to design his and his business partner's website.

Apparently there were disagreements on the design and layout; the site they came to a consensus on (below, in Figure 5.1) is one large picture. (I don't want to identify the site so I am only placing a little snippet of the site. There is some text underneath and above in the picture.)

Figure 5.1

It's a nice clean looking site with a spectacular picture on the first landing page. When I started discussing that he needed to have relevant readable text, RSS feeds, links, video, social media items, and more to increase his rankings, he stated, "Do whatever you want, but don't change the look."

Remember way back in Chapter 1 when I explained that Google and other search engines see can't read pictures? Here is what Google sees of this website (Figure 5.2):

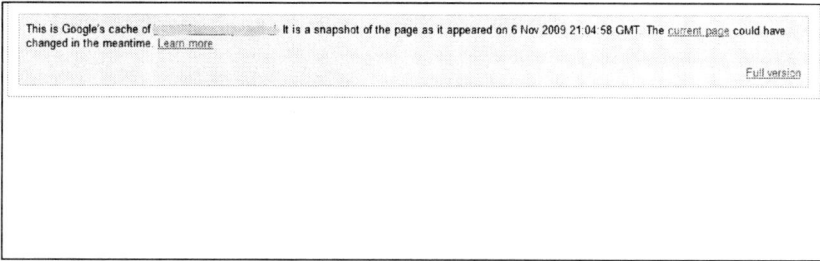

This is Google's cache of ░░░░░░░░░░░. It is a snapshot of the page as it appeared on 6 Nov 2009 21:04:58 GMT. The current page could have changed in the meantime. Learn more

Full version

Figure 5.2

That pretty picture on their website in Figure 5.1 is great, isn't it? No it isn't! Why? Because search engines cannot look at the text on pictures and index the information. They can't look at Flash or video either. Now here is the odd part. Having a little of each of those, including relevant text, pictures, video, and Flash, does increase the point ratio that increases your website's rankings on many of the major search engines.

So, am I going to turn a company that approaches me away for not allowing its website to be changed to optimize it? No. I am going to consult with them and tell them how to make their website increase its rankings, which is what I am paid to do. Then I am going to take their money and spend it wisely. I am an expensive person and if someone pays me for advice I am going to give it to them. If they choose not to use my advice, which others find very valuable, I will have no problem taking their money. They got what they paid for.

Also, this is something new that never came up before until this week. If you pay an SEO company to optimize your site during a site redesign, don't change the names of the pages that are indexed with the search engines. When a person does find you and the site file names have been changed, when they click on the link to your site, it won't work. There is a process to doing this if you really want do this later in this chapter.

What should come first, SEO or the design?

This really is the chicken and egg question of the internet marketing age. Depending on who you ask will determine the actual answer you receive.

A graphic designer will argue that in a majority of cases the design comes first, of course. Without an aesthetically pleasing design, a visitor will bounce off your site within a matter of seconds. Not so fast. How did they get to your website in the first place? A great-looking website is nothing if there is no one to look at it.

Even if you intend to employ Google Adwords, you will soon realize you are spending a fortune to make your sales. That is usually when the SEO expert gets called in because of some research someone did to see how to properly market a website. Then you learn from your poor design that it will take 6 months or so for the major search engine marketing campaign to try and rescue your website rankings.

Is this really the best way to go? The thousands of business owners that have been through this exact cycle will certainly argue that it most definitely is not the way you should go, especially when the owners of these sites realized when it was too late the amount of profit, potential, and clients lost because the design looked great to humans but was invisible to the search engines.

What is really laughable, though, is that if you actually read the sales pitch on any one of the myriad of web design companies own websites, many of them blatantly claim to be SEO experts as if it is a badge of honor or perhaps a must-have tick in the box. However, a quick check of their portfolios soon reveals that if they are search engine marketing experts, then it is clearly evident that their clients are definitely not on the receiving end of any claims they make.

 Can you implement site optimization into the design before you launch a website? Yes! The web design and SEO should go hand in hand. The thought process of optimizing a website and SEO-friendly website design should form the foundation right from the outset, so ultimately the content and design will capture free organic search engine traffic and also mark the website as a potential authority on the product or service.

You should remember that search engines don't care about what the site looks like: it's what's behind the scenes that makes the site so much more relevant to them. However, if we go back to the example above, my new client's initial chance to make the best impact on the search engine when the site first got indexed was wasted. In contrast, the extra time and money spent on predevelopment SEO, including the keyword research and SEO copywriting, gives an outstanding return on the investment of the website. This also gives you a far better chance of getting good website ranking from day one and even, in some cases, a page-one result faster than you might think.

If a web designer is not promoting web design SEO as part of your initial client brief, then they are selling you short. Now that you have read this book, even if you have only read Chapter 1, you know how to (look at?) the rankings of their referral sites to see if they know anything about SEO. If your web developers are not SEO experts or if they are not showing results in 6 months in terms of better rankings, the best practice would be to team up with an SEO professional to work with your web designer.

If you are implementing your own SEO, you need to set some SEO design goals for your website. Let's take a look at the different design or redesign goals for your website in the next sections to best design your website for both search engines and visitors.

Site Design Goals

If your website is a business, then your website most likely details the sales aspect of your business. Whether a visitor can buy right there online or has to contact you in other ways has to be addressed in the design. So when you design your website, optimizing your website is one goal, but making your website easy to navigate, getting more visitors, and getting leads are another.

Sidebar: Optimizing For Mobile Devices

SEO Tech Masters has recently started optimizing websites for mobile web devices. These devices include Blackberries, iPhones, and other mobile web devices that see things in a smaller screen. I haven't even seen this addressed in any books yet. But, as most companies are aware, the mobile Web is becoming more and more important in your web building efforts, which should translate into your SEO efforts as well.

As a company we have been doing Mobile Web SEO for larger enterprise companies for quite a while. As we have researched how to accomplish this, we have collected links on how to make your website mobile-ready:

- o **Bing Mobile:** discoverbing.com/mobile
- o **Google Mobile:** http://www.google.com/mobile/
- o **Google Mobile Sitemaps:** www.google.com/support/webmasters/bin/answer.py?hl=en&answer=34627
- o **Google Mobile Proxy:** www.google.com/gwt/n
- o **Mobile Search Marketing Guide:** www.mobilesearchmarketing.com/guide.php
- o **Tappity:** www.tappity.com
- o **Technorati Mobile:** http://m.technorati.com
- o **Windows Mobile 2003 Smartphone Emulator:** www.microsoft.com/downloads/details.aspx?familyid=8fe677fa7-3a6a-4265-b8eb-61a628ecd462

Add your mobile-optimized site to search engines and let retailers know (know what?) here:

- • **Abphone:** http://www.abphone.com and http://m.abphone.com
- • **Bing:** http:// discoverbing.com/mobile
- • **Bango:** http://www.bango.com
- • **Crispy:** http://www.crispyweb.com/submitmobile.htm
- • **Dotmobi**: http://mtld.mobi/sitesubmit
- • Google: Uhttp://www.google.com/addurlU (Put "Mobile" in comments)

- **JumpTap:** http://www.jumptap.com/content-publishers-submit-
  content
- **Medio:** http://medio.com/partners/addyourmobilesite/
- **Mobiseer**: http://www.mobiseer.com
- **Nokia:** http://europe.nokia.com/A4568518
- **Taptu:** http://taptu.com/a/submit?ps=Q1A9b
- **Sprint:** https://developer.sprint.com/site/global/home/
  p_home.jsp

You should focus on the results you want: more visitors, leads, and customers. Every decision you make should be focused on fulfilling those goals. Keeping that in mind, you might spend a bit less time worrying about the exact shade of blue on the callout background, and more time worrying about things that will improve your marketing results and keep visitors directed toward your goals.

There are countless ways a website design can negatively impact your results. In fact, I would say that more often than not, website designs done without an SEO professional tend to have a negative impact on marketing results.

Another problem occurs when you attempt to implement too many strategies in your SEO. For one, you won't be able to tell which of your strategies are successful and two, search engines don't like it when you lose focus. Most major search engines like to see each of your website landing pages centered around one topic.

Implementing one strategy at a time allows you to determine which strategies are working and which strategies are not. SEO campaigns are most successful when you concentrate on one effort at a time.

> **NOTE:** *One of the first things that attracts a search engine's attention is the actual design of your site. The Meta tags, links, navigational structure, and relative content are all focused on a single topic.*

If you have an existing website you usually have a lot of material that has accumulated over time. These items help your prospects find your website and help you turn them into leads and customers.

> **WARNING:** *When you do a site redesign, make sure you use the same links and file names for your new site. If you don't, the links that are on search engines will become useless. The proper way to change the site is to create the new pages with new file names. Use the Robot.txt file to tell search engines not to index the old links. In a few months you can get rid of the old files as they will no longer show on the search engines.*

The general rule is, the more content you have the more visitors you will have and the longer they will stay. This will in itself grow your business faster. A 100 page website will beat a 10 page website 90% of the time on search engine rankings. And a 500 page website is even better. if some of those web pages were written recently, that's even better. But remember, always keep the focus of each page as close as you can to a single topic and optimize that page, the Meta Tags, Title, and keyword density to that topic.

A little known rule that helps add to your imaginary point standings with search engine rankings is that the more often you update your content (while keeping it relevant to your website subject matter), the better.

NOTE: *Blogging makes creating new and updated content easy.*

You want your website design to attract new visitors and increase your conversion rate and the number of leads you get from your website. Over time you should constantly improve the effectiveness of your conversion tools, including your landing pages.

If you build a completely static website and have to go to a web designer, every time you want to set up a new landing page or to change an existing page, you are limiting your ability to quickly experiment and improve on the design. You should have a website that lets you edit content and build landing pages without having to know website code unless you know HTML, PHP, or XML well.

One of the rules you should live by is that you should spend money on resources and relevant content that attracts and converts as well as optimizes your site. You should not overdo a design that limits you to only one type of code, such as websites that include Flash. The code should be dynamic and easy to change. Of course, sometime the easily changed part costs a little more upfront, but not at the end.

If you follow the rules set forth in the last paragraph, you should be able to create ongoing content with a building strategy. When you have more content, you can grow your website. This will help you increase your visitors and grow your business faster.

When you have finished your website, you should constantly have conversion experiments. The key to driving your conversion rate and the number of leads you get from your website over time is to constantly improve the effectiveness of your website. Several sites can be used to test your website:

Website Grader (www.websitegrader.com) – Has a useful tool for measuring the marketing effectiveness of your website.

HubSpot Internet Marketing Blog (blog.hubspot.com) – Has articles about business strategies and inbound internet marketing. This site also has internet marketing software that helps you get found by more prospects and generates more qualified leads and sales.

The Basics in Our Design

We have already hit on the points here, but they fall into this chapter as well. So let's make sure our design or redesign has these points covered:

- Meta and HTML Tags
- Header Tag Content
- Body Text
- Links
- Alternative Tags
- Header Tag Content
- Other Items You Should Make Space For
- RSS Feeds
- Other Valuable Content
- Other Tips

Meta and HTML Tags

Meta tags are HTML tags; they just appear in very specific places on a web page. There are two Meta tags which are given more weight than the others on most search engines. Those are the keyword tag and the description tag.

Most of the Meta tags are also given some weight on less major search engines and directories. However, not all search engines take keyword and description Meta tags into consideration because in the past, these tags have been overloaded with keywords that were irrelevant to the website.

Header Tag Content

This is a simple attribute but about as commonly overlooked by web designers as the Meta tags are. The *header tags* are a bit different from other tags discussed earlier in this book. These are the attributes that set up the different levels of headings and subheadings on your website. There can be as many as six different levels of headings but typically search engines only look at the first four.

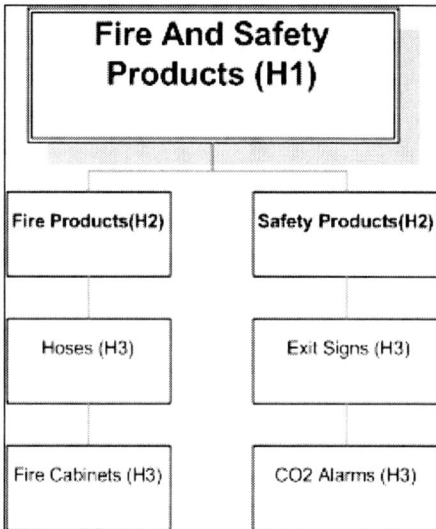

Figure 5.3

To help you understand this, the title or topic of a web page should be the H1 title that the human side can see. Subheading of the topic should be tagged with the H2 tag and so on–kind of like a tree (as shown in Figure 5.3).

So let's say you have a website that sells fire and safety products. The heading hierarchy in this example should look like this:

> H1: (Page Topic) Fire And Safety Products
> H2: (Main Topic) Fire Products
> H3: (Sub Topic) Hoses
> H3: (Sub Topic) Fire Cabinets
> …and so on.

If there is a new sub topic such as there is in the example, you would start again with an H2 tag.

> H2: (Main Topic) Safety Products

Headings denote important information and enable users to quickly skim the page to find the information they're seeking. The search engines use this in their scanning of web pages to determine what's vitally important.

Header tags on a web page should contain your most important keywords in a contextually appropriate manner. Specifically, search engine spiders, bots, and crawlers take into consideration the text within a header tags. Looking at the different levels of headings, first-level headings should contain the most important keywords on your web page.

> **NOTE:** *You should use your most important trophy keywords in the level-one heading, then lower-level headings (levels two through six) should contain decreasingly important keywords.*

The heading tags are similar in format to other tags that you've examined to this point and used after the <Body> tag of the website:

<H1>Header 1</H1>

<H2>Header 2</H2>

<H3>Header 3</H3>

<H4>Header 4</H4>

<H5>Header 5</H5>

<H6>Header 6</H6>

> **WARNING:** *Search engines are smart enough to know when your keywords are the same shade or color as your back ground and will penalize you for hiding the H1 tags or text that contains your keywords.*

Header tags should be included before the body-text tags of your website, and the text of the header goes in between the opening and closing tags.

Body Text

Like the Header tags, the *Body text* is also text that is visible to human readers of your site. When you look at the pages of this book, for example, the text that's between each of the headings would be the body text – the same way as it is for a web page.

The body text is another place where you want to include your keywords. A good rule of thumb is to use your keywords once in every paragraph as long as it makes sense to a reader.

Sidebar: Keywords in Text

Having your keyword strategically placed in your text on every page is one of the most important elements of any website. Of particular importance are the trophy keywords which we determined in Chapter 2. The trophy keywords need to be placed throughout the text on your primary landing page. It is of particular importance where those keywords appear and how often they appear on the page.

The keywords you choose must match the words and phrases that potential visitors will use when searching for the products or services your website provides.

You can also use additional tags to indicate special formatting in text. Those tags are as follows:

Bold
<i>Italics</i>

Strongly Emphasized
Emphasis
<li>New Line in List</li>

Each of these special tags indicates special formatting for the word or phrase in between the opening and closing tags, and the special emphasis makes a search engine crawler take notice of those words.

> **NOTE:** *You should try to use keywords within the special tags if possible. Only use keywords where appropriate, and avoid stuffing keywords into your site simply to improve your search engine rankings. If you use those tactics, they will most likely fail and may even get your site banned from some of the search engines.*

Sidebar: Things to Avoid

To make your website's body text visible to spiders, bots, and crawlers, avoid the following:

- Text embedded in JavaScript applications or Macromedia Flash files cannot been read.

- Text contained in images such as those with extensions .jpg, .gif, .png, and .bmp cannot be seen.

- Text that is accessible only on a submission form is not readable.

Most of these things make your site look flashy and cool. Site designers struggle with these issues and sometime choose looks over site optimization on purpose to make the site owner happy. There are only about 8 different fonts that can be used on a website without pictures because of the standards (whose standards?). Also, certain text styles cannot be indexed by search engines.

If search engine spiders, bots, and crawlers can't see your website text, then they can't index that content for visitors to find.

Links

You should have an area of your landing page dedicated to links. The links should be related to the content of the page and be active links to real websites. *Broken links* will lower your search engine rankings on major search engines.

Links have always been an important factor in how websites rank on the different major search engines. Most important are not only links from your site but to your site as well, as we discussed in Chapter 6.

Alternative Tags

Alternative tags for pictures and links are also important to have on your pages. These are the tags that are a brief description of a picture or graphic on a website to explain to spiders, bots, and crawlers what is displayed.

These Alt tags are also a good place to include additional keywords to make your site more relevant. Human users will never see your Alt tags unless they intentionally turn off images to enable web pages to load faster.

Other Items You Should Make Space For

Your website should have some of the below on its main landing pages. The more of these the better. Each one of these increases your site's value on different major search engines.

- A little flash
- Conversion page (submission page)
- RSS Feed
- Video (YouTube if possible. It is owned by Google.)
- Blog (BlogSpot if possible. It is operated by Google.)
- Facebook, MySpace, or Twitter Feed or Widget
- Links to other pages in your body text
- Text links to other pages in your website if you use pictures, maps, or Flash for buttons.
- Text that can change frequently.

Adding RSS Feeds

Really Simple Syndication(RSS) or it's sometimes referred to as Rich Site Summary is an XML-based content format for distributing news, headlines, content, and more about a website. It is almost a requirement now for higher rankings to have an RSS feed on your website or blog to rank well.

RSS Feed readers come in all shapes and sizes these days. The Firefox browser has one built right into the Bookmarks feature. I personally use Google Reader. (http://www.google.com/reader)

You can also create feeds for your own website so your audience can subscribe to them. If you update your content frequently and promote the feed effectively, it can help drive more steady traffic to your website.

Advantages of Creating RSS Feeds

This is an excellent way to bring repeat traffic to your site. Think about it, every time a web surfer opens their RSS reader to get the headlines for all the sites they monitor, they'll also see your site's updates.

Instead of relying on them to bookmark your site and return at a later date, their RSS reader keeps your site fresh in their minds.

Many entities are now pushing out their newsletters and switching to this method of content distribution because you don't have to worry about dodging the spam filters.

When you send an email newsletter more than half of those people won't even receive it due to spam filters or junk mail algorithms. With RSS feeds, you don't have to worry about that because you're not sending an email, your simply sending out a news feed for all the readers to pick up.

How to Create an RSS Feed for a Static Website

If you are novice in creating XML code, I recommend using www.feedforall.com for static websites. They have an easy-to-use feed builder that lets you create and manage all your feeds in one place.

Once you've created your feed you have to upload the XML file to your web server. FeedForAll.com will automatically convert your feed into the XML format so you don't need to worry about additional formatting or coding and make your RSS Feed URL something like:

http://www.yoursite.com/yourfeed.xml

Anytime you add a new article to your feed, that XML file is updated.

FeedForAll also has a built-in upload feature so you can upload the XML file right to your web server with their software, as long as your web host has FTP access.

Creating An RSS Feed From a Blog

Google allows you to create an RSS feed using their blog website Blogger.com. WordPress is another website type that offers a free blog equipped with and RSS feeds.

Other Valuable Content

Other Items that can be considered great content:

- A free whitepaper
- A how-to or manual
- A series of articles

- A YouTube video
- A podcast
- A badge or image
- A proprietary study
- A quiz, poll, or test
- A joke or cartoon
- A calculator or free software
- A blog or forum
- A wiki or knowledge base

Other Considerations for Your Website

For a website to rank well, the search engines must retrieve information from the website – not so much from the human side but from the coding side. The retrieval of data is a combination of the activity of the crawler, spider, or bots, the database, and the search algorithm used by each search engine. These three elements work together to retrieve web pages that are related to the word or phrase that a user enters into the search engine's user interface.

The algorithms change frequently, which is one reason this book is updated every year. In SEO, ranking is what you'll spend the most time and effort trying to change. Your ranking in a search engine determines how often people see your page.

How search engines rank a page or pages is a difficult science to figure out and changes frequently. Search engines don't want everyone to know the exact science. If it were known to everyone it would be tough to get on the first or second page of a search.

Ranking is such a large part in search engine optimization and appears frequently throughout book. There are some things that can give your website an advantage right from the beginning. Let's take a look at two: hosting location and frequency of keyword use.

Hosting Location

There are a lot of locations that we talk about in this book. In this section of the book, I will specifically refer to the location where you host your website. I have a customer who is in good straights now but had tried to handle his own optimization. No matter what he did he couldn't get his website off of page 68 on a Google search. At SEO Tech Masters, we do a complete SEO Report to find issues with the website. What we found was that the website was being hosted on the same server as several porn-related websites. In

SEO terms we call this being in a "Bad Neighborhood." That is where porn or blacklisted websites are using the same IP or IP Range as your website.

In this case, the website owner had bought his hosting on eBay for $42.00 per year. If you have a respectable business website, you have to be hosted on a respectable hosting provider. The Major search engines do not like to rank websites that contain pornography, racial comments, or other such content.

Frequency of Keyword Use

Websites must be relevant to the keywords you choose. So the frequency with which the keywords appear on a web page may also affect how a page is ranked in search results for that keyword. For example, on a page about office furniture, one that uses the words "office furniture" five times might be ranked higher than one that uses the words only two or three times.

When word frequency became a well-known factor, some website designers began using hidden words hundreds of times on pages, trying to artificially boost their rankings. Almost every search engine recognizes this as *keyword spamming* and ignore or even blacklist pages that use this technique.

Tips

- Don't repeat keywords in your title tags (give an example of this so the reader is clear about what you mean). Repetition can occasionally come across as spam when a crawler is examining your site, so avoid that in your title if possible, and never duplicate words just to gain a spider, bot, or crawler's attention.
- Include a call to action in your title. There's an adage that goes something like, "You'll never sell a thing if you don't ask for the sale." That's true on the Web as well. If you want your users to do something, you have to ask them. The title is never a bad place to ask. But include your trophy keywords there, too.
- Create a website that contains Meta tags, content, graphics, and keywords that help improve your site ranking.
- Use keywords liberally on your site, so long as they are used in the correct context of your site topic and content. Keep them relevant and search engines will keep you relevant.
- Include reciprocal links to your site from others as long as those links are legitimate and relevant to the topic of your website.
- Continuously encourage website traffic through many venues, including keyword advertising, reciprocal links, and marketing campaigns.
- Submit your website to search engines manually, rather than wait for them to pick up your site in the natural course of cataloging websites.

Keyword Density

One of the biggest design rules to keep is the number of times you use your keywords (known as *keyword density*). Most search engines allow a relatively low keyword density. Google is by far one of the more lenient in this regard when ranking websites. Google likes to see a keyword density of 5 to 7 percent – much lower or higher than that and your site is penalized. Bing, Yahoo!, MSN, and other search engines seem to be stricter and want keyword densities of about 5 percent.

Use a Word processing program to find out your total word count. Paste the HTML source code of the page into a blank document, then choose File, Properties, Statistics, Word Count. In Microsoft Office 2007/2010 it is found at File, Prepare, Properties, Statistics.

Let's move on. If you are optimizing that page for a single keyword, you need to figure out how many times that particular word is repeated within that 250 word total.

Manually scan the page and count every repetition of your keyword. If you have Microsoft Word 2007/2010, you should also have an Replace function under the Home tab all the way to the right. Paste in the code and then type in the keywords in both the edit box and the replace box. The program will replace each occurrence of the word with itself...and produce a total count for the number of repeats.

Let's assume for this exercise that you have used a keyword 10 times on your page. To calculate the keyword density - take that figure and divide it by the total number of words on your page. So in this case 10 divided by 250 = .04

Keyword density is always referred to as a percentage of the total word count for the page. So now you need to multiply .04 by 100 to get the percentage figure.

Your calculation would look like this;

.04 x 100 = 4%

The page has a keyword density of 4%.

For effective optimizing that will boost your pages into the Top 20 spots on the major search engines you are aiming for a keyword density of between 5-7%.

What you have just been shown is about as simple as it gets for working out the keyword density of a web page. To recap, the formula looks like this:

10 divided by 250 = .04 x 100 = 4% -or- keyword count divided by total word count x 100 = keyword density in percent. So you can add your keyword another few times without penalty on most major search engines.

Algorithms fluctuate constantly at the major search engines so it is much simpler to optimize a few pages for different weighting or densities. A few pages at 5%, 6%, and 7% keyword density will mean at least one of your pages should rank well on each major search engine.

Chapter 6 – Linking Up

It doesn't really take more any more research to show that the higher up the search engine results a site appears, the higher the chance of a searcher clicking through to your website. In other words for a business or it website it's "sink" or "swim". If you are on page 1 of a Google search for the keyword or keywords that relate to your website you get all the business. If you are on page 3 or later, you get no business.

As your ranking improves, so does your website traffic. The difference between even first and fourth page in the SERP rankings can make or break a business.

So how do the search engines decide the order in which sites appear in the results? Well there are a lot of sciences that go in to that. First is the science of on-page optimization which includes keyword density, outgoing links, social media, H1 tag, and more. Basically what the user sees.

Another is the Meta data science which we talked about in Chapter 2. Then there is the off-page sciences. Off-page there are a lot of items that are included in the metric that decides the placement of your website and this metric is ever changing. These include the content on your site, the domain name, the age of the website's domain name, and the relevancy of the site contents to the search query.

Google PageRank is based on Larry Page's (One of the co-founders of Google) that a website that has good content and is more important will be linked to by many. This is one reason that incoming and reciprocal links to your site are given a very high importance to its search engine rank.

Incoming links are links on other websites to your website. This metric is more reliable in search engines' eyes, because it is much harder to manipulate another person's website. If a link appears on the CNN home page, linking to your website with the term 'great travel website' in the anchor text, search engines can see that a highly respected site believes your website is worth linking to for the topic "Travel Websites". When it sees this it acts as if there is an imaginary voting system on the Internet and the link from CNN counted as a vote.

Not all links are created equal; therefore some link builders will spend months trying to get one strong link from a big, important, relevant site. Another link-building tactic would be to try to get thousands of links from smaller sites, which are presumably easier to get than a link on a highly prestigious site.

Once you realize the importance of relevant incoming links to the success of your website, you will understand the need to engage in link building and how a professional ongoing link building campaign is paramount to the success of your website.

Link building is one of the biggest SEO tasks. You can get your website to a Google PageRank of 2 without links, but after that your site needs to become relevant to the search engine with as many links as possible from sites that are in the same industry, related to you or news organizations.

There is a reason that search engines care about links to and from your website. Remember our imaginary point system from the early chapters? The search engines treat your incoming links from other relevant websites as a "point" for your site. The more you have the better. Some sites give you more points. News outlets such as LocalNewsDay.com, TheKnowOrlando.com, and CNN.com seem to help your rankings increase faster because Google sees them as an official news source. Other site types that seem to give more points are .EDU and .Gov websites that provide links to your website.

Just to give a little history, once webmasters figured out that links helped your rankings, all sorts of abuse started to occur. People started creating ways to beat the system including link farms, massive reciprocal link networks, automatically generated content with automatic links, and automated software that automatically posted to thousands of links on the Internet. Most of these links were never meant for a human visitor to see.

This is where the major search engines began to fight back. They didn't want junk in their results any more than searchers wanted to see it. Search engines started counting some links more than others, and discounting some links and types of links entirely. Then they started to ban websites for using these practices.

Now, link building is no longer a simple "more equals better" formula and the mathematics behind search results has gotten much more complicated. Meanwhile, the ability to use "right link building" has actually gotten a lot easier.

Right And Wrongs Of Linking

If your linking strategy is accomplishing the items in the Right Link Building column below in Table 6.1, you're heading in the right direction with your website linking.

How Link Building Affects…	Right Link Building	Wrong Link Building
Your Potential Visitors	Links that lead to good relevant content.	Links to content not meant for human eyes or deceiving content.
Search Engines	Links that improves search engine result quality.	Link that cause human visitors frustration and are unhelpful.
You	Links that are relevant and target your websites demographic, gives your website relevancy in your business or industry and ads credibility.	Links that don't drive relevant traffic to your website make your site seem cheap, fake, spammy or don't provide information related to the keywords used to find the site.

Table 6.1

How Many Links Does My Site Have?

There are several tools that can let you see what links are targeting your website. The two most accurate ones I recommend are Yahoo Site Explorer (https://siteexplorer.search.yahoo.com/mysites) and Majestic SEO (http://www.majesticseo.com). Google also has a limited link report now included in their Webmaster Tools console.

Places To Get Good Website Links

There are an infinite number of places you can get good links to your website that are relevant and will increase the your rankings. These are:

1. Websites in your industry (Experts, your suppliers, wholesalers, industry regulators, Industry training and certification sites.)
2. Charity websites, educational institutions, places you sponsor
3. Bhambers of commerce, BBB, Industry associations
4. Old sites with established domains
5. News organizations
6. Press release sites
7. Blogs and forums
8. Quality news articles
9. Websites from .gov and .edu sites
10. Social media and bookmarking sites
11. Customer review websites

12. Anyplace that you feel will bring you positive and relevant branding to enhance your company's credibility.

Tips For Creating Links

Anchor text is the visible, clickable text of a hyperlink (also known as link text). For example, if this were a website, then in this sentence, <u>this would be the anchor text</u>. You don't always have control over your anchor text. If someone links to you from their blog, or someone writes an article about you, the writer may not give you "keyword friendly" anchor text. In those cases, just be happy they linked to you. But, in other cases, you may be able to choose your anchor text.

Search engines pay particular attention to the anchor text that they are following. So, for your anchor text, use descriptive keywords and anchor text variants under which you would like to rank.

For example, if you own the site welding, you would want your anchor text . Especially when your text has your companies name in it and link it to your website. You need to vary your anchor text. Search engines view the links as more natural when you vary the anchor text. So, you don't want to use a link to your websites homepage every time your company name is mentioned. If they then talked about TIG Welders you might create a link that goes only to TIG Welders on your website or another.

> **NOTE:** *You should remember to use variants of singulars and plurals, your company name, and your website name.*

> **TIP:** *Pick up the phone and make a call to the administrators/editors for the website you want a link from. Such a simple concept, and one that's adopted by virtually every sales organization in the world, and yet the vast majority of link builders out there fail to utilize the phone, instead opting for mountains of emails or heaps of social network messaging.*

Build Links from Different IP Addresses

Now, if you're not link spamming, you probably don't have to worry about this one. But, if you are purchasing large amounts of links from questionable sources, and they say they'll put your links on 100's of unique domains, chances are they own all these domains. If they own all of these domains, then the domains are probably clustered on the same static IP address (The IP address of the server they host all their websites on.) Having a large number of links from the same IP address can be a warning sign to the search engines.

Link Juice

The term "link juice," refers to the voting power that a link passes to a page to which it links. The fact is only Google knows exactly how much link juice is getting passed on from each link on a page. However, there are some basic factors we can use to determine how valuable a given link will be. Look for links with these quality for better results:

- The page is relevant to your content.

- The link from the page to your page has good anchor text.

- The other outgoing links on the page look relevant and appear to be to quality sites.

- The text around the link that you will receive is relevant. The page has been recently cached by Google recently within the month. To check the cached date please see the instructions in Chapter 1.

- The page is a respected or authority page such as a charity, news, educational or government website.

The Orphan Page Link Test

An orphan page is a page that has no links from any other page and hence cannot be found by search engines. If you want to test if Google learns links. Please a link to the orphan page.

The next time Google indexes your page with the link to the orphan page, check to see if the orphan page was indexed by the search engines. If your orphan page gets indexed by Google, then there is a good chance the page you are testing is passing on link juice.

Linking Within Your site

It's easy to focus only on inbound links, but there are important best practices for linking within your site as well:

Site maps – Have one. If not for your visitors, for search engines. It's rough for search engines to have to drill down and find all that content. Make it easy for them. Oh, and keep it updated!

Anchor text within content – This may be even more important for onsite links that for offsite links. You have full control of your anchor text, so use it. Plus your site theme is already in place, so each link will have complete, natural relevance to the page it points to.

Breadcrumbs – Are a little piece of search engine love. Breadcrumbs are not only helpful for navigation, but search engines can pick up great anchor text from them. Breadcrumbs are the navigation elements that large sites use to help categorize content, and allow you to find your way back to core categories if you lose your way.

Featured products, news, etc. – Links from your homepage are, in general, considered more important than links from other parts of your site. So if you've got something you really want to show off, it makes sense to put it on your homepage, not only for usability, but for search engines as well.

Links to yourself – Link to your product or service pages from your own blogs, articles, resource sections, news releases, or any other relevant pages. Use the anchor text within each of these resources to send a little link love to your core pages. So, for example, if you sell toothbrushes, and you write a blog post about correct brushing practices, link the word <u>toothbrushes</u> from your blog post to your main toothbrush product page.

Directories

A directory is not a search engine, although the two types of sites are sometimes confused. A search engine finds its content by "crawling the web" via little roving programs called search engine spiders or robots.

A directory works completely differently than a search engine. A directory does not find content. It waits for you to bring the content to it. You submit your site, a human editor reviews and approves the site, and the directory includes your site URL under a category link (real estate sites, writing sites, baseball sites, whatever). Users can find sites by drilling down through categories and viewing lists of related sites. Many directories are *search*able, but that does not make them *search* engines.

Directories have been around for a long time, and submitting your site to directories used to be all the rage in search engine optimization. You'll still find plenty of services out there advertising that they'll submit you to 1000's of directories. But like all SEO practices that have been overdone, mass directory submission doesn't work like it used to. That doesn't mean, however, that directory submission is dead. It just means that you have to do your due diligence before submitting to directories. Some of the directories I suggest are:

- Best of the Web – botw.org
- Librarians Internet Index - www.lii.org
- Yahoo Directory – directory.yahoo.com
- Business.com
- Jayde.com
- Open Directory — dmoz.org
- Joe Ant — joeant.com
- Starting Point – stpt.com/directory

Social Bookmarking Sites

To get your links on social bookmarking sites, all you have to do is create a profile and post them. That part is pretty easy. Getting people to bookmark or vote for your links can be the tricky part.

To get people to bookmark or vote for your links, you need to be patient, and you need to be active on your chosen bookmarking site(s). Find other people with similar interests and colleagues that you already know. Share their links. They'll be more likely to pay attention to and vote for your links in turn.

Popular bookmarking sites include:

- del.icio.us - The oldest social bookmarking website and most popular. Users can also add people to their networks and share bookmarks.
- StumbleUpon.com – Has a browser add-on for saving and sharing websites. Works with IE, and Mozilla.
- Mister-wong.com - One of my personal favorites. The layout is nice looking and user friendly. Allows you to import/export.
- Digg.com - Digg allows you to submit stories, then digg users can "Digg" the stories, and make comments. Users can also upload videos, images and podcasts.

- Propeller.com - A social news and bookmarking portal that's part of the AOL network. Stories are submitted to specific channels, and then voted on by members.

- Simpy.com - Allows users to save, tag and search bookmarks, attach notes, and browse other user's links. Links can be public or private.

- Diigo.com - Allows users to bookmark, highlight parts of web pages, tag, add notes, and create and join groups. Diigo is also a collaborative research tool.

- Sphinn.com - Social bookmarking site for marketers. Allows you to share news, articles, etc., and participate in discussions

Directories

Search engines have not abolished directories. Google has simply gotten much stricter when it comes to acknowledging specific directories. Despite that, they are still beneficial for building page ranking and increasing traffic.

There are many different types of directories that can be of great value to your website or blog. You can search for directories on Google for good ones or for a small fee you can get your website submitted to thousands of directories by having services such as SubmissionComplete.com or WebsiteSubmitter.org do the work for you. These sites charge between $15 and $69 to perform the submissions. But it sure saves a lot of time.

Buying Text Links

This is definitely an example of what not to do. The major search engines do what they can to make sure a website's popularity is not increased by the use of paid links or link farm.

Buying links from sites that are very relevant to your website though will help you. If you've developed a reputable brand, a few paid or sponsored links could help drive traffic, and they are highly unlikely to hurt your rankings. When buying links, here are few things NOT to do:

- **DON'T** buy links from unrelated or poor quality sites.
- **DON'T** buy too many links at once. Make sure your link building looks natural (plan it out over time).
- **DON'T** purchase links from someplace that you wouldn't want to be associated with.

- **DON'T** purchase links from a page with a ton of other links on the page – try to keep the number of links on the page under 10.

Chapter 7- Optimizing for Major Search Engines

Optimization for Major Search Engines

- Optimization for Google
- Optimization for Bing, Yahoo!, MSN, and Microsoft Live

In general, search engine optimization basics are all the same. Each major search engine differs slightly in what it's looking for, however, so what makes you rank well with Google does not make you rank well with Bing (which, incidentally, provides the search results for MSN, Microsoft Live, and now Yahoo!).

It's still up in the air what will happen with smaller search engines that chose Yahoo! to do their search results but it looks like most will be allowing Yahoo! to forward Bing's results. These include:

- AllTheWeb
- AltaVista
- Go
- HotBot
- Lycos

So Bing is really a challenge to Google now.

In the next two sections, we will tell you how to optimize your website for better rankings with Google. Then we will explain how to optimize your website for better rankings with Bing. Included is a special report by Jason McCormick with SEO Tech Masters. He has done a three month study testing every aspect of Bing's search results using test websites which we have optimized and engineered specifically for testing search engine algorithms.

We will also include technical and content suggestions to help you rank higher with both Google and Bing.

Optimization for Google

This book has been focused heavily on Google, as it still maintains the lead in search engine searches. They have lost a lot of ground because of Bing and the millions Microsoft poured into an advertising campaign, but are still well above the fifty percent mark in internet searches.

Knowing this, how do you get Google to take notice of your website? What weights make your site rank higher? We are going to answer this question in this sections.

Google is traditionally, from my experience, the slowest of the major search engines to rank a new website – especially if you have a new domain name. Even if you manually register your site with Google using the steps in Chapter 4, it may take months before you can actually type in your domain name and see a result. That doesn't mean it is ranked either. Even with expert SEO it has taken me up to 8 months to get a new ranking on a site. Lately this has been around 3 months from notifying Google to actually getting the website indexed. I do this by putting plain text links on a few highly ranked websites.

Google Sandbox Period

The period between when Google is notified and it finally gets indexed is known as the "sandbox period".

How can you avoid the sandbox period when you need a new domain? My recommendation is to buy a domain name from GoDaddy Auctions(www.GoDaddy.com). Every domain you buy from the GoDaddy Auction is at least a year old and some have already had some pretty good SEO work done and there is already links to the domain. Domains are also available on just about any subject or industry.

One of the best things about buying a GoDaddy domain from their auction is the original date that the domain was registered on GoDaddy is the date that is listed when you do a WHOIS check. Google usually continues to index these domains and rarely puts the new purchased domain in a sandbox period.

Google doesn't sell organic placement, either. There are ads above and to the right side of the search results, but sponsored ads are the only placement that's available for purchase. That means that where your websites placement is based on your SEO and search engine marketing efforts.

Another heavy weight that adds votes to your website is the traffic to your website. You need to install the Google Analytics on your site to enjoy these additional votes to help improve the rankings on your website.

> **NOTE:** *Recently a lot of weight has been added to the Title Tag if it matches the first three keywords in the Meta Tags, the description contains the first three words, and the keyword density is around 7%.*

Sidebar: Google Caffeine

One thing that is new about Google is what is called Google Caffeine to improve how fast Google can index and deliver relevant new content. From early evaluations and hints dropped by Matt Cutts from Google, the algorithm hasn't changed but what is indexed and given to the algorithm has. One of the biggest changes is putting more relevancy on the "above the fold" area of the viewable content on each website page.

My recommendations to you is to make your website 100% relevant in the 800x600 viewable area at the top of each webpage. Place perfect keyword density, a relevant <H1> tag, all the links to your social media, and limit the pictures. If you do, Google Caffeine will be your friend.

Google PageRank

Google has a proprietary ranking algorithm and although they trademarked some parts of it, it changes frequently. An element of that algorithm is called Google PageRank.

Google explains PageRank like this:

> *"PageRank relies on the uniquely democratic nature of the Web by using its vast link structure as an indicator of an individual page's value. In essence, Google interprets a link from page A to page B as a vote, by page A, for page B. But, Google looks at considerably more than the sheer volume of votes, or links a page receives; for example, it also analyzes the page that casts the vote. Votes cast by pages that are themselves "important" weigh more heavily and help to make other pages "important." Using these and other factors, Google provides its views on pages' relative importance.*

Google PageRank is based on a balloting system that compares your site to all the other pages on the web that are of the same topic or topics. Then their algorithms take all the indexed information on those sites to determine which pages are most relevant to a search query based on numerous elements of the page.

An inbound link to a page counts as a vote of support, so links as discussed in Chapter 6 are very important. A page that is linked to by many pages with high PageRank receives a high rank if all the other components of optimization are in place. If there are no links to a web page, there is no support for that page. You will rarely find a page ranked by Google without inbound links. Know what the keyword density is or how well the other components of optimization are performed.

Google Instant

Google recently announced "Google Instant" in September and showed a new feature of the Google interface designed with a new search engine algorithm to improve the user experience. Google Instant is really about showing you more search results. Google Instant turns a search into a real-time stream of results which flow onto your screen as you type your query as shown below in Figure 7.1 as I start typing in a search for pocket knives.

Figure 7.1

With each letter you type, a whole new set of results displays on the screen. This is important for several reasons. First, you will now see many more search results than you would have otherwise. Most people never click through to the second page of search results so this is a way for Google to display several more pages of results.

If it is not in the first ten blue links (or really the first five or six), it might as well not exist for most people. With a Google Instant search, instead of people seeing only ten results, they may now see 50 or 100 (depending on how many letters they type and how far they get through each search query).

After testing the changes brought on by testing the results of Google Instant, several configurations clearly have an advantage. Those websites who have the key search words in their domain name or as the very first word(s) in the title that the users are searching for are not really effected by the change. Also those websites who have changed their pages to be completely relevant for only one keyword or one long-tail keyword are reaping the rewards of Google Instant.

I had theorized for a long time that Google would find a way to change the search to allow a page to be relevant for only one search term for quite some time and they found the way to deliver it.

From here on out you need to look at your pages either modify your current pages or add pages so that your pages are optimized for only a single search terms or the search term and the plural version. As an example, if your search term is a medical supply website selling beakers, you would make your title:

Beaker | Beakers

You should also have the keywords in your Meta Keywords tag and in the Meta Description tag as well. If you don't know what I am talking about, refer back to Chapter 2.

For many large websites creating new pages focusing on just one product, service, or keyword is a burden, but the sooner the changes are made, the sooner you will reap the rewards. Many companies are seeing their full keyword position not changing and do not realize they are losing visits because they are not optimized for Google Instant.

If you make changes right away, you will reap the immediate reward of being found in searches before others catch on to the changes they need.

According to Google, its classic search interface took nine seconds on average for each search results to be returned. The new interface utilizing Google Instant algorithm saves 2-5 seconds per search.

Optimizing Google Instant For Products

Research is important as well as the placement of the keywords in your Title and Meta tagging.

Use common sense when writing a post or optimizing for Google Instant. Always use keywords from the user perspective. What do I mean? Let's say you are selling a Motorola Droid X cell phone.

To research the users keyword or words, analyze the Google Instant search results about how users interacted previously with search terms by typing some related keywords for your product.

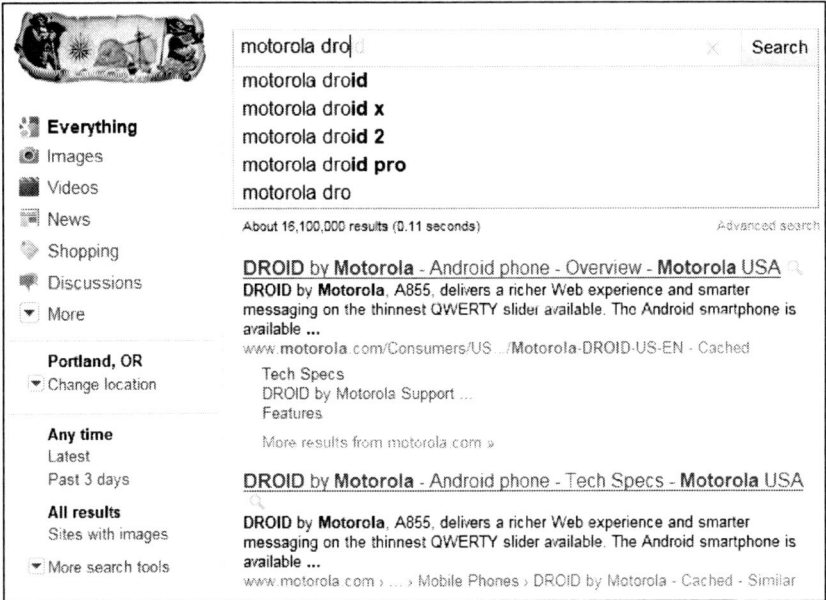

Figure 7.2

The above screenshot (Figure 7.2) is popping up some search results for the keyword "Droid By Motorola" which is based on previous search keywords used by the Google search engine users. You will notice that Google search suggestions are indicated as well and you can see that as you spell all the way to "Motorola Droid X". Every keyword that comes up in between would be an individual page I would recommend you optimize for that keyword.

If you are writing a review or a blog post it would also be better to include all those phrases or keywords as well in your post. If you include all the terms you researched in your post or page titles it will increase the probability of your website being listed under Google Instant search results.

Google Webmaster Tools

Google has some general guidelines if you want to rank successfully. These guidelines and recommendations are laid out on Google's Webmaster Central (www.google.com/webmasters) which we explained in Chapter 4. You will also find tools available at Webmaster Central that enable you to analyze your site to help make it more Google-friendly. Those tools include the following:

- **Site Status Wizard**: This tool helps you to determine whether your site is currently being indexed by Google.
- **Webmaster Tools:** A set of tools designed to help you improve the indexing and ranking of your site and adding a link to your website's site map.
- **Google Site Map Generator:** Under the Webmaster Tools you can find the Google Sitemap Generator to make a sitemap of your website.
- **Content Submission Tools:** This tools is used to submit your site to Google, or to add products to Google Base or content to Google Book Search.
- **Google's Webmaster Blog:** Here you can find tips and strategies for ranking well in Google. Also you will find information on how the Google algorithm has changed.
- Webmaster Help Center: If you don't understand something about Webmaster Central, here's where you'll find an explanation.

Some of the things that you should pay close attention to and follow through with is:

- Submit a sitemap of your site so Google knows what pages they should index.
- Tell Google what the canonical URL you want to use (site.com or www.site.com).
- Detect issues with duplicate title tags and meta descriptions.
- See a list of URLs restricted by robots.txt.
- Detect crawlability issues.
- Find 404 error pages.
- See the most common keywords people find your site through.
- Get a list of links pointing to your site.
- Tell Google how they should index your images.

iGoogle

Other useful tools for improving your search engine rankings are the various Google APIs (Application Programming Interfaces) that are available at iGoogle.com, as shown in Figure 7.3. These programming interfaces enable you to use Google technology to do many things, but most are geared toward improving the optimization of your website.

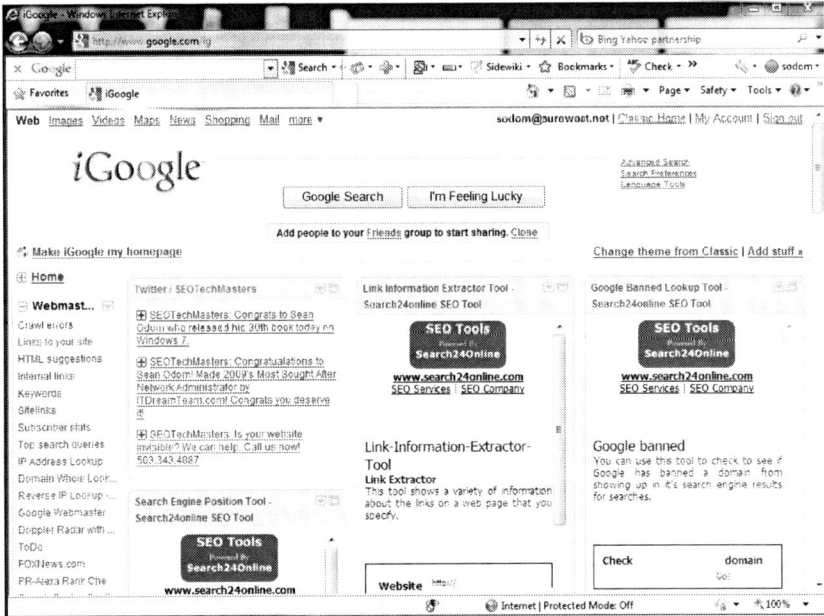

Figure 7.3

There are many help tools on the site to help you optimize your website. Many of them are pay-to-use tools, but usually you can find a free tool to do the same thing as the paid ones.

The use of Google APIs should be limited to creating applications and gadgets that your site visitors find useful. When you fulfill a need, visitors to your site continuously return, and that builds momentum. This in turn improves your search rankings simply on the merits of traffic and usability. That's a great vote for your site and Google will notice.

Pushing Your Google Optimization Over The Top

Along with great keyword densities and good Meta tagging, there are some things that can really push your Google optimization over the top.

1. Submit a video sitemap through the Google Webmaster Tool

> You should use the Google Webmaster tools provided by the major search engines. Among other wonderful things, they accept XML sitemap submission, which directly tells the search engine about every web page on your site you wish to be indexed. A

video sitemap does exactly what you think, it helps search engines find all your videos. For more information follow the instructions here:
(http://www.google.com/support/webmasters/bin/answer.py?h l=en&answer=80472)

2. Make sure your video format is supported by Google.

Google sitemaps only accepts the .mpg, .mpeg, .mp4, .m4v, .mov, .wmv, .avi, .asf, .ra, .ram and .flv files.

3. Use the Robots.txt file properly

Google doesn't ignore the robots.txt files for your website. If you disallow User-agent "Googlebot" anywhere on your website, Google will not crawl or index those pages. So it's important to be triply to be sure that all the URLs included in your site map allow Googlebot access.

4. Use a Content Delivery Network (CDN) or other means to speed up your website performance.

Hosting your own videos can help you outrank other websites or it can cause you to die in the rankings. If your website doesn't have the bandwidth or logistics to quickly display video, it can slow your website down. Using a content delivery network such as YouTube.com will help your pages load super-fast, which is now a major search engine ranking factor for Google. Google doesn't want to send searchers to slow landing pages.

5. Create a mechanically sound website.

Your website must be mechanically sound in every way. Google ranks sites now based on how good the coding of your website is. If your website is not completely compatible with all the available browsers, has broken links, errors in the code, stale or outdated coding, lacks W3C compliance, or any one of 400 other coding violations you may find it hard to rank at all on Google.

How do you know if you have these mechanical issues? You need to use a service such as **SEOAudits.com** or **AccuQuality.com**. They are the only tools I recommend and use to run over 400 tests on every page of your website and deliver a comprehensive report. They even spell check every page of your website and give you links or instructions on how to fix most of the issues in their reports.

New Google Features To Watch or Try

I have been watching Google experiment with their Auto-suggest algorithms and add it to multiple search services they run (including Google News, image search, etc). Here are the main Google Search Auto-Suggest sources and how they are different from one another.

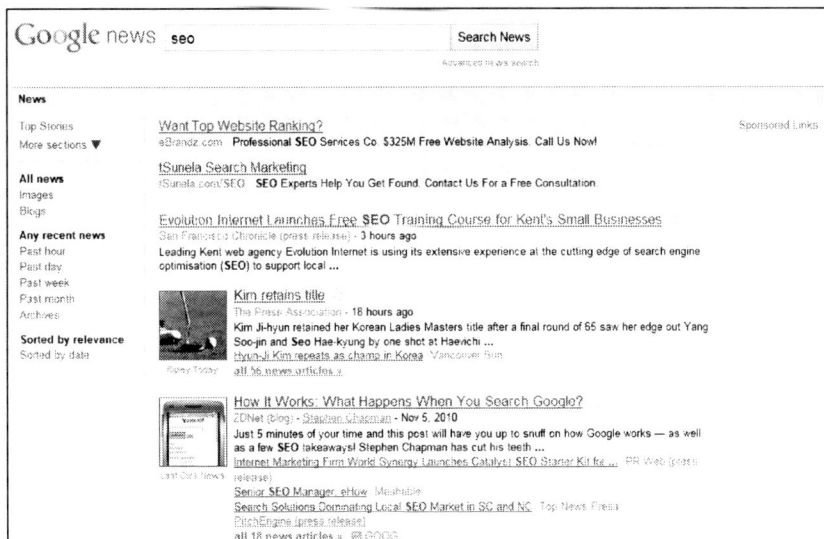

Figure 7.4

1. Google News Suggest

Google News Suggest was launched in late 2009. This is an invaluable tool for search marketers. The good thing about Google News Suggest is that it would suggest hot trends to you, so you may know what's hot without even searching the news (Google News Algorithm presents suggestions that are particularly relevant for **news-related queries**).

Here are the front page news and the suggestions that make it obvious as shown in Figure 7.4:

2. Google Image Suggest

One of the main reasons why website owners should keep an eye on Google Suggest is that Google Image Search is still the easiest way to get traffic, so be sure to target it carefully.

The Image Search suggestions include many specific words like "wallpaper", "cartoon", "photos", "landscape", "logo", "pictures":

3. Google Product Suggest

Google Product Suggest was launched in September 2009 and it is obviously an interesting tool for e-commerce focused projects. Type any search term and get up to 10 product suggestions.

4. Google Products/Google Shopping

Google Products and Google Shopping all start at http://base.google.com. This is a newer feature that allows for products to be sold on Google and have then appear near the top of search results. Google has placed a box which displays product suggestions in the SERPs as shown here in Figure 7.5 when I type in "hair dryer".

Figure 7.5

Here are the current recommendation for Google Shopping for Google Products.

> 1. Product Title - Primary keywords should be in title, not more than twice.
> 2. Product Description – make sure the keyword is listed once. Repeating keywords more than once may lead to penalties.
> 3. Freshness of feed - Products that are new and uploaded on a regular basis are listed above stale products. Upload product feed at least once a week, preferably 2x a week.
> 4. Place keywords in the URL of your products page.
> 5. Offering Google Checkout improves position and the frequency of the ad rotation.
> 6. Better Google Checkout reviews improves product showing frequency.

7. Also add the complete brand and model name in Alt tag your images on product pages.

8. Research your products at base.google.com.

9. If you are doing feeds to Google make sure the prices exactly match the prices on the product pages.

5. Google Video Suggest

In terms of video search, we are given two different options: Google Video search and YouTube Search. We have already described how with keyword research and brainstorming, Like YouTube Suggest, Google Video suggestions could work in certain niches for video optimization and keyword ideas (and inspiration):

6. Google Maps Suggest

Google "smarter" search suggestions were introduced in April of 2009 as well. They got smarter in two ways:

- Personalized suggestions (These are based on your search history and location). You should log out of Google before you check if your business pops up there.)

- Enhanced database (The search suggestions include additional information, such as the address of the business or the district that a place is in.

Google Technical Suggestions:

- ✓ Focus on only 1-3 keywords on a page. (Preferable one keyword per page.)
- ✓ Keep the keyword density for the first word around 7%, 6% for the second word, and 4% for the third.
- ✓ Put relative content including links to your social media accounts in the top 800x600 viewable screen for users to help Google Caffeine indexing.
- ✓ Make sure your domain name is registered for at least 5 years or more.
- ✓ Install Google Analytics to measure traffic to increase rankings.
- ✓ Use Google Webmasters Tools.
- ✓ Match the first three keywords on the Title tag, Meta descriptions tag, Meta keyword tag.
- ✓ Validate your HTML code.
- ✓ Make sure your website is compatible with all browsers and versions. Run either an **SEOAudits.com** or **AccuQuality.com** report to make sure.
- ✓ Avoid broken links.
- ✓ Ensure that you have allowed the GoogleBot to crawl your site and employ Robots.txt.
- ✓ Use static URLs wherever possible rather than dynamic URLs with multiple extensions.
- ✓ Interact with Google owned sites such as Blogger, BlogSpot, and YouTube.

Google Content Suggestions:

- ✓ Don't use a newly registered domain name if possible.
- ✓ Create valuable content.
- ✓ Use visible on-page text, include keywords.
- ✓ Keep pages down to a reasonable file size under 150K.
- ✓ Try not to cover more than one topic per page.
- ✓ Use static text links.
- ✓ Put keywords in text rather than in images.
- ✓ Don't hide text on a page.

Optimization for Bing, Yahoo!, MSN, & Microsoft Live

MSN and Microsoft Live are powered by Bing and there is now a new term for optimization of Bing. The term is DAO which stands for Decision Engine Optimization. In a short time Bing has become one of the top three search engines, and it's definitely not one that you should ignored – especially since Yahoo! partnered with Bing to produce Yahoo!'s search results and do advertising. This has made Yahoo! and Bing serious competition for Google.

This is one section that gives you a reason to throw last year's SEO books away for sure! As with other search engines, the basic optimization techniques that you've learned are the best way to get your site listed in Bing's database. Bing does not allow paid rankings, so your organic efforts will be the deciding factor for your rankings.

The one difference with Bing is that this search engine puts more emphasis on the freshness of content than other search engines. Specifically, sites that update high-quality, relevant content on a regular basis have a better chance of ranking high with Bing. Therefore, if you have not yet implemented a content renewal strategy and you want to rank well with Bing, you should plan and implement a strategy as quickly as you can.

Figuring out Bing's algorithm has been a task that two of our best SEO technicians here are SEO Tech Masters have been solely devoted to. More emphasis was given to this project when Bing announced it would take over search and advertising for Yahoo!. In the next section Jason McCormick, a Senior Search Engine Optimization Expert with SEO Tech Masters, reports his findings:

Bing Algorithm Summary of Overall Findings

Over the past three months I have done experiments with our test websites to figure out the key weights that Bing uses to decide rankings and return results from user searches. I have determined the following factors weigh more heavily in Bing's algorithms:

- Location Meta Tags in Long-tail Searches.
- Content and keyword density of around 6%.

- Excellent and continuously renewing content.
- Rich content (even more important on Bing than just about anything else).
- Keyword placement. Making sure you have your keywords in all the right places is imperative with the Bing search engine, especially page titles, H1 tags, and link text. They must all use matching trophy keywords.
- Authoritative inbound links. News organizations are especially ranked higher for inbound links. Inbound links are important for any major search engine, but Bing appears to act even more favorably toward inbound links, particularly those that are from sites that are news-oriented and have a high number of links.
- A technically sound, well-built site. Validating your code is important. You are penalized heavily for broken links.
- An XML Sitemap is absolutely required, as is a link to it placed under the website's listing in the Bing Webmaster Center.
- Bing recommends you create a Bing-specific mRSS (http://www.bing.com/toolbox/blogs/webmaster/archive/2010/05/29/a-king-s-feast-of-video-content-thanks-to-mrss.aspx) feed through Bing Webmaster Tools for maximal indexing.

Bing offers quite a few Websites and tools to help site owners ensure their sites are well positioned for indexing within the engine. Bing Webmaster Center, which we explained in Chapter 4, provides lots of helpful documentation and tools, including technical and content guidelines similar to Google's Webmaster Tools.

There's also a Webmaster blog, which contains a useful section on search marketing. As part of the Webmaster Center, Bing offers "Guidelines to Successful Indexing" to help Website owners ensure that the MSNBot can index all of your website's content.

Bing Technical Suggestions:

- ✓ Validate your HTML code.
- ✓ Avoid broken links.
- ✓ Set up redirects from old pages to new ones.
- ✓ Ensure that you have allowed the MSNBot to crawl your site and employ Robots.txt.
- ✓ Keep the keyword density around 5%.
- ✓ Use static URLs wherever possible rather than dynamic URLs with multiple extensions.

Bing Content Suggestions:

- ✓ Create valuable content.
- ✓ With visible on-page text, include keywords.
- ✓ Keep pages down to a reasonable file size.
- ✓ Try not to cover more than one topic per page.
- ✓ Use static text links.
- ✓ Put keywords in text rather than in images.

Chapter 8-Pay-Per-Click (PPC)

This chapter will focus on the top two Pay-Per-Click companies. Why? Because there were three – Google AdWords, Yahoo! Search Marketing, and Microsoft adCenter. Now however, Bing which is owned by Microsoft and is now doing advertising for Yahoo!

There are others, including MySpace and Facebook, but these are the two with the greatest reach for your money. Between the two they represent both a majority of the directories and search engines on the internet.

Pay-per-click marketing is an advertising method that enables you to buy search engine placement by bidding on keywords or phrases. When people search using your chosen keywords, and you have bid an amount that will place you on a page a user is looking at, your ad will appear in the sponsored listings to the right or above the organically-placed websites, regardless of how your site ranks on any search engine.

Now before we start, PPC management is an exact science and I don't recommend that you do this yourself. There is a reason why there are companies such as SEO Tech Masters (SEOTechMasters.com) that do PPC management for a fee.

If you aren't organically at the top of the search engines and you are a business that relies on your website for business, then you have to use PPC to draw in visitors to your website. PPC ads are paid ads which show up at the top or the sides of search engine listings and are sometimes called "Sponsored Listings." They also are placed on websites and other search engines associated with the search engine you are doing your marketing on.

Should I continue PPC after I have good organic placement?

The answer is yes! There are many reasons. Number one is you cannot guarantee that your organic placement will stay at the top. There are always other competing companies who will inevitably do their own SEO work to get ahead of your company. Sometimes a competitor will wind up in the news and all those news stories will show up before your company's listing. You could wind up on the second or third page for a month or two. Not only that, sometimes you drop down the organic list for no apparent reason at all.

This can really hurt sales and is sometimes not noticeable right away, unless you are checking Google and Bing every day for your keywords. However, if you are always running a PPC campaign to supplement your organic listings, you'll see your company name more than once on the screen. It also guarantees that no matter what happens with your organic placement, the keywords used on your PPC campaign will always be there.

If you are looking for a company to do your PPC campaign, there are some qualifying questions you should ask:

- How long has this company been around? You don't want a company that is new to the industry. Find out how much experience the owners have.
- What features and feature combinations does the company provide? Are there packages that include SEO, SEM, as well as PPC? Your company requirements might differ from other companies. Look at the different features and feature combinations that are offered.
- Do they have all inclusive packages or is this a service that has no fixed costs? If they don't have a fixed cost, you may be getting a bill for far more than you could ever imagine.
- How many campaigns can you run simultaneously? Some PPC management companies restrict the number of PPC campaigns you can run at any one time. Others have restrictions on the types of campaigns you can run as they only do local campaigns and not national or international ones.
- Does the company have client referrals? Client referrals are an often overlooked aspect of PPC company research. There should be a plethora of clients that are satisfied by the company. I know that with SEO Tech Masters I have a list of 20 clients or so I like to give as referrals. Each one will tell you that our services are unbelievable.

Some companies have dozens or even hundreds of pay-per-click campaigns running at any given time. Keeping up with all those ads and campaigns can be a real challenge; if it's not your core capability, it could take you away from activities that would be more profitable for your company.

In fact, I have two companies I manage which have two project managers to keep track of the campaigns. There are daily tasks that require companies to hire PPC management firms to take care of the daily tasks involved in running all those PPC campaigns.

It's not as easy as signing on to Google and giving them your credit card. You can do that but you will be wasting thousands of dollars for very little results. Just like SEO, PPC is almost an exact science and it changes frequently as well.

For instance, there is keyword research, writing ad copies, tracking analytics, determining the return on investment (ROI) for each campaign, and any of the other tasks that attend pay-per-click campaigns.

Return on Investment (ROI) Formula

Return on investment (ROI) is a term that you'll hear frequently throughout this chapter. It is associated with keyword advertising. PPC advertising is becoming increasingly expensive – you need a way to justify your keyword investments with solid returns and a way to measure the PPC campaign's effectiveness.

There are a number of formulas for determining the ROI. For my customers, I use a straight forward formula:

ROI = [Contribution] / [Cost]

To calculate Contribution for a PPC campaign:

([Your average profit per sale] x [Estimated number of Conversions]) – [PPC Cost]

To demonstrate, let's take the following example:

Monthly PPC Cost:	**$1,500**
Average Profit per Sale:	$ **50**
Number of Conversions (Sales) per Month:	**75**

This would make the break down the following:

($50 x 75) – $1500 = $2,250

So your ROI would be:

$2,250 / $1500 = 150%

The services provided by PPC management firms can cost you anywhere from about $500 per month for basic services to as much a $250,000 flat fee for a complete campaign-management package over a specified amount of time. The question is whether it's worth it for you to pay this fee to free up your time and get the right expertise involved.

For a successful campaign, the answer is most likely "yes." A PPC management firm might be just what you need to help reduce the burden of managing single or multiple PPC campaigns and doing the job right. Just make sure you know what you're getting into before you sign a contract.

Since there is no contract yet, let's look at how to start your own campaign with Google AdWords and the Microsoft adCenter in the next few sections.

The funny thing about this section is that it went through major changes in 2009 and virtually every new SEO book I picked up, even the ones for 2010 have the old AdWords screens in their books and giving all the wrong information.

Oh, and another thing that people sometimes get confused about. Many people mistakenly believe that PPC and paid-inclusion (PI) services are the same type of marketing, but there are major differences. For starters, paid-inclusion services are used by some search engines to enable website owners to pay a one-year subscription fee to ensure that their site is indexed with that search engine at all times.

This fee doesn't guarantee any specific rank in search engine results; it only guarantees that the site is indexed by the search engine. PPC costs money when a searching user clicks on a link advertised in the sponsored listings of a page. You pay each time a user clicks on the link to your site or landing page.

Google AdWords

Since Google still has a leading edge over all the other major search engines combined, it makes sense that AdWords is the PPC component you hear the most often. AdWords is a challenge even for the most informed and talented. I cannot tell you how many times an I.T. guru from a company came into SEO Tech Masters to inquire about having us manage their ad campaigns. They tell of how they have spent thousands on AdWords campaigns and got a lot of clicks but never a sale or very few sales. Why? Because it is again almost an exact science from the keywords you choose, the wording of your ad, bidding for placement, all the way to the landing page that each ad goes to.

Most think they can learn it all from an eBook they bought online or bought at a store. It is very easy to give your credit card to Google and wind up with a $1200.00 bill and not a single phone call if you don't know what you are doing.

One of the biggest stumbling blocks is when you choose too broad of a keyword. I will give you an example. One of my clients owns a private gym here in Tualatin, Oregon. He tried his own PPC campaign and chose every keyword he could think of remotely related to gyms, exercise, and equipment. Less than two weeks later he noticed his credit card had been billed $500 (Google bills the card every time the amount reaches $500) seven times for a total of $3,500 by the time he got his credit card statement, with not one call that he could think of. He had been expecting to spend around $250.00 per month.

You can imagine his frustration and disbelief. It didn't deter him, but he tried some other things and set limits. Month after month he increased those limits until it matched what he was spending on telephone book ads, which did nothing for him anymore. Month after month, no results but lots of clicks. To the tune of $2,000. Which was spent usually within the first 10-14 days of the month.

He sat down with us and we took a look at some of the things he was doing with his PPC campaign. He was using 44 keywords which we reduced down to only 12. Because he had no clue about researching keyword costs he chose keywords that were at a national level and not local, but also had so much competition that he spent up to $25.00 for a single click!

Keep this rule in mind. Placement costs for ads is based on how much competition there is for a keyword. You actually bid on placement for those keywords. If there is a lot of competition you can spend a fortune quick.

His next major problem was that he chose words such as "exercise equipment" and "gym membership." These are great keywords on a national level but you have people all over the nation clicking on his ads and they live in other states or nowhere close to Tualatin, Oregon. So he wasted his money on people clicking on his ads who would never become a customer or even bother to call.

Next issue is that "exercise equipment" is too broad and there is too much competition. Someone searching for "exercise equipment" might be looking to buy exercise equipment, to repair exercise equipment, or to donate exercise equipment. They might be looking for new exercise equipment or used exercise equipment. The list goes on. The point I am trying to make: very few of those clicking were looking to get a gym membership.

Keep in mind that he had 30 more words that had similar or less critical flaws. I didn't mean to make this sound like a sales pitch but the fact is, if you are not expert, don't try to make yourself one overnight.

I now handle all of SEO and PPC campaigns for Mark Romine, the owner of the gym I mentioned above. Mark spent virtually every hour of his workday for an entire two months to try and get his campaign done right and failed. He graciously allowed me to use his name in this book on the condition that I printed this statement:

> "If you use my name, make sure your readers know that as a business owner, they should spend their time doing other things selling and growing their business. I wasted more than $7,500 trying to do an AdWords [campaign] before one of my customers recommended Sean Odom at SEOTechMasters.com.
>
> You guys get the results I wanted and more for about $500.00 per month. I get 500 times the business from my website then I do from the *** telephone book which I spend $2,100 per month on by the way."

He went on to state why he still had to keep an ad but basically it was because he has a senior demographic which is about the only demographic besides the telephone ad sales people that crack open a telephone book.

Now being the biggest doesn't always mean being the best. When you're evaluating the different PPC companies you might use, be sure to check not only the traffic rate, but also the conversion rate, if possible. It's great if your ads receive a lot of impressions. If those impressions don't turn to clicks, you'll find that your PPC campaign is not at all effective.

> **NOTE:** *An impression is every time someone performs a search on one of your chosen keywords and your ad is displayed on the screen. Google tracks this information as well as the clicks. Also tracked are the numbers of times a particular keyword was clicked on, the ad that was used when it was clicked, and the cost.*
>
> *Another thing to note is that if you have more than one ad for the keywords you use, Google will alternate between them in the beginning. If, however, a particular ad is clicked on more often, Google will automatically show on the more popular ad a greater percentage of the time and will sometimes stop creating impressions of the non-performing ad altogether.*

One thing that many people don't know is that Google also offers TV, newspaper, and embedded-video advertising. Even the radio and phone models of AdWords are charged on a bid-per-keyword basis. To make things even more complicated, AdWords is linked to Google's AdSense program, which is an advertisement publishing program whereby website owners place ads on their websites with similar relevancy to your ads – sometimes competing sites. When users click through those ads and make purchases, the website owner is paid a small amount. Many website owners use this service to help offset the cost of having a site or to make money.

So if you place an ad with Google, your ad may show in the results of an AOL search, Ask.com, and Netscape as well. This helps give Google AdWords one of the largest markets available for keyword advertisements.

A larger market, however, does not necessarily mean better results or a guarantee of higher-quality leads. With Google AdWords, it's essential that you pay attention to the details that help place your ads, and use them to your advantage so they are the most effective. As an example, when doing research for a fire and safety company that I do the SEO and PPC for, we realized that there was so much competition and the cost was so great on Google that Microsoft's adCenter made more sense.

The competition for the fire- and safety-related keywords was primarily focused on Google and was quite low on Bing and its related search engines. Although there are less clicks, the ratio of competing websites to clicks gave my client an advantage. We still use the keywords on Google AdWords but we focus on Microsoft adCenter results and it is really paying off for the client, who now has a 5 to 1 ratio some months – at a much lower cost. Giving the customer a great ROI.

Signing up for Google AdWords

Signing up for Google AdWords is quick and easy. You can get there by going to http://www.google.com/services and choosing the link to AdWords or the "Get Started" button, as shown in Figure 8.1.

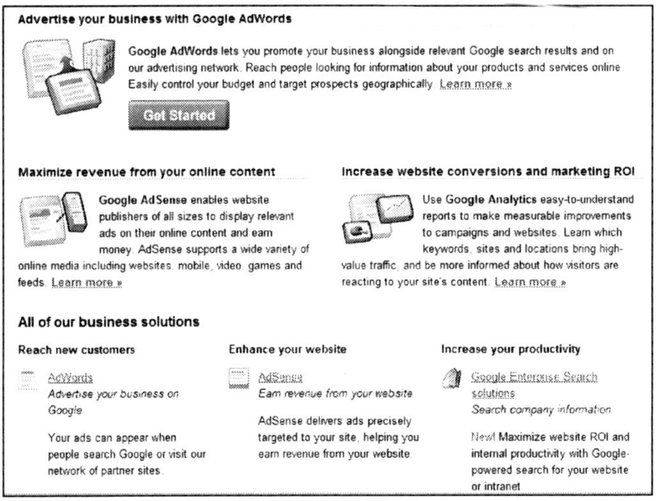

Figure 8.1

If you have a Google account you can enter it and sign it. Otherwise you need to choose "Start Now" and create an account, as shown in figure 8.2.

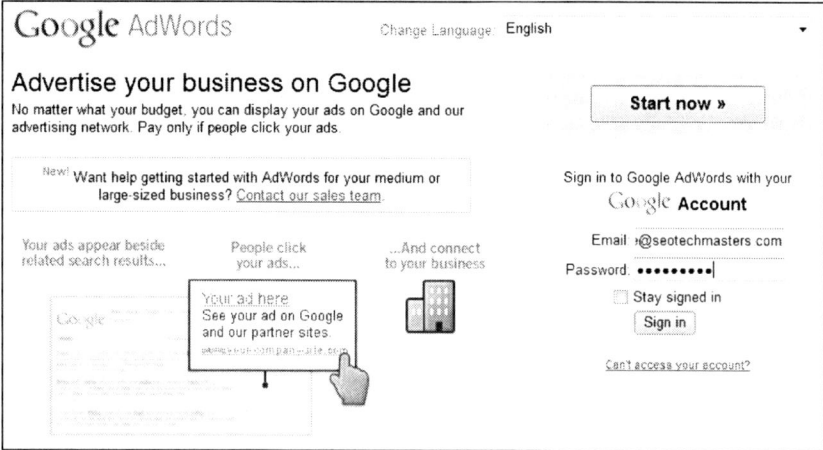

Figure 8.2

If you press "Start Now," you are given the option of using an existing Google account or creating a new account specifically for AdWords. After selecting, login as shown in figure 8.3.

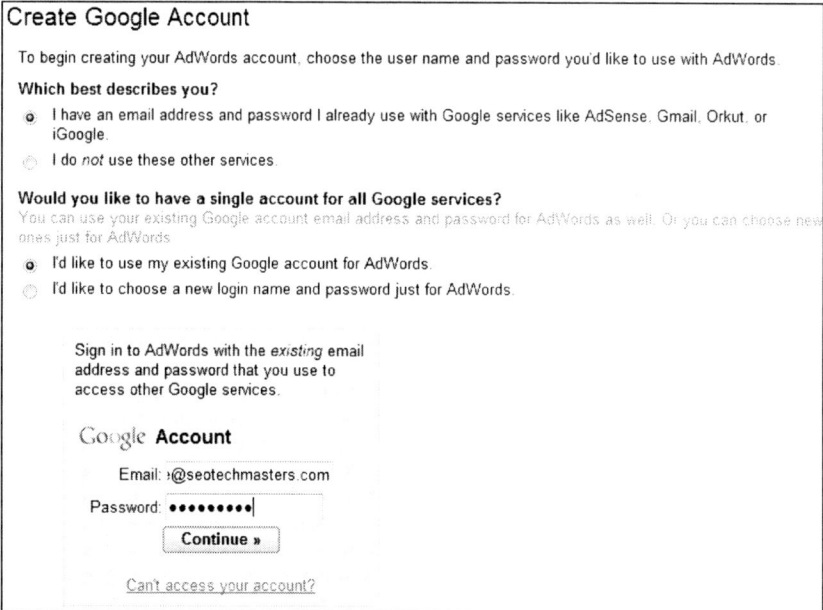

Figure 8.3

Your next screen allows you to set the country, time zone, and the type of currency you use, as shown in figure 8.4. You have to remember that Google is a worldwide search engine and not just a U.S. search engine.

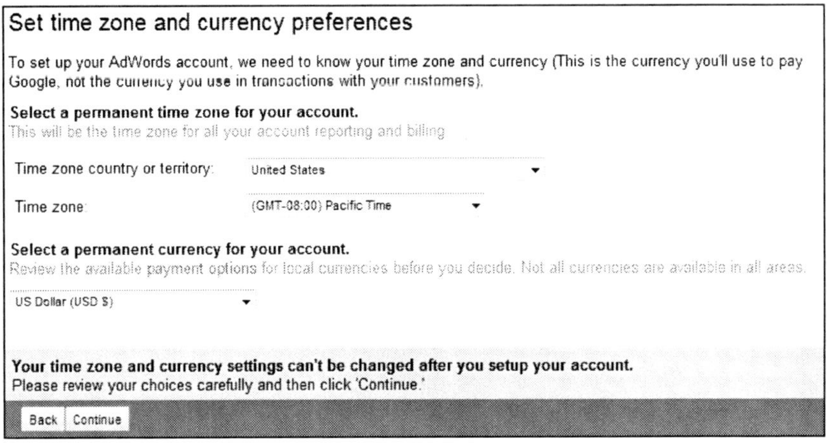

Set time zone and currency preferences

To set up your AdWords account, we need to know your time zone and currency (This is the currency you'll use to pay Google, not the currency you use in transactions with your customers).

Select a permanent time zone for your account.
This will be the time zone for all your account reporting and billing

Time zone country or territory: United States   ▼

Time zone: (GMT-08:00) Pacific Time   ▼

Select a permanent currency for your account.
Review the available payment options for local currencies before you decide. Not all currencies are available in all areas.

US Dollar (USD $)   ▼

Your time zone and currency settings can't be changed after you setup your account.
Please review your choices carefully and then click 'Continue.'

Back   Continue

Figure 8.4

After you press "Continue," your AdWords account is created, as shown in figure 8.5.

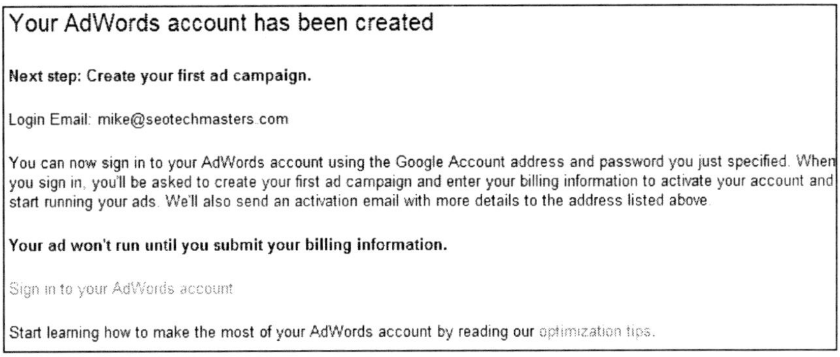

Your AdWords account has been created

Next step: Create your first ad campaign.

Login Email: mike@seotechmasters.com

You can now sign in to your AdWords account using the Google Account address and password you just specified. When you sign in, you'll be asked to create your first ad campaign and enter your billing information to activate your account and start running your ads. We'll also send an activation email with more details to the address listed above.

Your ad won't run until you submit your billing information.

Sign in to your AdWords account

Start learning how to make the most of your AdWords account by reading our optimization tips.

Figure 8.5

Press the link "Sign into your AdWords account." You are redirected to login, as shown in Figure 8.6.

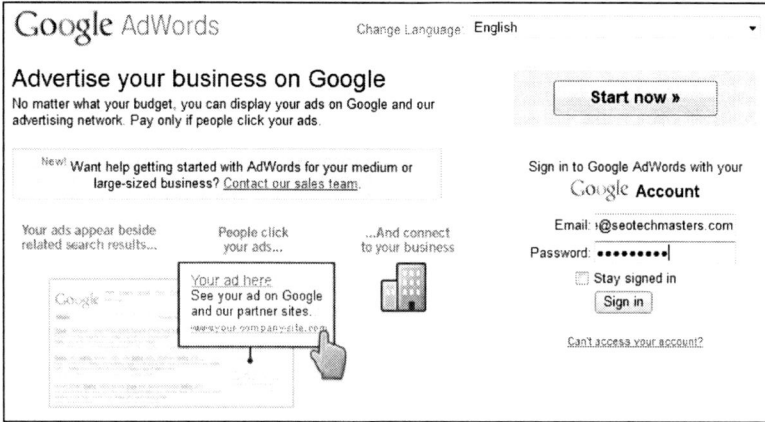

Figure 8.6

When you first login, it will give you the option to learn more about Google AdWords in Figure 8.7. Keep in mind that there is useful information on the links, but in my opinion, it gives you just enough information to be dangerous. The instructions teach you get the broadest range of clicks that makes Google the most amount of money.

Figure 8.7

If you look at the right of the screen, you have the option to create your first campaign. Click here and begin, as shown in Figure 8.8.

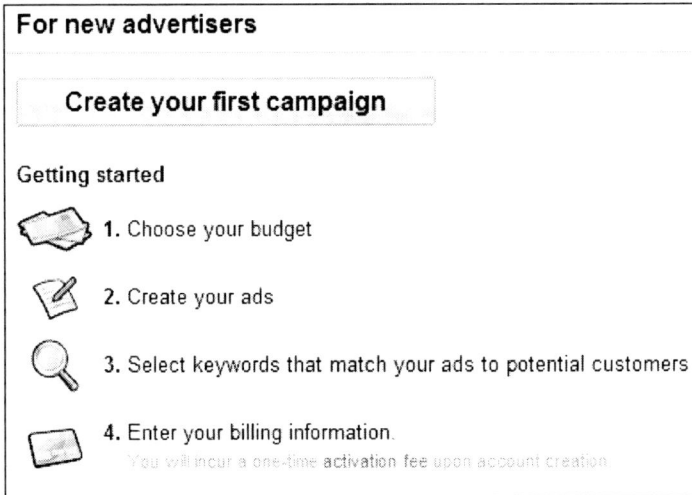

For new advertisers

Create your first campaign

Getting started

1. Choose your budget

2. Create your ads

3. Select keywords that match your ads to potential customers

4. Enter your billing information.
   You will incur a one-time activation fee upon account creation

Figure 8.8

Keep in mind, this is one of Google's primary income sources and there are a lot of stockholders to pay.

Then you begin the registration process, which configures the basic edition of AdWords. The basic edition is great if you've never used a PPC program before. It includes one set of keywords, basic reporting capabilities, and basic targeting.

> **Note:** *At the bottom of the screen of Figure 8.8 there is an option to create Advanced Campaigns. This type of campaign is for very experienced users and creates multiple sets of keywords and more advanced targeting and reporting, in addition to a few other tools.*

You can begin with the basic starter edition, then you can graduate to the an advanced campaign when you're ready. When you do, your starter campaign will be moved to your new AdWords account, so you don't lose any of your existing advertisements.

Next, Google wants to know about your business, as shown in Figure 8.9. This is to give you advice on the types of ads you should run.

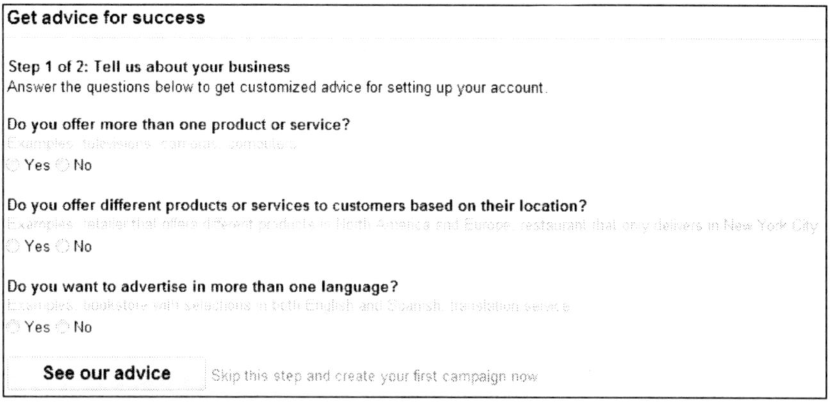

Get advice for success

Step 1 of 2: Tell us about your business
Answer the questions below to get customized advice for setting up your account.

Do you offer more than one product or service?
Examples: televisions, cameras, computers
Yes No

Do you offer different products or services to customers based on their location?
Examples: retailer that offers different products in North America and Europe, restaurant that only delivers in New York City
Yes No

Do you want to advertise in more than one language?
Examples: bookstore with selections in both English and Spanish, translation service
Yes No

See our advice Skip this step and create your first campaign now

Figure 8.9

The questions in figure 8.9 are primarily for novice users. There is a link to disregard Google's advice and go straight to the campaign. I am going to move on and create a campaign for my spectacular, make-believe excavating company called "Sacramento Excavating Contractors, Inc." as shown in figure 8.10.

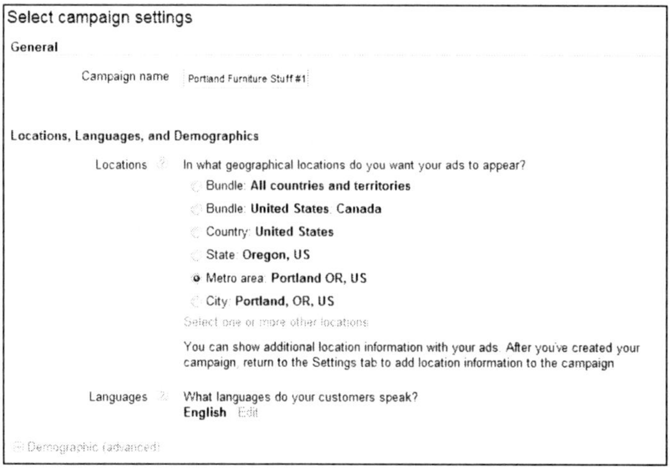

Select campaign settings

General

Campaign name Portland Furniture Stuff #1

Locations, Languages, and Demographics

Locations In what geographical locations do you want your ads to appear?
Bundle: All countries and territories
Bundle: United States, Canada
Country: United States
State: Oregon, US
● Metro area: Portland OR, US
City: Portland, OR, US
Select one or more other locations

You can show additional location information with your ads. After you've created your campaign, return to the Settings tab to add location information to the campaign.

Languages What languages do your customers speak?
English Edit

Demographic (advanced)

Figure 8.10

I can also choose an additional demographic such as ages, locations, occupation and much more by clicking on the "Demographic (advanced)" option.

Next you choose where you would like your ads to be seen, as shown in Figure 8.11. This screen can also protect you from click fraud. (We will discuss click fraud in more depth later in this chapter.) If you find yourself the victim of click fraud, you can change your "Network, devices, and extensions" setting based on where the fraud is occurring.

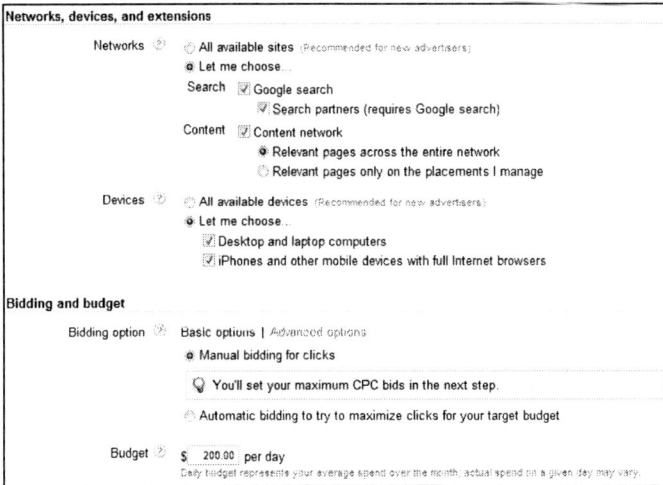

Networks, devices, and extensions

Networks ⑦ ○ All available sites (Recommended for new advertisers)
           ⊙ Let me choose...
           Search ☑ Google search
                   ☑ Search partners (requires Google search)
           Content ☑ Content network
                   ⊙ Relevant pages across the entire network
                   ○ Relevant pages only on the placements I manage

Devices ⑦ ○ All available devices (Recommended for new advertisers)
           ⊙ Let me choose...
               ☑ Desktop and laptop computers
               ☑ iPhones and other mobile devices with full Internet browsers

Bidding and budget

Bidding option ⑦ Basic options | Advanced options
                  ⊙ Manual bidding for clicks
                      💡 You'll set your maximum CPC bids in the next step.
                  ○ Automatic bidding to try to maximize clicks for your target budget

Budget ⑦ $ 200.00 per day
          Daily budget represents your average spend over the month; actual spend on a given day may vary.

Figure 8.11

In Figure 8.12, there are some optional advanced settings. For instance, you can choose where you want your ad to show and the delivery method. The defaults are shown.

Next, you can change the dates your ad run, set the rotation frequency, and place a limit on the number of times your ad can be shown in a given time period. Why would you want this? Let's say that you have a strong ROI and too many impressions send you too much business. You can set a cap so you don't get 100 calls to your one-man business within 20 minutes after the ad begins.

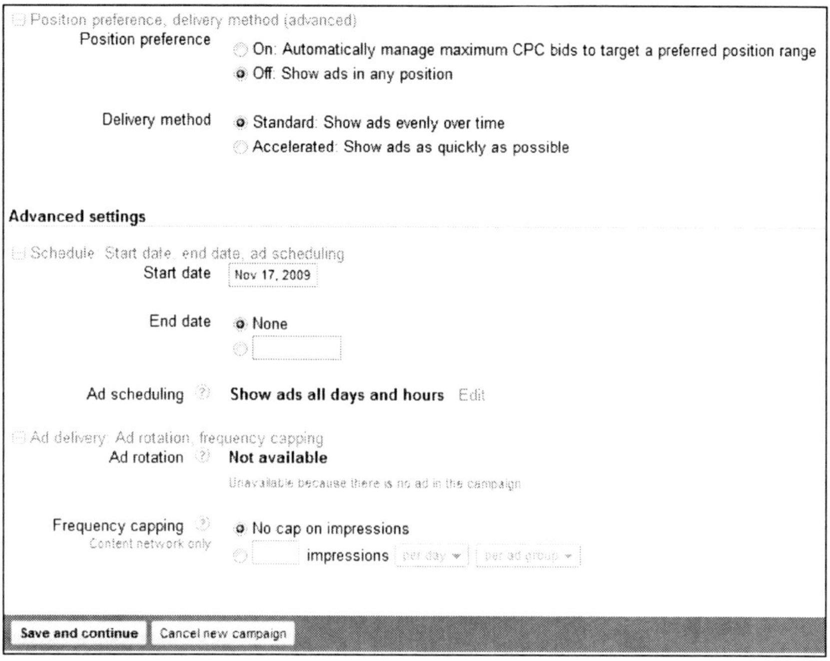

Figure 8.12

Next is the hard part – trying to decide what you want your AdWords ad to say (figure 8.13). If you don't have experience with this, you should get professional help. It is another absolute science to determine the words that draw people to click on one ad versus another. It is industry specific.

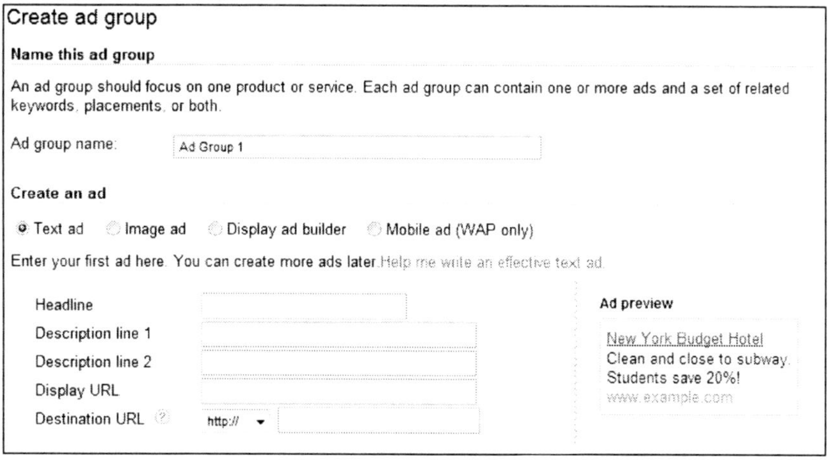

Figure 8.13

Next is the keywords. Now you may want to just use the ones you decided in Chapter 2, but you can supplement them with other keywords, even if they have a lot of competition. Keep in mind, though, that some of these keywords can be pricey and you might want to do some research using the Google's Keyword Tool we also talked about in Chapter 2. In Figure 8.14, you can see where to enter your keywords. Be sure to add them one per line.

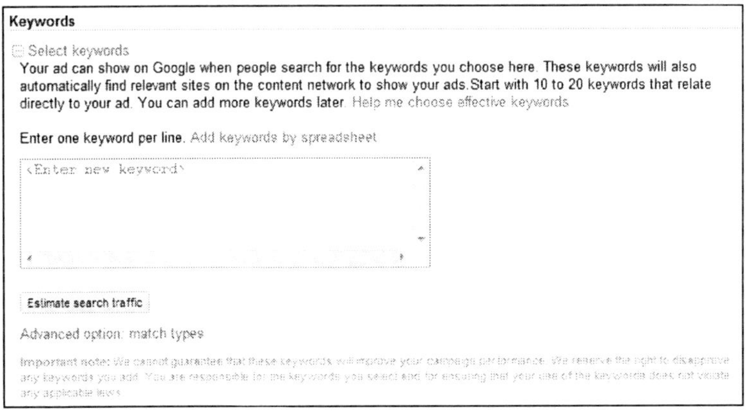

Keywords

☐ Select keywords
Your ad can show on Google when people search for the keywords you choose here. These keywords will also automatically find relevant sites on the content network to show your ads. Start with 10 to 20 keywords that relate directly to your ad. You can add more keywords later. Help me choose effective keywords

Enter one keyword per line. Add keywords by spreadsheet

<Enter new keyword>

Estimate search traffic

Advanced option: match types

Important note: We cannot guarantee that these keywords will improve your campaign performance. We reserve the right to disapprove any keywords you add. You are responsible for the keywords you select and for ensuring that your use of the keywords does not violate any applicable laws.

Figure 8.14

In Figure 8.15, you see where you enter in the maximum amount you wish to bid for first page placement of Google search results. Keep in mind that if you leave the spaces blank you are writing a blank check. You will automatically outbid your competition. It will add up quickly, trust me – especially for those competitive keywords.

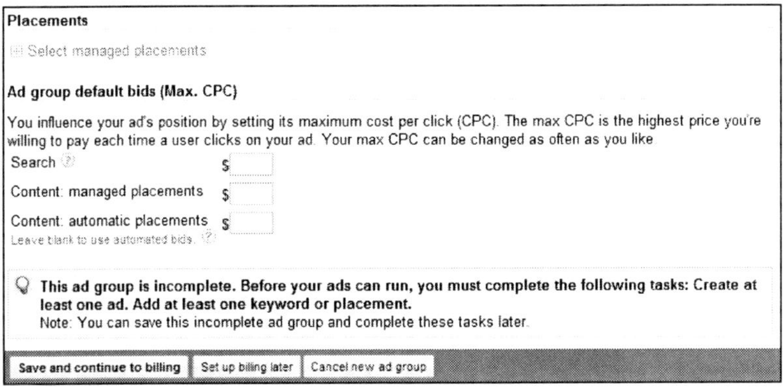

Placements

☐ Select managed placements

Ad group default bids (Max. CPC)

You influence your ad's position by setting its maximum cost per click (CPC). The max CPC is the highest price you're willing to pay each time a user clicks on your ad. Your max CPC can be changed as often as you like

Search ? $ [____]

Content: managed placements $ [____]

Content: automatic placements $ [____]
Leave blank to use automated bids. ?

♀ This ad group is incomplete. Before your ads can run, you must complete the following tasks: Create at least one ad. Add at least one keyword or placement.
Note: You can save this incomplete ad group and complete these tasks later.

| Save and continue to billing | Set up billing later | Cancel new ad group |

Figure 8.15

Next you have to fund your account by clicking "Save and continue to billing" (Figure 8.15). Billing simply means that you provide Google with a credit card number that they can use to charge your monthly advertising costs.

I would like to say that once you fund the account, your ads will begin showing immediately. But that is not true. Typically it takes Google about 2-3 days to approve or reject your add based on the content of your add. Google wants the ad to contain no foul language or email addresses, as well as many other published and unpublished rules.

Once your ad is approved, it will start immediately. However, in my experience, you only get a few hundred impressions the first week or so before it really kicks in and starts working. So don't expect to start AdWords today and get calls tomorrow.

Monitoring Your Campaign

The Campaign Management tab is where you'll perform most of the tasks to manage your account and see the results of your money and control the costs of your ads, as shown in Figure 8.16. This tab contains an overview of the campaigns that you have running, as well as links to an account snapshot, tools for managing your accounts, conversion tracking tools, and a website optimizer.

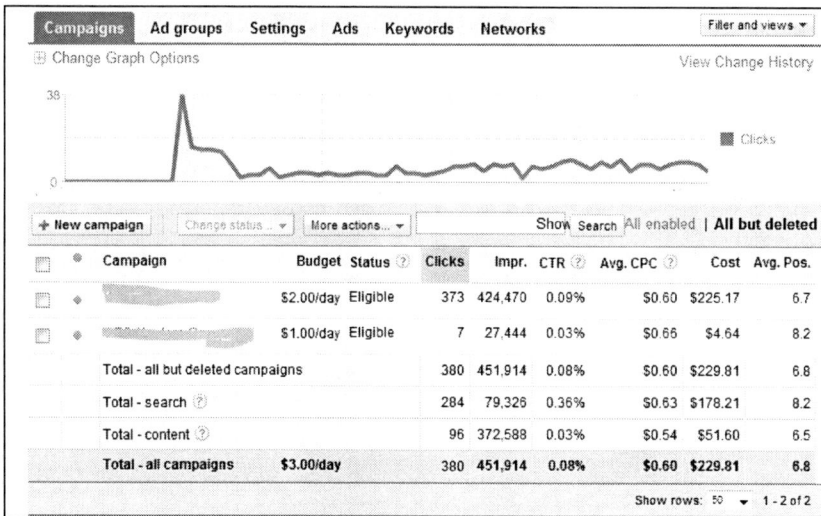

Campaign	Budget	Status	Clicks	Impr.	CTR	Avg. CPC	Cost	Avg. Pos.
	$2.00/day	Eligible	373	424,470	0.09%	$0.60	$225.17	6.7
	$1.00/day	Eligible	7	27,444	0.03%	$0.66	$4.64	8.2
Total - all but deleted campaigns			380	451,914	0.08%	$0.60	$229.81	6.8
Total - search			284	79,326	0.36%	$0.63	$178.21	8.2
Total - content			96	372,588	0.03%	$0.54	$51.60	6.5
Total - all campaigns	**$3.00/day**		**380**	**451,914**	**0.08%**	**$0.60**	**$229.81**	**6.8**

Figure 8.16

The Ad groups tab allows you to create groups for ad campaigns and see a more detailed look at the monetary settings, as shown in Figure 8.17.

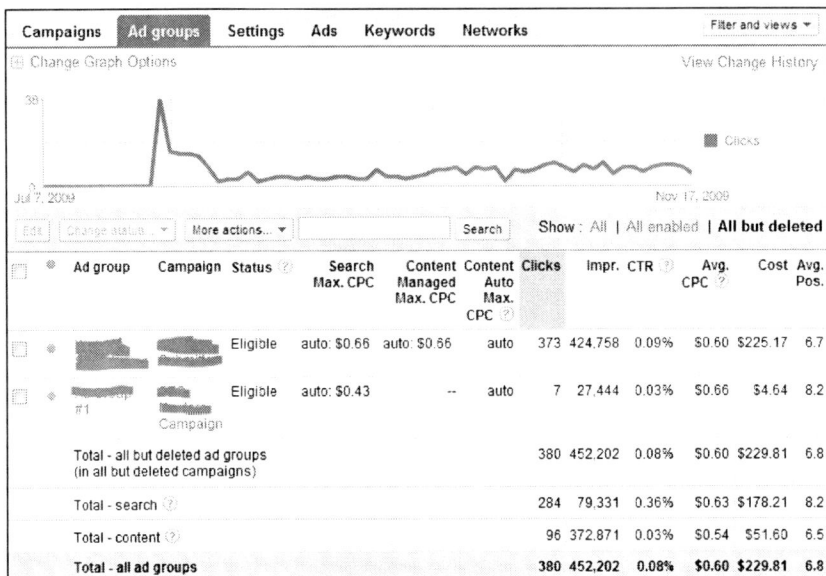

	Ad group	Campaign	Status	Search Max. CPC	Content Managed Max. CPC	Content Auto Max. CPC	Clicks	Impr.	CTR	Avg. CPC	Cost	Avg. Pos.
			Eligible	auto: $0.66	auto: $0.66	auto	373	424,758	0.09%	$0.60	$225.17	6.7
	#1	Campaign	Eligible	auto: $0.43	--	auto	7	27,444	0.03%	$0.66	$4.64	8.2
	Total - all but deleted ad groups (in all but deleted campaigns)						380	452,202	0.08%	$0.60	$229.81	6.8
	Total - search						284	79,331	0.36%	$0.63	$178.21	8.2
	Total - content						96	372,871	0.03%	$0.54	$51.60	6.5
	Total - all ad groups						380	452,202	0.08%	$0.60	$229.81	6.8

Figure 8.17

The Settings tab shown in Figure 8.18 allows you to change all the settings that were displayed in Figure 8.17. Simply click on any of the Budget options and it will allow you to change them.

The Ads tab shows the ads you have and how many clicks each ad received.

The Keywords tab allows you to see what keywords were clicked on and how many times they were shown. You can also change the keywords you are using by adding or removing them.

The Networks tab (as shown in Figure 8.18) shows information on where your ad was click on and whether it was on Google.com or another one of their partner sites.

All online campaigns					All time Jul 7, 2009 - Nov 17, 2009			▼

Messages ▽ Alerts (1)

Alerts
▽ Increase traffic with new keywords (80) View | Dismiss

Campaigns	Ad groups	Settings	Ads	Keywords	**Networks**		Filter and views ▼	
				Clicks	Impr.	CTR ⑦	Avg. CPC ⑦	Cost	Avg. Pos.
Search				284	79,347	0.36%	$0.63	$178.21	8.2
Google search				222	40,942	0.54%	$0.62	$137.77	8.1
Search partners ⑦				62	38,405	0.16%	$0.65	$40.44	8.3
Content				96	374,140	0.03%	$0.54	$51.60	6.5
▨ Managed placements ⑦ show details				0	0	0.00%	$0.00	$0.00	0
▨ Automatic placements ⑦ show details				96	374,140	0.03%	$0.54	$51.60	6.5
Total - All networks				**380**	**453,487**	**0.08%**	**$0.60**	**$229.81**	**6.8**

Figure 8.18

At the top of the Google AdWords screen there are a few more options. In the next few sections, let's take a look at the Reporting tab, the Billing tab, and the My account tab.

Reporting Tab

Click on the Reporting tab, and then choose Reports. You'll arrive at the Report Center screen, as shown in Figure 8.19. You can see existing reports and the links to create new reports.

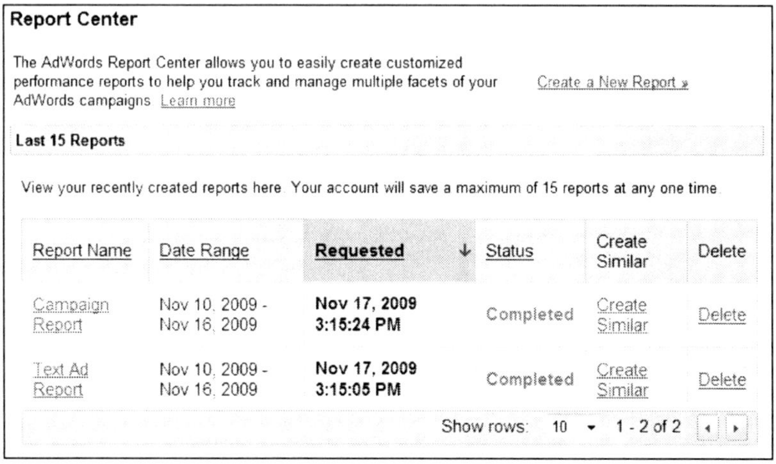

Report Center

The AdWords Report Center allows you to easily create customized performance reports to help you track and manage multiple facets of your AdWords campaigns Learn more

Create a New Report »

Last 15 Reports

View your recently created reports here. Your account will save a maximum of 15 reports at any one time.

Report Name	Date Range	Requested	↓	Status	Create Similar	Delete
Campaign Report	Nov 10, 2009 - Nov 16, 2009	Nov 17, 2009 3:15:24 PM		Completed	Create Similar	Delete
Text Ad Report	Nov 10, 2009 - Nov 16, 2009	Nov 17, 2009 3:15:05 PM		Completed	Create Similar	Delete

Show rows: 10 ▼ 1 - 2 of 2 ◄ ►

Figure 8.19

There used to be only three reports you could run: the Statistical, Financial, and Conversion reports. Google has come a long way, as you can see in

Figure 8.20, which shows all the reports that are currently available. Each report is also customizable with many options.

1. Report Type

Choose a report from the following options: Learn more about report types

	Placement / Keyword Performance	View performance data for keywords or placements you've specifically targeted.
	Ad Performance	View performance data for each of your ads.
	URL Performance	View performance data for each of your Destination URLs.
	Ad Group Performance	View ad group performance data for one or more of your campaigns
	Campaign Performance	View performance data for your campaigns.
	Account Performance	View performance data for your entire account.
	Demographic Performance	View performance data for sites by demographic.
	Geographic Performance	View performance data by geographic origin.
	Search Query Performance	View performance data for search queries which triggered your ad and received clicks.
	Placement Performance	View performance data for content network sites where your ad has been shown.
	Reach and Frequency Performance	View reach and frequency performance data for your campaigns.

Figure 8.20

Billing Tab

This tab allows you to keeping track of your invoices, billing information, account access, and account preferences.

This tab provides you with two options. Select either Billing Summary (which shows your payment type, the amount of the last payment, your current balance, and the current charges for each campaign), or Billing Preferences (which allows you to change the way you are billed or the credit card information on file).

My Account Tab

This tab allows you to change those Google accounts that can access your AdWords account and reports, as shown in figure 8.21. It also allows you to change your time zone, language, PhamacyChecker ID, or tracking options; get the Google AdWords terms and conditions; manage your business hosted page at Google Sites; or cancel your AdWords account altogether.

Account Access

If you manage this AdWords account with others, see who has access to sign in. Invite others to create their own login email and password to access this account by clicking 'Invite other users.' Learn more

+ Invite other users

Users with account access

Adwords user	Last logged in ?	Access level ?	Actions
	Nov 16, 2009	Administrative access	Actions ▼

Figure 8.21

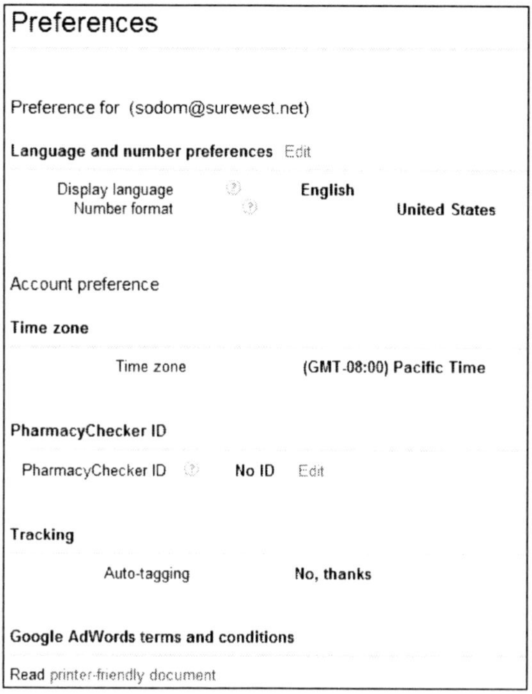

Figure 8.22

Common AdWords Issues

No one really likes to be told they're doing something wrong. Over and over again however, I see our clients making the same mistakes over and over when they set up their accounts for AdWords, Here is a list of the most common mistakes.

1. **Using geo-modified keywords in your geo-targeted campaigns**

   What does this means? If you have a pizza restaurant in Sacramento California and you are using geo-targeted campaigns leave the word "Sacramento" out of the "pizza restaurant" key term.
   This can result in a lot less traffic, since there is a strong chance the ads will not display due to a "geo-targeting mismatch." One solution for this: use geo-modified keywords only in campaigns *not* using geo-targeting.

2. **Duplicating keywords across ad campaigns**

   What does this mean? When you run more than one campaign selling something don't target the same keywords. If you have two ads competing for the same keyword you are bidding against yourself and bringing the cost up for that keyword for both ads.

   When you have a good keyword, it may seem like a smart move to spread the goodness around to all of your ad groups and campaigns. However, duplicating keywords won't help your performance.

3. **Jumping the gun**

   What does this mean? Give your bids a chance. Many times, we've seen advertisers make bid adjustments, or pause or delete keywords well before enough data has been collected to make an educated decision. For example, your cost-per-acquisition (CPA) target might be $30, and because you think your keyword isn't giving you enough impressions or clicks, you pause it or increase your bidding amount. Our experience has shown that many advertisers do this too quickly. A good rule of thumb is that if you haven't reached your $30 or the amount was you set for your target wait and judge.

4. **Putting your phone number in your ad**

   What does this mean? Why wouldn't you want to give your prospects another way to contact you and save money on a click? At first it sounds like bad logic, however a phone number in your ad can decrease your click-through rate and quality index score, which in turn drives up your cost-per-click and pushes the ad further down in Google results.

   The basic rule is that Google displays ads that get clicked on more often and charge them less.

This book isn't really about PPC campaigns and we just barely touched on Google AdWords. There is so much to learn. Now let's take a look at the Microsoft AdCenter .

Microsoft adCenter

Microsoft adCenter, formerly MSN AdCenter, is Microsoft's advertising program. PPC ads through Microsoft adCenter are distributed on Bing, MSN, Live, Yahoo and many other smaller search engines.

Go to http://advertising.microsoft.com/home to setup an account, as shown in Figure 8.23.

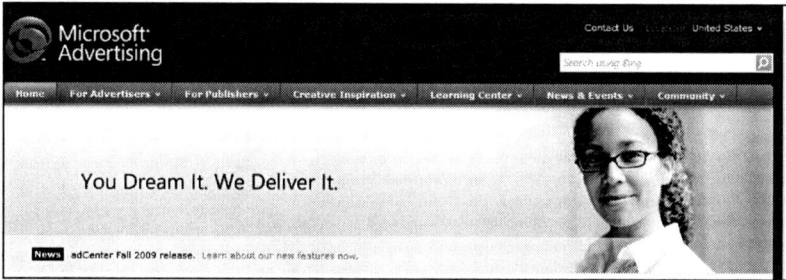

Figure 8.23

If you already have an account, go to https://adcenter.microsoft.com/Default.aspx, as shown in figure 8.24.

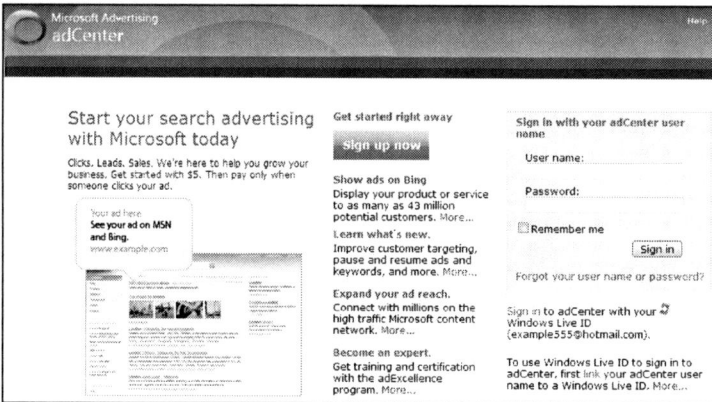

Figure 8.24

There is a new guide which explains all the new features of the Microsoft adCenter: *http://advertising.microsoft.com/wwdocs/user/en-us/learningcenter/adCenter_2009_Fall_Upgrade_Feature_Guide_US.pdf*

In Figure 8.25, you see a list from Microsoft.com which explains the new features of the Microsoft adCenter.

Top 5 Features

- **Search Query Performance Report**

  The Search Query Performance Report will pull reports that contain the actual queries that users perform that resulted in your ad being clicked. This report will provide you with information to help you manage your keyword lists by adding keywords that are aligned with actual user queries, in addition to identifying potential negative keywords to add.

- **Default Time Zone**

  The Default Time Zone feature will allow you to set a default or preferred time zone at the account level. Additionally, this feature will require a campaign level time zone to be selected in order to proceed with campaign creation if a default time zone has not been entered at the account level. This allows you to have the appropriate time zone aligned with every campaign.

- **Ad Preview Tool**

  The Ad Preview tool was added in advance of the Fall 2009 Upgrade, but it is being moved from the Campaigns tab to the new Tools tab with the fall upgrade. The Ad Preview tool assists you in confirming that your ads are showing on Bing without incurring unnecessary impressions or accidental clicks.

- **Agency Invitation and Termination**

  adCenter advertisers will be able to invite an agency to manage their adCenter account. When an advertiser invites an agency to manage their account, they will be inviting the agency to manage all of their accounts; there will be no capability to invite an agency to manage only specific accounts or campaigns.

- **Managing Multiple Accounts**

  The Customer Selection page included in the Fall 2009 Upgrade will ease the pain of agencies, SEMs and large organizations, and help them efficiently manage all of their accounts in adCenter.

Figure 8.25

Setting up your Microsoft adCenter account is slightly different from setting up a Google AdWords account. One of the first differences is that Microsoft wants $5.00 and your billing information up front, even before you create a first campaign ad. The setup fee of $5.00 is charged to the credit card you provide for payment and charged immediately to your account.

Once you've provided billing information, you can begin to set up your first Microsoft adCenter campaign ad. When you sign into adCenter, you're taken to a general page that includes five tabs, which you can use to manage your adCenter ads. These tabs are Home, Campaign, Accounts & Billing, Tools, and Reports as seen in Figure 8.26.

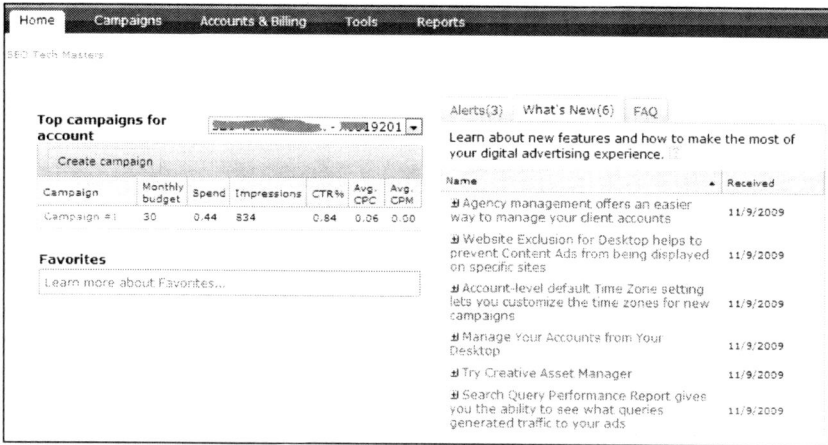

Figure 8.26

Home Tab

In figure 8.26, you see the Home tab which shows your campaigns, account information, Alerts, What's New and FAQ's. This is the screen you see when you immediately go into your Microsoft adCenter account.

Campaign

The Campaign tab in the Microsoft adCenter (as shown in Figure 8.27) is similar to the Google AdWords Campaign tab. When you click the Campaign tab, you're given an overview page, where you can create or import PPC campaigns. To create a campaign, click the Create Campaign button to start the creation process.

Figure 8.27

To keep you from getting bored, I am not going to walk you through the creation process because you are asked to provide all the same information that we just went through for creating a Google AdWords campaign.

One thing is a little different in the adCenter campaign creation process, however: the importing capability is unique to the Microsoft adCenter. Using this capability, you can import PPC ads that you've created in Microsoft Excel or another spreadsheet program. If the ads were not created in Excel, you need to save the file as a .csv file for importing.

Accounts & Billing Tab

The Accounts & Billing tab is where you'll find the financial information for your PPC accounts. From this page you have access to access and configure your company information, create a Business Page, configure users, change payment methods, get your billing statements and identify a client-agency relationship to identify a company that is handling your PPC campaign.

Tools Tab

The Tools tab is used for maintaining your PPC campaigns with research and other tools. The Tools tab in adCenter gives you tools to help generate a keyword list, an ad Preview Tool to see what your ad will looks like, and a Microsoft Excel 2007 Add-in tool to create campaigns.

Reports Tab

The final tab in the adCenter console is the Reports tab. When you click the Reports tab, you're taken to the Create New Report page, where you can do just that. Once you've created a first report, it will appear on the Recent Reports tab with any other reports that you may have created.

You don't need to create a new report type each time you need to generate one. Simply save the report as a template; and then the next time you want to run a report, select the template during the report creation process. The list of reports you can create is shown in Figure 8.28.

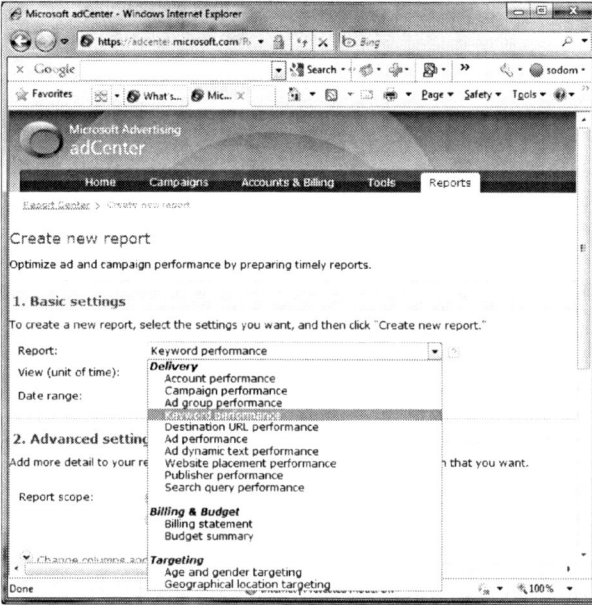

Figure 8.28

There are certain instances where Microsoft adCenter can outperform Google AdWords, particularly since so many people formulate their marketing efforts toward Google and have not taken advantage of Microsoft's adCenter.

Many organizations use more than one PPC campaign provider. Using multiple PPC vendors means better coverage with your PPC ad, which can lead to better conversion rates and a better ROI.

Before You Begin Using PPC

There are several things to consider before you being a PPC campaign. Because you're paying for placement or advertising space for your keywords, you're not necessarily going to get the best results with all the keywords or phrases that you choose.

In some cases you must continuously test and evaluate to see which keywords draw in the demographic that will buy your product or service. I recommend that you begin small, with a minimal number of keywords, to see how the search engine you've selected performs. You can also see the results and determine what it costs for first page placement of your sponsored ads.

You should also be able to gauge what it costs to run a campaign in terms of the amount of traffic it delivers and how well that traffic converts into paying customers as well. Even if you make two sales you can gauge and average how many clicks it took to make a sale and the cost.

Having a method in place that enables you to track your return on investment is imperative. If your goal is to bring new subscribers to your website, you'll want to track the conversions, perhaps by directing the visitors funneled to your site by your PPC link to a landing page set up just for them.

You can then monitor how many clicks came to that page in Google Analytics. This is easy to track if you have a special phone number or sales page setup for users coming from your PPC campaign. All this together will allow you to quickly track your ROI and to determine how much you're paying for each new conversion or sale.

Questions to Ask Before You Begin a Campaign

Before investing a lot of time and money into a PPC service, you may want to review a few different PPC Management services to determine which is the best one for you. If you choose to do it yourself you can gauge your readiness by seeing if you can answer these basic question:

1. How many searches are conducted each month through the search engine for which you're considering a PPC program for the keywords you have chosen?
2. What is the competition versus the number of searches for each keyword you have selected?
3. Does the search engine have major partners or affiliates that could contribute to the volume of traffic you're hoping to get?
4. How does the search engine or PPC program prevent fraudulent activity?
5. Is there recourse to get a refund or help with the investigation if click fraud occurs?
6. Do you know what to look for to determine if click fraud is occurring?
7. How difficult is it to file a report about fraudulent activity and how quickly is the issue addressed?
8. Do you have control over where your listing appears on the search engine?
9. Can you choose to have your listing withheld from affiliate searches or websites?
10. Can you limit the amount you spend by day or by a particular search?
11. Do you know what your PPC campaign budget will allow?

12. Do you have time to learn PPC in depth?
13. Do you have the time to monitor your PPC campaign daily?

Some search engines and websites have strict guidelines about how sites appear in their searches, on their website, how partners and affiliates calculate visits, and how fraud is handled.

You need to think of these before you start. If you cannot answer the questionnaire with reasonable certainty that you can handle the task, it is more cost effective to have a professional run your PPC campaign.

If you are not up to the task, you could be stuck paying for clicks that didn't actually happen or are of no use and cost more than you can afford.

PPC Advertisement Text

The text of your PPC advertisement is the single most important element in determining the success or failure of your PPC campaign. Don't get confused. The optimization of your site for SEO and PPC advertising are two *separate* activities.

In fact the closest thing that ties them together are that they both use the same keywords. Choosing those keywords for both your SEO and PPC campaign does determine your success or failure in both.

Those chosen keywords should lead your targeted demographic (also known as qualified visitors) to your site through direct links. A successfully researched and implemented SEO strategy defines and optimizes your site for keywords relevant to the site topic that help visitors to find you by using search engines.

The combination of SEO and PPC ensures that your site is drawing *qualified visitors*. Once you understand the relationship between PPC and SEO, you can begin to consider what it takes to make PPC ads successful. It all starts with the right advertisement text.

In PPC you should never use category words which are broad. Category words are those that can relate to many things that your website doesn't provide. Let's consider the example we used earlier where one of the keywords for the local gym was "exercise equipment." Well, that broad category keyword could get people to see your ad and click if they are trying to buy equipment or sell equipment or repair equipment. Want to pay for the useless click from those people?

Product words are more specific (think long-tail), and these are the words that people search for when they're ready to make a purchase. For example, keywords that make up a better long-tail word for a Sacramento Gym are "sacramento gym," "sacramento racketball," or "sacramento fitness center":

Sidebar: Avoiding negative keywords

Negative keywords are words that cause a PPC ad *not* to be shown. These are words that can be associated with the topic that you're targeting, but not with the specific product or service that you're trying to advertise.

For example, if your website sells classical music, you should never use keywords such as country, heavy metal, or "rap." Most of the search engines are now smart enough to flag those words as negative keywords and reduce the number of times that your ad is shown.

It's important to keep your keywords grouped together if you are using different landing pages of your website. It's these words that you'll be working with as you create your keyword advertisement text for each set of keywords.

Note: *Using your keywords in your advertisement text can increase your advertisement click-through rates by as much as 50 percent.*

It always helps if you write down several clear sentences that express the message you want visitors to see. Just brainstorm and get the ideas written down. Make sure you include the benefits of your product or service as well. You should also write down several benefits that might draw in your searching demographic.

There is a way to cheat. See what words and phrases your competition are using by researching your keywords on Google or Bing and looking at the ads your competition is using.

Writing Your Ad

Now that we have your list, we need to set the tone for the demographic we are looking for. For example, there is a big difference between the teenage generation and the senior generation. If you're trying to reach teens for video game sales, you'll want to write your advertisement in a language that attracts them. On the other hand, if you are trying to reach seniors, your slogan might be something more old-fashioned.

You shouldn't try to reach everyone with a single ad. If you do, you'll probably be reaching no one at all. Each demographic should have its own unique guidelines for ad text, and you should take the time to learn the requirements for the PPC campaign you need to create.

You should write and create your ad to be relevant and compelling. Here are some tips to help you:

- Include keywords in your ad text.

- Tell your potential visitors exactly what you offer and why they want it.

- Don't exaggerate claims regarding the benefits of your products or services.

- Instruct your potential visitors to action saying things like "Click now!"

- Create a sense of urgency if possible. Such as "Discount today only," "limited availability," or "offer expires soon."

- Draw valid demographics, not views. The purpose in PPC advertisement is to draw potential visitors to your site, not just get clicks.

- Use long full sentences and abbreviate when possible. Try to cut only non-keywords.

- Use strong, motivating words – you'll have a very limited amount of space in which to write your ad.

- Experiment endlessly. If your PPC ad is perfect right out of the gate, it will truly be an anomaly. Trust me.

You'll likely find yourself readjusting the ad you create frequently because of changes in your products or services. Set aside at least an hour or two a day to put into your PPC ad campaign, especially in the beginning. Only through experimentation and testing can you achieve PPC success and not break the bank..

Getting the Most out of PPC

As a website owner you are always trying to get new and old customers back to our site. We want those human visitors to come to our websites and to buy what we are selling. To entice new customers to your website you cannot rely on your site being on the top of the search engines with no competition all the time.

Having a consistent PPC campaign is essential. Not only that but you can target your PPC campaign toward many more keywords than you can optimize your site for and make changes quickly and effectively.

We have learned in this chapter the effectiveness of the PPC Model, which is the most popular advertising model. Pay-Per-Click is exactly what it sounds like. The advertiser bids on keywords and tells the advertising company that they will pay a certain number of cents or dollars for every click on the ad that you place on the search engine or its partner websites.

There are more places for PPC advertising than you might think. All these websites have advantages in one way or another and might be effective for your websites advertising. Here are some websites you might consider for your PPC budget:

> http://adwords.google.com/
> http://www.content.overture.com/d
> http://www.411web.com/
> http://www.7search.com/
> http://www.abcsearch.com/
> http://www.adbrite.com/
> http://www.ask.com/
> http://www.brainfox.com/
> http://www.enhance.com/
> http://www.kanoodle.com/
> http://search.looksmart.com/
> http://www.lycos.com/
> http://advertising.microsoft.com/home
> http://www.miva.com/
> http://www.search123.com/
> http://www.searchfeed.com/
> http://turbo10.com/

NOTE: *Yahoo no longer makes the list because they are now operated by Microsoft adCenter.*

There are some disadvantages to PPC as opposed to organic SEO listings, including the high cost of bids for certain keywords, poor conversion rates on purchased clicks, and click fraud which we discussed earlier.

Impressions in Cost Per Thousands (CPM)

The Cost Per Thousand Impressions Model (CPM) is often associated with banner advertising, but can now be purchased for text ads as well. This type of advertising is available from these sources:

- http://adwords.google.com/
- http://www.realtechnetwork.com/
- http://www.joetec.net/

Generally, per click, CPM advertising is much cheaper than PPC. It's cheaper because its effectiveness is usually less. As with any other type of advertising, you need to track click-through and conversion rates to determine if the advertising is effective for your business.

How much cheaper is it? Well, using Google AdWords, you can sometimes buy CPM advertising for as little as $2 per 1000 impressions. The major appeal of CPM advertising is its perceived low-cost, with rates ranging between $2 – $3 per 1000 impressions. Watch out though. Google could have 10,000 impressions for popular keywords in two days.

Just make sure to keep an eye on your advertising budget. From firsthand experience, I can vouch that it may appear inexpensive, but in a short time it can add up quickly.

Pay-for-Inclusion Services

Another tool that you can use to get paid results on a search engine is a service known as *paid inclusion*. Sometimes this is also called *pay for inclusion (PFI.)* Similarly there is another term called *pay per inclusion (PPI)*. It is similar although there is a small difference between the two. PFI is a strategy whereby you pay a fee small fee to be included in a search index. This fee doesn't guarantee your ranking on the search engine. It's a simple flat fee that's usually paid annually.

PPI is a strategy in which you pay a small fee to have your websites URL included on a search engine. There is a twist however. The fee that you pay for PPI is based on the number of clicks you receive as a result of that inclusion on the search engine. Again, PPI does not guarantee your ranking on the search engine. Your only guarantee is that you will be listed on a search. Moreover, that per-click fee can often be comparatively high, in the range of $.25 to $.50 per click to your website.

Click Fraud

Say you own a website that allows Google AdWords to appear on the site. Knowing you make a profit the ads are clicked on, you go to the site whenever possible and click on the ads. Cha-ching! Money in your pocket. This would be what is known as click fraud.

Sometimes click fraud happens when a person, group of people, or automated script clicks on PPC advertisements. Because the concept of PPC is that advertisers pay each time someone clicks on their ads, this drives the cost of ads higher and higher without resulting in any conversions.

Sometimes there is no immediate monetary benefit. For example, your competition might do it just to make your costs higher. Some advertisers also believe that PPC providers commit and even encourage click fraud to drive profits. This might not be so far from the truth. Several court cases have resulted in settlements when PPC providers such as Google and Yahoo! were sued for contributing to or allowing click fraud.

Unless all the clicks come from the same IP address, it's hard to prove that click fraud is actually happening. There are many software programs, called clickbots, that can create clicks from what appear to be spoofed or different IP addresses.

In many cases, there are indicators of click fraud such as an inflated number of clicks without conversions, clicks that all occur from the same IP, the same city, or if the time of clicks is unusual. These can all be signs of click fraud.

Another good indicator for me is when the level of clicks from Google partner websites are more than half the number of clicks on the actual Google search engine website. That is a big red flag for me and when that starts happening I know to turnoff the ads on affiliate websites.

If you suspect that you're being targeted by click fraud, immediately contact the fraud department of your PPC provider. If you don't receive satisfactory results from reporting the activity, then you should consider pursuing some type of legal action or discontinue the ads that are suspect.

Click fraud in the end can cost your company thousands, even tens of thousands, of dollars and ultimately destroy your PPC advertising campaign altogether. Only close monitoring of your stats for any signs of click fraud will help prevent it.

Look at this chart in Figure 8.29. Because of constant monitoring we picked up on what appears to be an automated click fraud on day two of the fraud. Look at the figure. Can you tell the day?

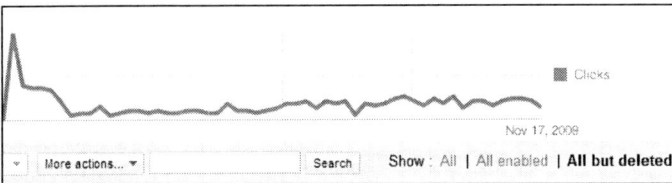

Figure 8.29

We noticed the day this happened right away. We went to Google to see where they were all coming from and it was several affiliate websites. It was easy to see the huge increase in clicks. Halfway through the next day we eliminated the problem. It hurt initially but at least we didn't go bankrupt not knowing the problem was there.

Click Fraud Is a Crime

Click fraud is a crime, whether you are falsely inflating the number of click-throughs on PPC ads either for personal gain or simply as a way to harm the competition.

In an effort to insulate themselves from criminal charges and to create as many problems as possible, some advertisers will employ what are called "clickbots." These are software programs that search for and click on PPC links to drive up prices. These "clickbots" are usually automated and very often almost impossible to trace back to their owners.

Another form of click fraud are called "Paid-to-Read" searchers, also known as PTR's. Businesses actually hire readers to read and click through PPC ads online. It's much harder to track multiple individuals than to track a single individual at one location using repetitive activity or "clickbots" to commit click fraud.

Search engines are being made to answer for click fraud, and the associated costs that PPC users are having to pay because of it, causing search engines to crack down on the problem. If you get caught conducting a click-fraud scheme, you could face stout fines and possibly even a criminal prosecution that could result in jail time.

Now that your head is about to explode with all this information on PPC campaigns, let's switch gears and look at how social media can help rankings in the next chapter.

Chapter 9-Social Media

Let's go back to my analogy in the early chapters where everything you do adds to the imaginary points value that Google and other major search engines use to assess your rankings. The more you make your website interactive, the longer people will stay. The general thinking is, the more *social media elements* you add, the more often visitors will visit and find your website relevant to its subject matter.

Search engines believe those rules mentioned in the last paragraph, so you should make social media play a big role in your website's optimization. If you're a novice you might be asking right now, "what are social media elements?" When you understand what social media elements are, it's not a long leap from there to *social-media optimization*.

Social media is content created by people using highly accessible and scalable publishing technologies. A better definition might be that social media elements are works of user-created video, audio, text or other multimedia that are published and shared in a social environment, such as a blog, wiki, or video hosting website. Well known sites that engage in social media are BlogSpot, Blogger, Twitter, YouTube, Flickr, LinkedIn, and Facebook.

Creating your own social media elements such as blogs on your website or participating in other social media websites is what brings traffic to your website and adds to your websites content. One of the best things about social media is that in general most elements are free in terms of monetary investment. There is, for the most part, no cost to participate in these networks except for your investment of time, which depending on how involved you get could become substantial.

When correctly tapped into social media, marketing spreads like a virus. This is why it is sometimes called viral marketing Viral marketing is a not a bad thing. When you participate in social-media, you can almost guarantee that your marketing will soon have that viral quality you're seeking.

Unfortunately, social-media optimization is not as simple as going to a website and signing up or starting a one paragraph blog and waiting for people to come to your website. For the most part, they won't.

Approaching social media in that manner will waste your time, and by the time you figure it out the bad reputation you may leave behind may haunt your website or domain name. Managing your reputation on the web is called *reputation management* in SEO circles and I could write another book just on this topic. I have hundreds of stories on what to look out for and stories of companies ruined on the web because of social media.

The basics to keep yourself from having a bad reputation in social networking is this: when you provide input using social media methods, make sure you do the following:

1. Provide only relative content and no exaggerated claims.
2. Add positive comments and don't make it appear as though you are trying to outdo someone else or are advertising your services. People don't forget when a faker tries to jump in their midst for purely marketing purposes. You are marketing but this is social networking. You are making friends.
3. If you're an expert, make sure your claims are accurate. There are real experts on every subject who will point out your flaws with actual data.
4. Don't ignore people's issues with your product or service. Address them immediately or you are inviting everyone who has ever had a small issue with your product or service to add their two cents.
5. Don't bad mouth a competitor – your only inviting a tidal wave of retribution from your competitor and others.

Seems easy enough, right? Social-media optimization is about first joining communities and creating relationships or friends. It's by going through the process of becoming part of the community and providing relevant and helpful information that your brand will begin to be recognized by other community members. That's when you can announce that your website has useful information, and your efforts will begin to pay off.

Social Media's Value

Some sites have obvious value in social media. Websites such as MySpace, Twitter, YouTube, and Facebook are all websites that no one thought would amount to anything when they began, but they each suddenly took off in their own way, becoming some of the most popular sites on the internet.

Internet users like something to do and to be a part of something bigger. They love to be a part of the community, and that includes online communities as well. The generation that has just entered the workforce and those growing up right now are very computer and internet savvy. For the most part, this generation has been a part of those social networking sites during their schooling. These sites have provided everything from evaluations of teachers, classes, entertainment events, self advertising, keeping up with the latest school rumors, and even schools providing their school event calendars.

When this generation is out of school they become involved in all kinds of activities online, from shopping and downloading music to participating in social networks. The kids are networking socially for different reasons than adults, but both have learned to participate.

Social-Media Strategies

So you have a website and you need to market it. Using social media is different than most marketing techniques you are taught in economics or marketing in college – At least until they stop using 15-year-old text books. Now there are thousands of sites and you can make your own social media components, but the goals are the same. In the end your goals are to:

- **Know how to target your audience and deliver the right message:** If you approach the wrong audience with the wrong message, you'll learn a quick lesson in reputation management when the court of opinion attempts to destroy your reputation.
- **Create valuable content:** Good content is key to social-media marketing. If you make it a point to create fresh, unique content regularly, visitors will come to you because they know they can find the current information they need. If you're afraid of giving away all your eggs except on a one on one sales call, you will get your message out very slowly.
- **Be a valuable resource, even if it doesn't help you monetarily:** If you try to help without expecting anything in return you gain points and you can gain a good reputation which will, in turn, draw users to your website. Always wearing your salesman hat works in the corporate world, but online it is a death sentence.
- **Be a user resource**: Internet users, and especially those users who participate in social media and social networking, expect you to provide information that is useful and relevant to them. If you're not providing accurate and helpful information, they'll go to someone who is and bad mouth you on the way.
- **Help your content spread:** One way of advertising your website's services or products discreetly is to use your trophy and long-tail keywords in your helpful tips and comments on social media sites. Search engines also index this information and

when people use search engines to search on those keywords, your blog or other social networking submissions show up. Another good tip is to collect or group your helpful information into other online content such as a PDF, an audio file, or video file which you can provide links for.

- **Increase your linkability:** You want useful information that other site owners find valuable enough to put a link on their website to yours. The linkability of your site is determined by the amount of content that you have available to users who might come from social networks. Old information that rarely changes will not help, so make sure your content is updated regularly.

- **Make bookmarking your site easy:** Don't make users try to figure out how to add your blog or site to their content feed. Post your URL or code for visitors to add you to their important links or their website. Use a tool called RSS Button Maker at www.toprankblog.com/tools/rss-buttons to create a button.

- **Reward helpful users:** If you have users that are helpful and/or send business your way, find a way to reward those users so they will continue to be helpful, especially if you made the sale.

- **Don't be afraid to try new things**: Use your creativity to do something different as often as possible. In social-media optimization, creativity is rewarded.

Social media marketing is a great tool if used wisely. It can also be a terrible one if you use it wrong. Using the wrong tactics or using them only half way will render your efforts worthless. You can also expect that it will be very hard to rebuild the trust that you destroy on the web.

There are some rules of etiquette to follow that will help you keep out of trouble. Let's take a look at those in the next section.

Social Media Etiquette

As an SEO expert, I find that companies come to me frequently because their web reputation has been injured, many times unintentionally by their own staff and sometimes through no fault of their own.

Let's take a look at a few rules of etiquette that you should follow to keep yourself from becoming a statistic in the bad category:

1. Spend some time listening to your audience before you join the conversation so you can gain an understanding of the language, the tone, and the expectations of the conversation participants.
2. After you begin to interact with social media elements, use the information that you gather watching and listening on a social

networks to ensure that your strategy is targeting the correct people and that the responses to your input are positive.

3. Track your site metrics to see if there are any sudden spikes or dips in your web traffic which could indicate that your involvement is effective or ineffective.

4. Provide only content that adds value to the conversation. If your content doesn't add anything or is inaccurate, the other participants will either ignore you or begin to destroy you.

5. Use RSS feeds. RSS feeds instantly update those who have chosen to watch your content. This means that your links will spread faster than you could ever imagine.

6. Keep in mind that social media is all about relationships. Both engage in and be willing to encourage participation.

7. Make an individual approach as an expert in your service or product. Approaching as the business or company will automatically create suspicion. They may think you are just there to sell something. If you don't have the time yourself, consider hiring bloggers or others to handle your company's social-media participation.

Social Media Outlets

There are many types of social media elements out there in the web world for you to tap into. It is sometimes referred to as Web 2.0 and is definitely the major shift in SEO right now. Web 2.0 is all about the social nature of the internet, and if you don't tap into that social aspect, the SEO on your site will quickly be out-of-date and ranked very low on every major search engine. Using social-media elements, however, you can get a jump-start on your social-media strategy.

So where do you start? Here are some suggestions on what sites you should visit and incorporate into your website:

- ✓ **Blogger:** www.blogger.com
- ✓ **Blogspot:** www.blogspot.com
- ✓ **Crunchbase:** www.crunchbase.com
- ✓ **Delicious Bookmarks**: www.delicious.com
- ✓ **Digg:** www.digg.com
- ✓ **Furl:** www.furl.net
- ✓ **Twitter:** www.twitter.com
- ✓ **MySpace:** www.myspace.com
- ✓ **Facebook:** www.facebook.com
- ✓ **LinkedIn:** www.linkedin.com
- ✓ **Merchant Circle:** www.merchantcircle.com

- ✓ **Micro Persuasion:** www.micropersuasion.com
- ✓ **Propeller:** www.propeller.com
- ✓ **StumbleUpon:** www.stumbleupon.com
- ✓ **Reddit:** www.reddit.com
- ✓ **Newsvine:** www.newsvine.com
- ✓ **Fark:** www.fark.com
- ✓ **Clipmarks:** www.clipmarks.com
- ✓ **Shoutwire:** www.shoutwire.com
- ✓ **Smogger Social Media Blog:** smogger.wordpress.com
- ✓ **YouTube:** www.youtube.com
- ✓ **Wikipedia:** www.wikipedia.com

Note: *See Appendix C for a more complete list of the top social media websites.*

These sites each have a different social media element which can be incorporated into your website. But here is a little tip! In SEO circles the saying goes, "Have more to do with Google and Google will have more to do with you." It couldn't be more true in social media either. Why am I telling you this? Well from that list above, Google owns and runs Blogger.com, Blogspot.com and YouTube.com. So if you're just starting with social media elements, which do you think will give you the greatest rankings on Google? You're right, brain scientist, the ones owned by Google.

Twitter Shunned By Google?

Well Twitter on steroids has appeared from Google in the form of Google Buzz. Is this because Google is upset with Twitter? Up until recently Twitter was more of a data pusher, but could they be deliberately moving in to a search engine?

Google itself is already designed like a social network. As a Google "publisher" your goal is to be listed and get the attention of as many others as possible. If you are successful, your content is shared via links that Google users (searchers) can click on.

For most Google users, when they find something they like, they link to the website. This can be in the form of creating bookmarks, subscribe to the site's RSS feed or e-mail newsletter, and if you are a website owner creating a link to the content from your own website. Without realizing it, you become a "follower" of that website. Similar to the concept of Twitter only a search engine does this in a massive quantity.

Twitter's has a new advertising system of sponsored topics and searches. When you visit Twitter you new see a sponsored topic at the bottom of that section (at right). And when you search Twitter, you'll find sponsored tweets at the top. Does this look familiar to you Google users?

There are rumors floating around that these sponsored listing are costing in the tens of thousands of dollars. I am sure this will soon lead Twitter to heavily promote its new advertising making their sponsored listings more attractive to advertisers and big bucks to Twitter.

I don't think it is too much of a stretch to think Twitter won't get in to the same business that Google is in. It's not too hard to create a bidding system of keywords and phrases for top positions on Twitter search. Just like I have mentioned throughout this book, use keywords and phrases, hashtags, aim for retweets and use the correct keyword density for your target search engines.

The more you can brand your Twitter account and keywords with users, the better prepared you will be when competitors start buying your keywords for a Twitter search.

Chapter 10-Setting SEO Goals and Making a Plan

For most people the goal is simple, outdo what your competition does for the same keywords and beat their rankings. So I guess the chapter is done. Well, maybe it's not that simple. Maybe I should break it down just a little.

Before we begin, you should have a search engine optimization plan in place. This will help you create your SEO goals. This will help your focus as the purpose of making critical changes to your website for optimization.

Your SEO plan should be updated every 3 months based on what your competition is doing versus what your previous changes have accomplished. In the next chapter, we will look at website analytics which will help you understand where your needs are. It will also help you see where you need to concentrate your efforts at any given time.

Before reading this chapter, however, you should have a good understanding of your trophy keywords and the other keywords you want to focus on. If you don't, you should visit Chapter 2 and make sure you know the keywords your company needs to use and the competition that is competing for those keywords.

In the beginning, you're most likely going to be focusing your SEO on getting your site listed on all the search engines. For this part, Chapter 3 should be your first stop. If you haven't done all the steps outlined in Chapter 3, then you should stop now and jump back there and make sure that your website's URL is listed on all the hand submissions and you have your website being submitted through automation to all the other smaller search engines and directories.

By now you should be familiar with the focus of the other chapters. We have already talked about adding your keywords into the content of each page and making each page focused on one subject, getting relevant links to your website, adding keywords to the content of each page, adding Meta tags, adding correct titles with keywords, adding multimedia, adding social media, and providing the correct word density on each page for a focused search engine.

Each one of these components is a must on your website and is all a part of your SEO strategy. These are all a part of your SEO plan and all of these components are an "add it once and forget about it" type of deal. You need to continuously monitor what is working, what is not, what your competition is doing, and make adjustments as necessary to maintain and update the elements of SEO that help you rank well.

The basic rule here is that your efforts will change, but they will never end. You need to plan to continue using, modifying, and updating your website to help your SEO rankings, and changing your strategies based on search engine changes, new internet components, etc.

For instance, last year having Twitter and RSS feeds on your website did virtually nothing for rankings. The year before having a YouTube video on your website did almost nothing for rankings. This year they are an absolute must-have to increase rankings.

This year a major change took place. Bing didn't even exist last year and our recommendation was to focus your SEO strategies only on Google with Yahoo! as an afterthought. Now because of all the changes, you might actually get more business by optimizing for Bing than your ever realized. Bing has a major market share now. With a majority of the website optimized for Google and not Bing, there is market share to gain by optimizing for Bing, especially in the very competitive keyword arena where the competition is higher than most for a keyword.

Today, every major search engine focuses on many components of a website in ranking a website. Only a few of the smaller search engines focus on a single aspect of a website their rankings. This means that over time, if you are focused only on a single keyword or links for your website, you will find that your SEO efforts will begin to fail quickly.

You have to keep your efforts up and not let down your guard. You can spend a year getting your website's rankings high and be on the first page for any search with your keywords only to lose everything in a week. The fact is you can spend months getting your rankings up and they can be lost in a fleeting moment if you are not careful.

Let me give you an example. There is a very large software company that I do the SEO for. I spent a year and a half getting them to a Google ranking of 8 out of 10. It was one of my most prized accomplishments and I jumped for joy and bragged to everyone I worked with the day I looked and their website ranking was an 8/10 on Google. Only a month later they were a 2. So what happened?

Someone took over their website development who didn't have a clue about SEO. The new designer worked with the owner of the company to create a flashy new website without any consultation from me. In fact, my point of contact with the company didn't even know it was being done. The new website was all Flash and looked great.

The trouble is that when it was created, none of my SEO work was incorporated into the website. Even worse, the new web designer changed all the page file names for every page that was indexed with the search engines. So when users on the search engines searched on their keywords and clicked on a link to their website, there was no page. Rather, there was an error saying the page didn't exist. They were now invisible on the internet. Sales dropped to all time lows in a single month. It was two weeks before someone at my office noticed what was going on and contacted the company. By then it was too late.

When you went to their "About Us" page that used to be named "aboutus.html" it went to an error page because the new web developer named the file "about_us.php". This happened four months ago and they have reverted back to the old site as the SEO work I needed wouldn't incorporate into the new site. Search engines don't like websites that change their URL of their pages and ranking really is based on URL and not actually by website. Each page on your website has its own ranking from Google based on it relevance and all the other items we discuss in this book.

Today, the software company website that was once on the first page of every major search engine for their keywords is on page 3 of Google and has a ranking of 4/10. Their sales went from averaging 150-200 sales per month to only 63 last month. This was a catastrophe for them. They were on an uphill trend adding new employees and growing all because of the SEO work I was doing for them. Today they are four employees fewer and just barely staying in business.

A website needs constant growth and relevant material constantly to maintain its SEO status and keep the site from becoming what is known to search engines as a stale website. (A website where the material never changes.) Those changes, however, need to be looked at from an SEO optimization perspective from every angle. Most outsiders think that every web designer is familiar with SEO. From my experience, very few have any knowledge of it. It is a specialization that most web designers and developers know little or nothing about.

So what should your SEO Plan include? Let's look at this in the next section.

Time and Effort in an SEO Plan

The first thing your plan needs to include is lots of time. Then add more time to that. This is one of the main reasons that most companies sub out their SEO work. Not only because it takes someone who lives and breathes SEO to keep up on the latest trends and technology, but because of the amount of time involved.

Simply adding new content here and there on your website and changing a Meta tag or two won't help you increase your rankings on the major search engines.

> **NOTE:** *If you are doing the SEO yourself, to keep pace and save some time, you might consider designing your site similar to a blog where content is easily changeable.*

Your SEO plan should be considered a dynamic document that changes all the time based on your needs assessed from monitoring not only your website, but the search engines and your competition on the search engines. If you can't figure out what your competition is doing to one up your SEO work, then you need to call in a professional and you need to do it fast because what you do today has virtually no effect on search engines for months. In essence, you are planning today what you want to happen on the search engines 3-6 months from now. An SEO plan will help you stay on track.

Now that you understand how important it is to put time into your website's SEO, we need to create a clearly defined goal built around your business needs. Virtually every business has different needs and at different levels even when two different company websites are in the same industry.

A small local business would focus only on the local area long-tail keyword searches, whereas a large business selling nationally or in a large geographical area would need to invest time, money, and considerable effort into increasing the exposure of their website to potential customers outside its geographic region on a larger level using more generic shorter keywords.

For example, if you sold sports equipment in Sacramento, you would target a local campaign using the keyword of "sacramento sports equipment." If your website sold sports equipment nationally you would target a much harder SEO keyword with more competition such as, "sports equipment". The fewer the words, the harder it is to get your site listed higher in the search engines. The broader the keyword, the more competition there is for that keyword.

In Sacramento there are probably 40 websites competing for sports equipment and maybe ten percent do any professional website optimization. However, nationwide there are probably thousands vying for first place with those keywords and if only ten percent do website optimization, you have a lot of competition to beat.

Both the smaller company and the larger company need to implement an SEO plan. The larger company that needs to concentrate on a national level with lots of competition will require more than this book can offer (unless you are just starting your website).

If you are trying to do a national campaign with lots of competition, most likely your competition is employing powerhouse professional help. This is not the time to experiment. Your revenue (The money you make from your website) is an important factor. Your SEO plan and goals should not only focus on increasing your website visits, but also on increasing your revenues. You can track revenue by funneling your website visitors through individually targeted sales transaction pages while they are visiting your website.

You should make sure the goals you set are realistic. It's very easy to become unfocused with your SEO efforts and get discouraged when those efforts don't meet your goals or expectations. It's very easy to spend gobs of money on SEO and never accomplish anything.

Your SEO goals and the plan you create must be flexible and grow with your organization.

SEO Plan Details

Now that you have a set of goals in mind for your website, it's time to create an SEO plan. The SEO plan is the document that you'll use to help you stay focused as you try to implement your individual SEO strategies.

Keyword Research

Continuous keyword research should be your second line item after your time entry on your SEO plans details. Google Analytics (discussed in the next chapter) has a way of looking to see what keywords were used to find your site. Many times it becomes clear that there are a market of people who find your site that you didn't even know.

I will give you an example. My SEO website targets many keywords, but I noticed that several people searching for better website rankings searched using the keyword "search engine help" and found my website way down on the list of a search engine. After a few of these in one month, I added the keyword to my PPC campaign. After getting about 80 hits from that in one month, I optimized a landing page just for that keyword. I now get about 200 hits per month from that term which is business I never would have gotten had I not been analyzing the keywords people were using to access my site.

It was a minor change in the bigger picture. I was already creating content for the site, but by focusing on some of the most logical and well known keywords. I didn't crawl in the mind of a prospective searcher but Google caught it for me. I just had to interpret the results.

You should never discount the little things. Even minor details, such as refocusing and changing your keyword efforts or modifying the tagging on your pages can have a major impact if it is done right. For every website that I do SEO, I find a little niche on a monthly basis that my clients' competition never catches and I capitalize on that. Using those little niches in the right places can make a major difference in the amount of traffic that your site receives.

Reputation Management

The next item you should have in your plan is reputation management, which is a critical part of any online business. If you Google anyone of my SEO client's URL's, you see nothing but good or neutral press. The top 10 results of a search are usually corporate sites, blogs, press releases and other landing pages I optimized or created for them. This is no accident. Many clients who do any volume of online sales will get a disgruntled customer or two and sometimes a negative news article or blog entry or other problem can affect their online reputation.

Sometimes this bad press is known when it comes out in a news article that everyone sees and talks about. Sometimes, however, a disgruntled person can place negative information on blogs, as comments, and many other places that can be indexed into the search engines and work to destroy your online presence little by little. If you do not take time to monitor you SERP (Search Engine Results Page), you may miss the reason you are dropping in sales or hits to your website because of the negative that is displayed. In one case I had a customer who owned a large mortgage company. Their company does about 8,000 loans per year and have to turn down some clients for a loan, often at the last minute because of some unforeseen issue such as the client used a credit card or bought a car and dropped their credit scores, disqualifying them for the loan product for which they had been approved. It was inevitable, like it or not, that those few disturbed clients who posted their comments on blogs managed to fill up four of the top ten spots on a Google search for many of their important keywords.

Then the inevitable happened. The web visits stopped and the phone calls stopped coming. This is a good example of what can happen if you don't have monitoring your online reputation a part of your SEO plan. You're probably saying, this is nice to tell me but where do I start if I find negative links or information about my company?

Before this ever happens, you should identify key editorial contacts at industry and business publications, ezines, and press release portals that can help to place positive press in its place. Make a separate page in your plan to log these contacts. You should always be looking for opportunities to post comments on relevant articles and place links to your company's URL.

Today, you can publish stories in minutes, versus days, weeks or months. So when you do post content, it not only appears on the Website, but on search engines, syndicated content sites, and news search engines as well.

You should always create targeted press releases that can be linked-to from a variety of sources. The press release should also be optimized for the best relevant keyword density so it appears as high as possible in related searches. If you skipped learning about keyword density, there is an index in the back of this book. I would recommend learning about how to use that to your advantage.

Launch your own blog and become friendly with other bloggers, because bloggers are the most publicized arm of social online media. Bloggers are increasing their credibility with the consumer, which means their opinions really do matter. This is somewhat like a "Third Party Endorsement." Having bloggers post negative comments about you or your brand can spell disaster. Be prepared to get into the conversation by posting comments on blogs with negative content about your product/services and link back to your own press release or blog.

Another very effective tool is the use of sub-domains. Google sees them as separate websites, but they do still carry the authority and trust of the root domain. When you create a sub-domain, you must not simply copy content from your main domain. The content must be different. The new sub-domain must have useful, unique content. It does not need 100 pages; just ten or so pages per sub-domain will do. All you need is two to three well-optimized sub-domains.

Sign up for a Twitter account and place the Twitter Wiki on your website, but keep updating it with relevant information about your site. You might also consider MySpace and Facebook, or other social bookmarking network entries. And of course, post links to your press releases using keywords in your text links.

Managing your reputation requires the creation of relative content on your own website, distribution of positive content, as well as strategic participation in online discussions. When you combine these strategies, an integrated search engine reputation management program is in place and ready for action in the event a negative piece of information is indexed about your company or URL.

PPC

Monitoring your PPC account is, of course, important. Whether you use Google AdWords or Bing's AdCenter or related pay-per-click programs to get your message out there you need to constantly monitor which keywords are working for you and which ones get a lot of clicks but don't turn into sales. Too broad of a keyword, as we learned in previous chapters, can cost you a lot of money with very little results.

In terms of reputation management, a PPC campaign can help as well. While optimized press releases and related content may take days or weeks to appear high in relevant search results on search engines, paid text ads are virtually instantaneous and provide total control over placement (by keyword) of your message.

Reprioritizing Pages

In the beginning, prioritizing your web pages is easy. Give priority to the pages that focus on each of your keywords, and in the same order that your keywords are in. You should prioritize your efforts on the pages that support those trophy words and draw the most amount of traffic and sales.

These are top-priority pages and visitors should naturally gravitate to those pages. These should be focused landing pages that utilize all the optimization techniques, including social media and keyword density optimization. The content should remain relevant and constantly be updated so it never gets stale.

Pages such as your home landing page or those that will generate the most traffic or revenue should be a road map and included in your SEO plan and goals should be set for your marketing efforts. If four of the web pages on your site are your top priority, those should encompass a majority of your time and efforts in your SEO plan.

Additional Plan Items

After you have prioritized your sites web pages, you should assess where you stand and where you need to be with your current SEO efforts. Make a checklist and dedicate time to assess all the pages in your website. Those that should be checked more frequently are the following:

- Keywords
- Keyword density
- Title tags
- Social media elements
- Site/page tagging
- Page content relevancy
- Replacement of stale content
- Frequently changed content
- Blogs
- Social media optimization
- Social bookmarking
- Site linking
- Press release writing
- Article submissions
- Video optimization
- RSS Feeds
- Search engine placement
- PPC

Items that can be checked less frequently:

- Site map accuracy
- Longevity of domain registration
- Robots.txt optimization
- Site map
- HTML source code and errors
- Alt tags
- Link development
- Manual link requests to related sites
- Directory listings
- One-way links/two-way links
- HTML design
- ASP. and other coding such as Java and Flash
- Linked URLs

Completing the Plan

At this point you should have collected all the information you need to put into your SEO plan. You should also have a good idea of the priority of each item and what needs to be done frequently and which ones can be done on a less frequent basis to increase or maintain your website's search engine rankings.

Now it's time to put all of the information that you've gathered into a comprehensive plan comparing your available time and determining the SEO efforts you should be making to best utilize that time. Your SEO plan is more than just a simple picture of what's included in your website and what's not. This is the document you should use to help determine your website's current search engine rankings, reputation management, your needed marketing efforts, capital expenditures, time frames, and how you're going to keep your website from becoming stale.

The plan should look much like a business plan when you are done. It includes your goals, a work plan, marketing information, how you will grow your business, plans for managing problems, and much more.

Those strategies can include efforts such as manually submitting your site or pages from your site to directories and planning the content you'll use to draw search engine bots, spiders, and crawlers. It should also outline which pay-per-click programs you plan to use and a time line for the testing and implementation of those efforts, as well as regular follow-ups.

I always recommend that you supplement your SEO with a well-managed PPC campaign. But the goal is to maintain your URL on the first page of a search engine's search using organic SEO to maximize those naturally occurring elements. When you build on each internal and external element on your website to create a site that will naturally fall near the top of the search engine results pages (SERPs), you achieve high SERPs rankings free — other than the time it takes to implement your SEO plan.

Achieving each ranking point for organic SEO can take anywhere from three to eight months if you implement the right SEO plan. Don't get upset if you don't see immediate results from your SEO efforts. Stick to your SEO plan. If you don't see changes within 3-6 months or your rankings get worse, you should reevaluate your SEO plan or seek professional help.

Chapter 11-SEO Toolbars, Tools & Plug-Ins

If you search the internet you can find a plethora of SEO tools for sale. However, from experience I can tell you there is a free tool for just about everything. Not only that, but ninety percent of the tools that you have to pay for may also do the following:

1. Separate your money from your bank account.

2. Get information from you on how to contact you so someone from India or Pakistan or some other offshore entity can hard sell you on their SEO services, tools, or whatever you're searching for at ridiculous amounts. I might add that there are some legitimate SEO services in Middle Eastern countries but you will find the fraudulent ones much easier. They usually contact you.

3. Con you into paying for SEO tools that many times are free.

4. Con you into paying for a tool that works worse than the free tool.

Lucky for you, you are reading a book by two authors who have pretty much been there and done that for all of the above. Be very skeptical of any SEO option not included in this book or on one of our blogs. In this book, we outline free alternatives that work just as well for every type of tool. Many of the times these free tools work better than the paid alternative.

This is the section in many other SEO books where I am very disappointed because endorsements for software galore are given and the free alternatives are left out. In fact while we were writing this book, we had a company offer to pay us $5,000 for an endorsement in our book for their analytics software and another offered us $2,500 for endorsing their SEO website full of different SEO tools which are pay-per-use.

Both wanted us to leave out different free products, especially Google Analytics and Google Keyword Tools. Unfortunately for those websites and software companies, we have our own reputation management to maintain and we decided early on to make this a true SEO reference guide and not endorse any paid product unless there wasn't a better free alternative. You can be assured that we have accepted no paid endorsement fees for this book and contracted that with the publisher. This means you can trust what we write.

In the next few sections I will be looking at many different toolbars, free plug-ins, extra buttons, and software and website tools to help you with your SEO efforts. Let's start in the next section, called Toolbars and Plug-ins.

Toolbars and Plug-Ins

In site optimization and monitoring, browser toolbars are especially useful. Best of all, the ones you really need are free. In this section, I will talk about the Alexa Toolbar and go more in depth on what you can do with the Google Toolbar using plug-ins. If you did not read how to install the Google Toolbar in chapter 1, you should go back there and read that section first.

Since the Google Toolbar will encompass most of this section and has plug-ins to learn about, let's take a look at this first. Now I am assuming that you read and followed the instructions in Chapter 1 and already have the Google Toolbar installed with the PageRank icon sitting in the bar. Now, my Google Toolbar looks like the one in Figure 11.1.

Figure 11.1

I bet your wondering what all these little icons in Figure 11.2 are and how they got there. You're probably also asking yourself, "What do they do and how can they help me?"

Figure 11.2

Google has many plug-ins that can be accessed by pressing the "Adjust Toolbar Options" (the icon that looks like a wrench) on the Google Toolbar and selecting the Custom Tools option. When you do this you will see a screen similar to the one in Figure 11.3.

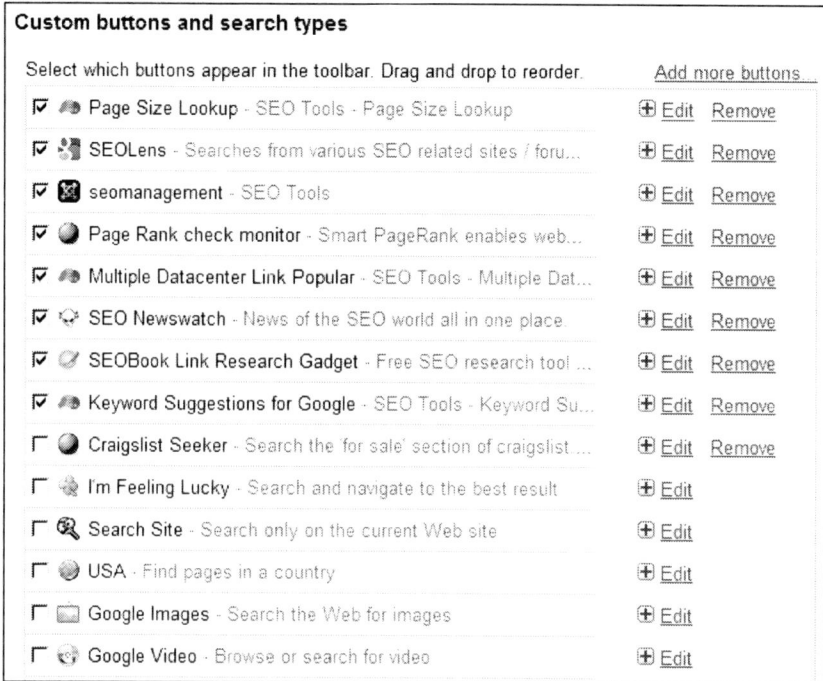

Custom buttons and search types

Select which buttons appear in the toolbar. Drag and drop to reorder.   Add more buttons

☑	Page Size Lookup · SEO Tools · Page Size Lookup	⊞ Edit	Remove
☑	SEOLens · Searches from various SEO related sites / foru...	⊞ Edit	Remove
☑	seomanagement · SEO Tools	⊞ Edit	Remove
☑	Page Rank check monitor · Smart PageRank enables web...	⊞ Edit	Remove
☑	Multiple Datacenter Link Popular · SEO Tools · Multiple Dat...	⊞ Edit	Remove
☑	SEO Newswatch · News of the SEO world all in one place	⊞ Edit	Remove
☑	SEOBook Link Research Gadget · Free SEO research tool ...	⊞ Edit	Remove
☑	Keyword Suggestions for Google · SEO Tools · Keyword Su...	⊞ Edit	Remove
☐	Craigslist Seeker · Search the 'for sale' section of craigslist ...	⊞ Edit	Remove
☐	I'm Feeling Lucky · Search and navigate to the best result	⊞ Edit	
☐	Search Site · Search only on the current Web site	⊞ Edit	
☐	USA · Find pages in a country	⊞ Edit	
☐	Google Images · Search the Web for images	⊞ Edit	
☐	Google Video · Browse or search for video	⊞ Edit	

Figure 11.3

To add SEO plug-ins and search Google for additional SEO tools, select the "Add more buttons…" link at the top right of the screen. You must first download and install the plug-ins which are accessible by clicking on their associate buttons on the Google Toolbar. They will install into your web browser without any coding from you. Most SEO plug-ins are designed to work with the Internet Explorer, Google Chrome, and the Firefox browsers. You will find that you get the most functionality using the Firefox browser; it usually becomes the browser of choice for most people in charge of SEO.

> **NOTE:** If you use Chrome, you'll find that many of the plug-ins available are not compatible. You can go to go to a website called ChromePlugIns.org to find many of the SEO tools that are compatible with the Google Chrome browser.

Choosing Plug-Ins Wisely

There are hundreds of SEO plug-ins that are available. Few plug-ins monitor more than one element of optimization, so in order to have multiple facets of your SEO strategy measured, you need multiple plug-ins. The key is determining what you need.

This is where I will put a big warning!

DO NOT BUY ANYTHING OR SIGN UP TO GET A FUNCTIONAL GOOGLE TOOLBAR PLUG-IN. DON'T GIVE A CREDIT CARD OR BANK ACCOUNT INFORMATION TO ANYONE EITHER!

In texting, when you use capital letters you are yelling. And in a sense I was. Many of the plug-ins on Google are placed by people wanting to sell you their version of a plug-in. Most of the times it is just a modified version of a free one already available.

For websites, you can choose among several different plug-ins, each usually monitoring something different. Some monitor links, while others monitor PageRank or keyword density, and still others monitor several elements. The selection process, then, begins with understanding what's available and what you can do with it.

So we have now hit the "Add more buttons…" link under Custom Tools on the "Adjust Toolbar Options" on the Google Toolbar. "So what do I do now?" you may be asking. Well, that's easy. In the search box, simply type "SEO" or "SEM" and press enter. You will see a list such as those in Figure 11.4.

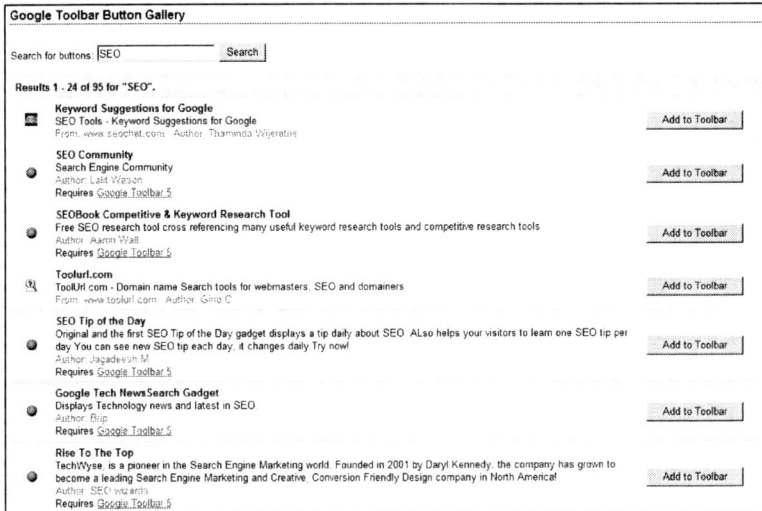

Figure 11.4

That search turns over 90 different SEO related buttons that you can add to the Google Toolbar. I recommend the following for good SEO Analysis:

1. Keyword Suggestions for Google

2. SEOBook Competitive and Keyword Research Tool
3. Google AdWords Campaign
4. SEO News
5. SEO Search Engine
6. Toolurl.com
7. Multiple Datacenter Link Popularity Check
8. SEO Tip of the Day
9. SEOBook Link Research Tool
10. SEOLens
11. Page Rank Check Monitor
12. Website Traffic
13. Code to Text Ratio
14. Page Size Lookup

As you can see from this list, there are a variety of different tools that you can plug into the Google toolbar. Everything from keyword research tools to SEO news and blogs is available. All you have to do is decide which ones are most useful for you and your SEO needs.

Each one has its own set of instructions but for the most part they ask you just to enter very little information such as a URL, IP Address, or keyword to get results.

Now let's take a look at the Alexa Toolbar and how that can help us in our quest to get better rankings.

Alexa Toolbar

The Alexa Toolbar, shown in figure 11.5, is tied into Alexa's web-traffic statistics, so the numbers that you'll find when you use this toolbar are a little skewed.

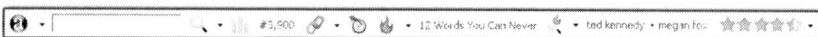

Figure 11.5

However, Alexa provides enough information to make the toolbar useful. Also, Alexa's results are a major influence on rankings found on the major search engines.

As you can see, the Alexa Toolbar looks quite a bit different from the Google Toolbar, and offers some good information. Once installed it also tracks where you go on the internet which helps Alexa determine the average traffic to a site. So visiting your own websites frequently will help to improve the rankings on a Alexa.

Installing the Alexa Toolbar

To install the Alexa Toolbar, type http://www.alexa.com/toolbar into your browser, as shown in Figure 11.6 and 11.7.

Figure 11.6

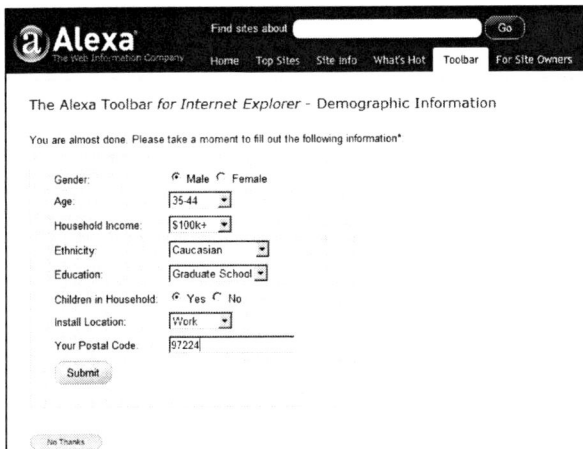

Figure 11.7

After you are done entering the demographic information and pressing "Submit," you will get a success message, as shown in Figure 11.8.

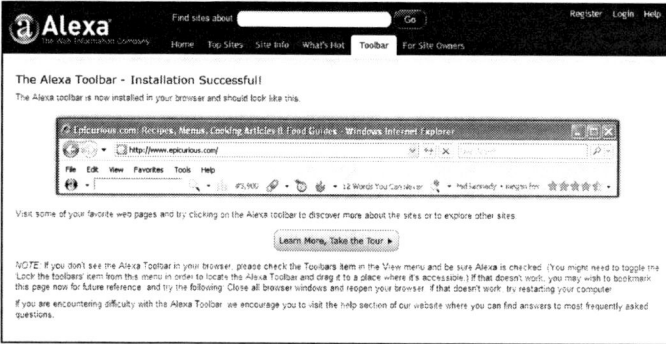

Figure 11.8a

You will now be given an option to take the tour that explains all the features of the Alexa Toolbar, as shown in Figure 11.9a and 11.9b.

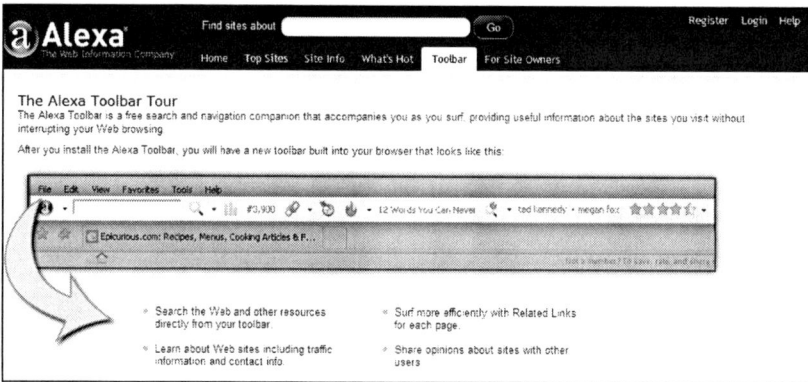

Figure 11.9a

Features of the Alexa Toolbar

Web Search

The Alexa Web Search is a whole new way to search the web. Begin by typing your search term into the box then press enter. You will be transported to a world of behind-the-scenes information about each site on the web. Don't waste time sitting through lousy sites. Use the Alexa Web Search and know before you go.

Site Info

Alexa's exclusive Site Information allows you to peer behind the scenes of each site on the web. Get access to contact information, site stats and user reviews of web sites. Plus you can even write your own reviews.

Related Links

Alexa's Related Links are a great way to discover new sites. As you surf the web, the toolbar is constantly updating with information about where other users visit.

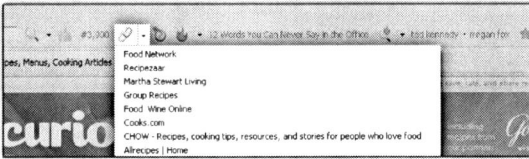

The Wayback Machine

Having trouble getting access to your favorite site, or want to see what it looked like in the past? The Wayback Machine can transport you back in time to see archived copies of your favorite sites. Click the Wayback button, select a date, and go!

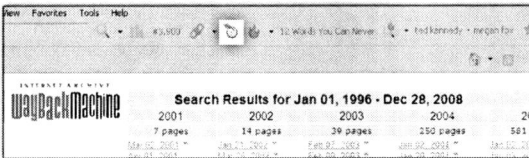

Figure 11.9b

Analytics

Analytics are used to determine all kinds of things about the traffic to your website. There are many packages that can cost stacks of money, but most do not track or report half as well as Google. Their sales techniques to sell their inferior software are interesting and usually pretty much the same when they compare their web analytics programs to Google Analytics.

I recommend using Google Analytics. You can always look for better products but watch out if these are their only claims:

    A. "Install on your own server"

    B. "Restore historical data from files"

    C. "Can track behind a firewall"

    D. "Track robots, crawlers, and spiders"

Google Analytics is a free website statistics application that you can use to track your website traffic. You can begin using Google Analytics by going to www.google.com/analytics. You must have a Google user name to access the program.

If you do not have a Google user name, you can create one when you sign in the first time by provide an e-mail address and a password. Type the verification word from the graphic provided, and then agree to the Terms of Service by clicking "I accept. Create my account."

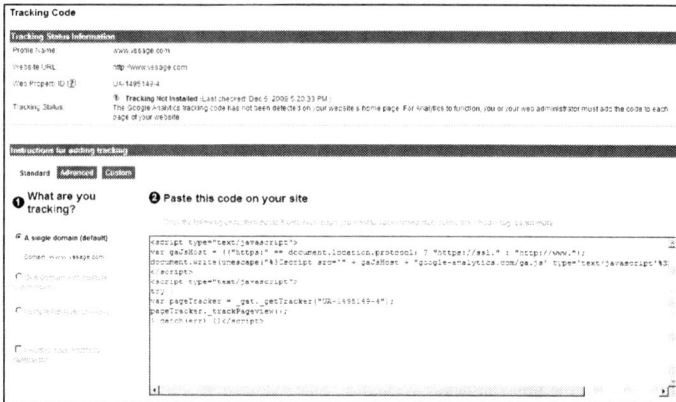

Figure 11.10

Once you've created your user name and password, accessing the tracking capabilities of Google is easy. You'll need to copy a small piece of code that Google gives you onto your website pages just before the closing Body tag: "<\Body>". Let's take a look at the text that Google provides for the coding of your website (Figure 11.10).

After you've added the code to your website, it will take a few days for Google to gather enough information to provide reports about it. More useful information will come after a full month of analytics.

Google Analytics is a service provided by Google that allows you to view and interact with detailed statistical information about the visitors to your website. After you have given Google some time to collect information about the visitors to your website, you can formulate that into reports.

The information from Google Analytics allows you to see who is visiting your website, how they are getting there, how long they stayed, what browser the visitors used, what keywords were used, and most importantly, what the visitors did once they were on your website.

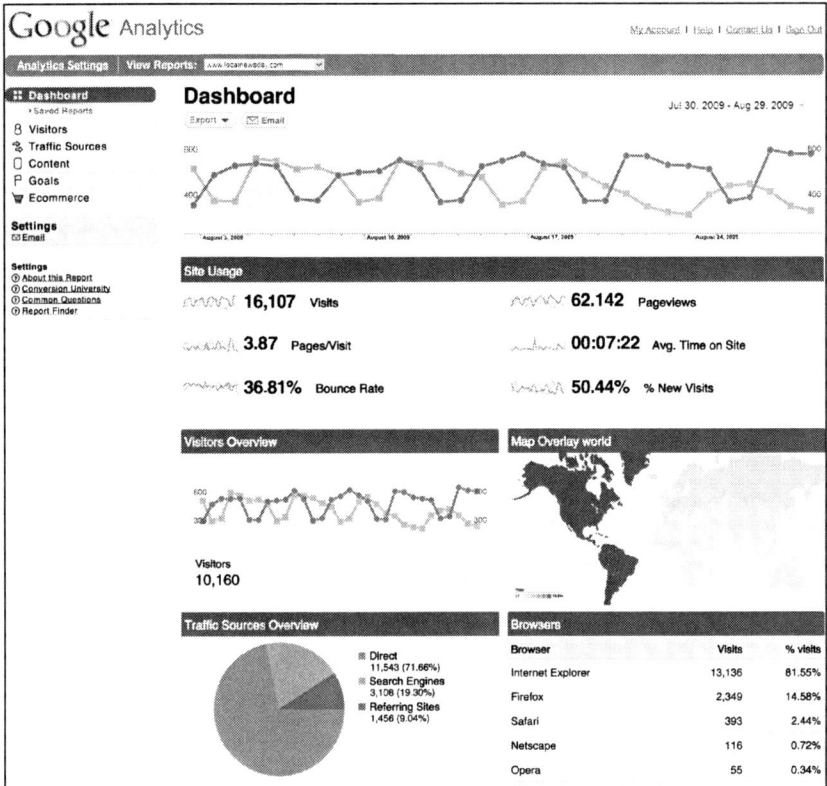

Figure 11.11

Being able to quickly access relevant information about your website visitors is important because it will allow you address a range of marketing issues, relating both to your website and your business as a whole. You will be able to track online and offline marketing campaigns, understand what your customers and prospective customers are looking for, and pinpoint areas of your website that need improvement.

192

When you first login to Google Analytics and select the domain you want to view, if you have more than one, you are presented with a Dashboard view of your domain, such as the one showing LocalNewsDay.com (Figure 11.11).

Most website owners could only wish for over 16,000 visits in a single month such as those pictured here from the monthly report for LocalNewsDay.com. However, there is a story here. When I took over their website's optimization two years ago, the monthly visits only averaged about 800-900. It is absolutely amazing what being at the top of Google and Bing for your keyword searches can do. This is why you need SEO for your website.

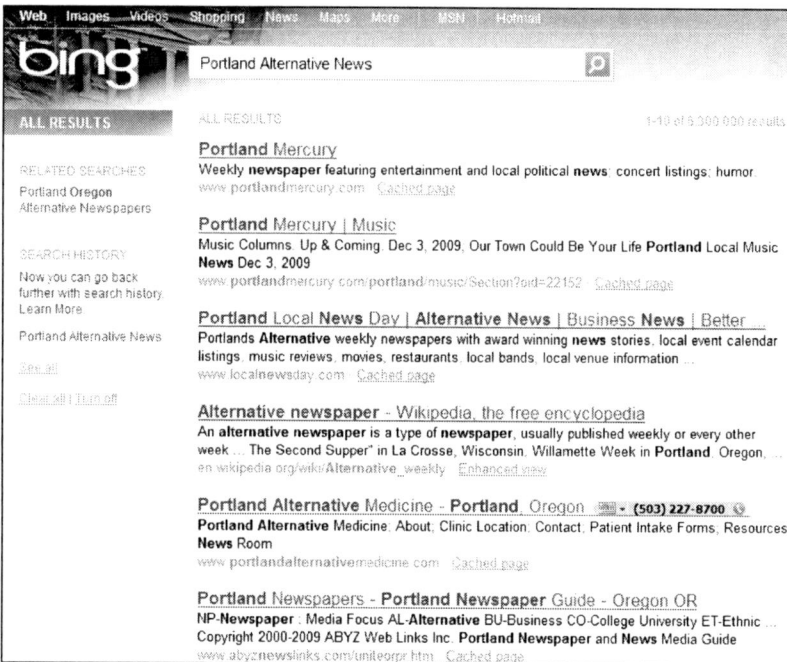

Figure 11.12

Notice a search on "portland alternative news" on Bing or Google places LocalNewsDay.com on the first page of every major search engine, as shown in figure 11.12. Understanding and utilizing relevant analytics about your website visitors will allow you to make your website work harder for you, increase your ROI, increase your search engine rankings, generate more sales leads and allow you to better allocate resources.

Now let's take a look at some of the reports and information you can obtain from Google Analytics to help you.

Analysis in Action

Access to visitors' statistics is one thing, but the true value of analytics comes in the form of analysis and action. Improvements to your website should come out of a defined process and a decision based on information and knowledge. Analytics allows you to make those decisions and then measure the results. Below is a list of some of the most informational analyses from Google Analytics:

- Visitors
- Traffic Sources
- Intelligence Reports
- Expanded Goals
- Site Engagement Goals
- Advanced Table Filtering
- Expanded Mobile Reporting
- Share Advanced Segments
- Share Custom Reports
- Multiple Custom Variables

Google Analytics gives you many technical graphs, but value is only gained when that data is used to drive action to improve your website. So how do we begin to analyze results in Google Analytics?

Firstly, you need to understand what your website is about and what it actually does for your business. This may seem like a obvious place to start, and hopefully you know this by now.

So what is the purpose of your website? Is it to generate leads? To sell products or services? To register subscribers? To provide support?

Once you identify the purpose of your website you can begin to identify ways to improve your website. Generally your initial focus will either be content or a specific process you want to optimize.

The most important ways to improve your website content is by analyzing Google Analytics reports in the next section.

Analyzing the Keywords Report

The first report after viewing how many visitors you received should be the keywords information under Traffic Sources. Do the keywords align with the purpose of your site or business? Are there keywords that are not optimized but are drawing relevant visitors?

Figures 11.13a and 11.13b can both help you with this.

If you identify an organic keyword that is important to your business, but has a high bounce rate, then develop content that specifically targets visitors using that keyword.

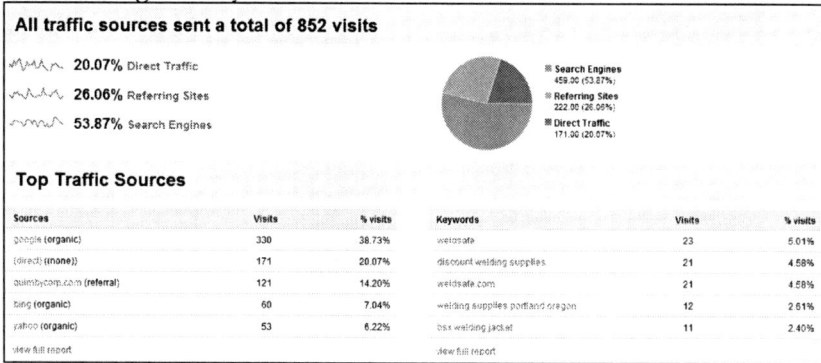

All traffic sources sent a total of 852 visits

〰 **20.07%** Direct Traffic

〰 **26.06%** Referring Sites

〰 **53.87%** Search Engines

▦ Search Engines
459.00 (53.87%)

▦ Referring Sites
222.00 (26.06%)

▦ Direct Traffic
171.00 (20.07%)

Top Traffic Sources

Sources	Visits	% visits	Keywords	Visits	% visits
google (organic)	330	38.73%	weldsafe	23	5.01%
(direct) ((none))	171	20.07%	discount welding supplies	21	4.58%
quimbycorp.com (referral)	121	14.20%	weldsafe.com	21	4.58%
bing (organic)	60	7.04%	welding supplies portland oregon	12	2.61%
yahoo (organic)	53	6.22%	bsx welding jacket	11	2.40%
view full report			view full report		

Figure11.13a(Top)

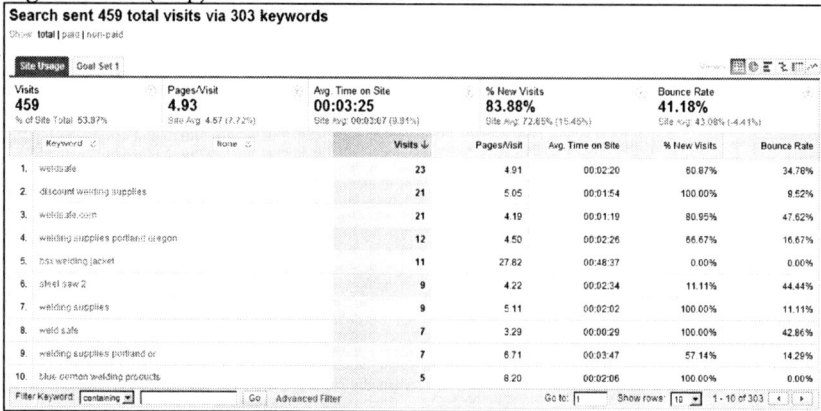

Search sent 459 total visits via 303 keywords

Show: total | paid | non-paid

	Visits	Pages/Visit	Avg. Time on Site	% New Visits	Bounce Rate
	459	**4.93**	**00:03:25**	**83.88%**	**41.18%**
	% of Site Total: 53.87%	Site Avg: 4.57 (7.72%)	Site Avg: 00:03:07 (9.91%)	Site Avg: 72.65% (15.45%)	Site Avg: 43.08% (-4.41%)

	Keyword	None	Visits ↓	Pages/Visit	Avg. Time on Site	% New Visits	Bounce Rate
1.	weldsafe		23	4.91	00:02:20	60.87%	34.78%
2.	discount welding supplies		21	5.05	00:01:54	100.00%	9.52%
3.	weldsafe.com		21	4.19	00:01:19	80.95%	47.62%
4.	welding supplies portland oregon		12	4.50	00:02:26	66.67%	16.67%
5.	bsx welding jacket		11	27.82	00:48:37	0.00%	0.00%
6.	steel saw 2		9	4.22	00:02:34	11.11%	44.44%
7.	welding supplies		9	5.11	00:02:02	100.00%	11.11%
8.	weld safe		7	3.29	00:00:29	100.00%	42.86%
9.	welding supplies portland or		7	6.71	00:03:47	57.14%	14.29%
10.	blue demon welding products		5	8.20	00:02:06	100.00%	0.00%

Filter Keyword: containing ▼   Go   Advanced Filter   Go to: 1   Show rows: 10 ▼ 1 - 10 of 303 ◄ ►

Figure 11.13b (Bottom)

Analyzing the Site Search Report

Setup Site Search as shown in Figure 11.14 to identify gaps in content. Are people searching for something that your site already answers? If so, you should look at your navigation system. Can they get there easily? If Site Search contains search terms that you know won't bring up relevant content on your site, you need to ask yourself why. Do these search terms identify opportunities to generate new content or fill the desires of your website visitors?

Site Usage	Goal Conversion			
Total Unique Searches (?)	Results Pageviews/Search (?)	% Search Exits (?)	% Search Refinements	
114	1.41	26.32%	35.40%	
% of Site Total: 100.00%	Site Avg: 1.41 (0.00%)	Site Avg: 26.32% (0.00%)	Site Avg: 35.40% (0.00%)	

Search Term		Total Unique ↓ Searches	Results Pageviews/Search	%
1. contact details		55	1.00	

Figure 11.14

Analyze the Top Content Report

When you look at top content report in Figure 11.15 are there any pages that have a low average time on page or a high bounce rate? This generally indicates that a page isn't giving visitors what they are seeking. Review the pages that have the lowest time on page and highest bounce rate.

			Views:	
Time on Page (?)	Bounce Rate (?)	% Exit (?)	$ Index (?)	
00:01:21	53.42%	36.77%	$0.00	
Site Avg: 00:01:21 (0.00%)	Site Avg: 53.42% (0.00%)	Site Avg: 36.77% (0.00%)	Site Avg: $0.00 (0.00%)	

Pageviews ↓	Unique Pageviews	Time on Page	Bounce Rate	% Exit	$ Index
75	67	00:00:31	46.67%	36.33%	$0.00
71	67	00:06:51	81.54%	80.28%	$0.00
68	53	00:00:29	31.58%	26.50%	$0.00

Figure 11.15

Sidebar: What is the bounce rate?

Google Analytics can tell you how many of your visitors are *bouncing* from your site. This is labeled as your "bounce rate," which is the percentage of visitors coming to your site and leaving immediately.

High percentages of bounces is an indication that your site is not optimized properly or relevant for what the visitor is looking for. If the bounces happen on landing pages that are designed to greet visitors, contain a lot of information, or are for marketing URLs. Visitors who bounce from your site are not finding what they thought they would find, based on the search engine results or advertisements they clicked through may lose ranking or get a bad quality score.

You can begin to see how to analyze results in Google Analytics based on the purpose of your website. Once you understand how your site works as a business tool, you can use Google Analytics to inform your process.

Google Analytics With Intelligence Reports

How would you like to have 24-hour a day access to a dedicated assistant who is focused exclusively on your site's analytics? Your assistant would be so diligent and detailed that they wouldn't miss a thing. Sound too good to be true? We're giving you one. Say "Hello" to Analytics Intelligence.

Your new hardworking assistant, Analytics Intelligence, can't replace you or a professional analyst. It can, however, find key information for you and your professional analysts so that your team can focus on making strategic decisions, instead of sifting through an endless sea of data.

Analytics Intelligence constantly monitors your website's traffic. Anytime something significant happens, it adds an automatic alert in your Intelligence reports. If your bounce rate suddenly jumps on one of your referrals, Analytics Intelligence creates an alert. Of course, it's up to you to go find out that the bounce rate jumped because someone inadvertently changed the landing page or for some other reason. But you might not have noticed that there was a problem that needed fixing if your trusty assistant hadn't alerted you. Figures 11.16 and 11.17 show the alerts screen in Analytics Intelligence.

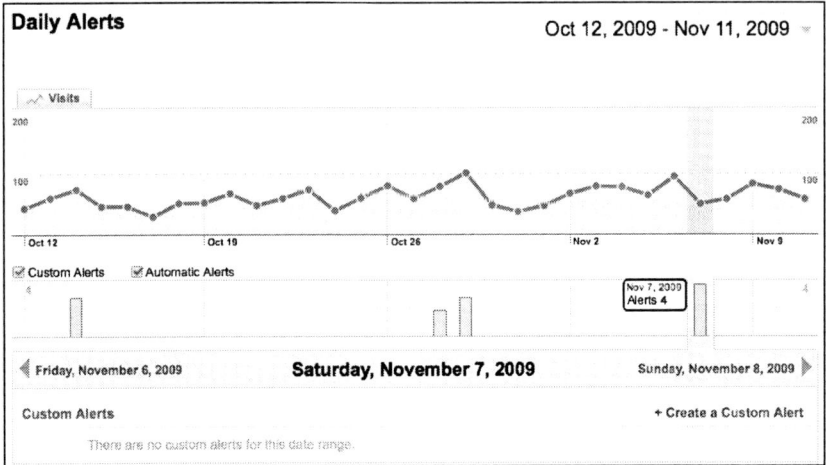

Figure 11.16

Figure 11.17

The automatic alerts will give a webmaster immediate information about traffic jumps or changes according to the configured thresholds you create. This can include major traffic changes to certain pages on the website, a change in a page's bounce rate, page views, or a higher or lower than usual visitor stream from a specific country, state or region as shown in the automatic alerts in figure 11.17.

Figure 11.17
This gives the webmaster a quick overview of traffic developments on a specific web project or website.

There are built in alerts that you can choose, but you can take Intelligence reports to the next level with Custom Alerts. These allow you to define your own alert triggers and receive an email alert. For example you can create a Custom Alert to notify you when your Google AdWords campaign traffic meets a revenue target or when your organic keyword terms from your SEO efforts has resulted in a certain number of visitors to your site.
There is almost a limitless number of alerts you can configure. Now it's time to set some goals in Google Analytics in the next section.

New Feature of Google Analytics Goals

A website goal is a high value action that you would like your website visitors to perform. On a content or lead generation site, this could include subscribing to an email newsletter or completing a contact form. On an e-commerce site this could be the completion of a checkout process. You can access goal data across numerous reports within Google Analytics, plus you will have access to goal specific reports under the 'Goals' tab.

If you have ever set up optimization or visitor goals in Google Analytics, one feature that you may have wanted is the ability to set more than four goals per profile. Now, Google Analytics profile can be setup with 20 goals. These are also now conveniently arranged in four groups containing five goals each.

Another new feature is the addition of site engagement goals. Standard goals are great for reporting on particular actions you want your visitors to take (buying online, filling out a contact form or registering for your email newsletter), but what if your primary objective is providing quality content and an engaging experience for your visitors?

Site engagement goals is your answer. Now you can set a goal conversion for time on site or pages per visit allowing you to access the power of goal reports within Google Analytics. If you are a SMB (Small to Medium Business), non-profit, government, or any organization with a content- or branding-focused site you should definitely begin using site engagement goals.

Mobile Reporting in Google Analytics

Google Analytics now allows for improved tracking of mobile devices, so you can now track interactions within your iPhone and Android apps to measure usage and engagement.

A new tracking code for mobile sites built using PHP, Perl, JSP and ASPX will also become available, allowing you to track all web-enabled mobile devices (not just mobile devices that run JavaScript).

Tips to Help You Utilize Google Analytics

1. Setup e-commerce tracking. If you have an e-commerce website make sure you enable e-commerce tracking within your Google Analytics website profile and add appropriate e-commerce tags to your website. If you don't have an e-commerce website you can still use e-commerce reports to associate a dollar value to particular website visitors.

2. Link your Google AdWords account to your Google Analytics account. Once your accounts are linked you will have access to AdWords visitor data within Google Analytics.

3. Track your marketing campaigns. Campaign tracking is a crucial element in understanding how your marketing campaigns are performing. By tagging online and offline campaigns you can begin to evaluate and compare the effectiveness of your marketing initiatives. Tag everything!

4. Manually tag your CPC (Cost Per Click) campaigns. If you use a CPC system other than Google AdWords, you will need to manually tag your campaign URLs. CPC campaigns that are not tagged will be logged as "organic" (or unpaid) searches within Google Analytics.

Chapter 12 – What Not to Do

I have so many instances and references where I myself have made mistakes or where others have fallen before me and I have learned from their mistakes. In this chapter we will talk about:

- Abnormal Keyword Placement
- SEO Spam
- Doorway Pages
- Meta Jacking
- Page Cloaking
- IP Delivery/Page Cloaking
- Link Farms
- Spamblogs
- Page Highjacking
- Sybil Attacks
- Link Bombing
- What to Do If You Have Been Banned
- Problem Pages and Work-Arounds
- Validating Your HTML

Abnormal Keyword Delivery

The reason I am discussing this first is because it is the most common occurrence. I read all the time on SEO blogs that a person got his website on the first page of Google by placing his keywords a hundred times at the bottom of his website landing page in text that was the same color as the background of his website. The person is so excited that he discounts and ignores all the professionals who comment that he shouldn't do this. Sometime the blog creator or commenter who has his site on the first page of Google even bad mouths the SEO professionals trying to help him.

I come back and read all the time how just a few short months later, the same guy that was so excited that his website was on the first page of Google has written, "You guys were right. Google banned my URL for doing this." It is easy to temporarily be the most relevant site on Google the wrong way. But Google and the other major search engines have ways of figuring it out quite quickly. And once you are banned, you better call in the pros to help you. There is a section dedicated to this as the end of this chapter.

SEO Spam

SEO spam is the SEO version of email spam. Email spam pops up in your inbox where it's least wanted and those who are sending it believe that the law of averages is on their side. They think if you send out enough messages, eventually someone will respond.

SEO spam uses the same principle, except SEO spam fills the search engine results pages on search engines with results that have little or no value to the searcher. This can get you quickly banned. Imagine if you went to Google and every time you did a search you got results that were for something totally different than you searched for, or if the top 10 spaces of the search results were filled with the same company. If that happened you would switch to Bing in a heartbeat to get better results. Right?

Google and the other major search engines don't want this to happen. So if you do something that a search engine sees as spamming, your search rankings will be penalized. It's now even more likely that you'll be removed from search rankings entirely. If Google bans your URL it's as if you website has been removed from the internet. It is almost invisible.

A term for some SEO spam is called *black hat SEO*. Black hat SEO refers to the use of aggressive SEO strategies, techniques and tactics that focus only on search engines and not a human audience. Some examples of black hat SEO techniques include keyword stuffing, link farms, invisible website text and doorway pages, which we will learn about later in this chapter.

Black Hat SEO is more frequently used by those who are looking for a quick financial return rather than a long-term investment on their website.

> **NOTE:** *Black Hat SEO will most likely result in your URL being banned from major search engines. However, since the focus is usually on quick high return business models, most experts who use Black Hat SEO tactics consider being banned from search engines a somewhat irrelevant risk. Black Hat SEO may also be referred to as Unethical SEO or just spamdexing.*

To make things a little more perplexing, search engines change their definitions of spam regularly. What works and is acceptable today may well be classified as spam tomorrow. This can have a profound effect on your rankings. One day you may be ranked high and on page one of a search and the next you may find that you're on page 8 of the results all because of the links you maintain.

The easiest way to monitor search engine changes is to keep up with what's happening in SEO on the Google Webmaster Central Blog (http://googlewebmastercentral.blogspot.com/). You can also learn about what's changing on ISEdb–Internet Search Engine Database (www.isedb.com), High Rankings Advisor (www.highrankings.com), and SEONews.com.

The general rule is, if you're doing something on your website that you have to worry might get you banned from major search engines, you probably shouldn't be doing it.

If you read anywhere that SEO spam techniques are okay, or that you won't get caught because search engines don't pay attention, ignore this advice at all costs. The penalties differ according to the search engine, but if you are caught spamming even once, most search engines will delist you from search results immediately. I have seen it a hundred times and have had it happen to me on accident when I went overboard experimenting. Yes, even the experts make a mistake or two. But we learn from them.

Here's what is definitely considered spam:

- Trying to make your site appear more relevant to the search engines by embedding hidden keywords in your website.
- Artificially generating links to your website from unrelated sites for the purpose of increasing your ranking based on link analysis.
- Artificially generating traffic to your website so that it appears more popular than it really is.
- Submitting your website repeatedly for inclusion in the rankings.

NOTE: *You should submit your site once and then wait at least six weeks before submitting it again.*

Doorway Pages

Doorway pages are created to do well for particular phrases. They are also known as portal pages, jump pages, bridges, gateway pages, entry pages, and by other names as well. Search engines have developed ways to easily identify these pages. They are primarily to make a page seem more relevant for search engines, and not for human beings.

You should always have your pages designed for human eyes and not just for a search engine. There are various ways to deliver doorway pages. The low-tech way is to create and submit a web page that is targeted toward a particular phrase or keyword.

These pages tend to be very generic. It's easy for people to copy them, make minor changes, and submit the revised page. Sometimes these are so similar that the search consider these duplicates and automatically exclude them from their listings.

Another problem is that users sometimes arrive at the doorway page. Say a real person searched for "welding supplies" and the doorway page appears. They click through, but that page probably lacks any detail about the welding supplies that you sell. To get them to that content, webmasters usually propel visitors forward with a prominent "Click Here" link or with an automatic page redirect.

Some search engines no longer accept pages using any redirects (sometimes referred to as fast Meta refresh). This has led to some black hatters doing a bait-and-switch, or "code-swapping," on the search engines. Some black hat webmasters submit a real web page, wait for it to be indexed and then swap it with a doorway page.

The trouble is that a search engine may revisit at any time figure out what you have done.

Meta Jacking

Meta jacking is the taking of the Meta tagging from one page and placing them on another page hoping to obtain good rankings and relevance. However, simply taking Meta tags from a page will not guarantee a page will do well. In fact, sometimes resubmitting the exact page from another location does not gain the same position as the original page.

Agent Delivery

When you target a single doorway page to a single search engine this is called "agent delivery." Each search engine reports an "agent" name, just as each browser reports a name.

Agent delivery pages are tailored pages that direct users to the actual content you want them to see. It also has the added benefit of "cloaking" your code from only the search engine you are targeting. The major search engines have gotten wise to this, though. They change the name they report specifically to help keep people honest.

IP Delivery / Page Cloaking

To avoid the agent name changing, you can also deliver pages to the search engines by allowing only the search engines IP address. If a bot, crawler, or spider visits your doorway page and reports an IP address that matches the search engine's or the IP resolves to a certain host name, it can see the code of the website.

Link Farms

Link farms are simply pages of links that are created just to artificially boost a linking strategy in an effort to speed the appearance of the website in the top search ranking positions. Typically you pay money to join them or buy software that allows you to mass send your links.

Spamblogs

These are software or machine-generated blogs which have only one purpose – increase search engine rankings.

Page Highjacking

Page hijacking occurs when very popular webpage coding is stolen and used to represent your website to the search engines. When users perform a search and see your webpage in the search results, they click through the link only to be taken to your actual page.

Sybil Attacks

Sybil attacks are when a spammer creates multiple websites that are all interlinked for the purpose of creating a false link structure. These are sometimes called incestuous links.

Link Bombing

One anchor text tactic to avoid is link bombing . Link bombing refers to the methods used by black hat SEOs to artificially inflate their website ranking by connecting an unrelated keyword to a specific website. For link bombing to work, more than one website designer must be willing to participate in a link exchange.

What to Do If You Have Been Banned

If you have been banned from the major search engines, you may find it the worst experience of your life, especially since the internet is now the official yellow pages for most and being banned from the major search engines is like locking your business doors and taking the phone off the hook.

Most of the time you will know what was done that got you banned. In this case, it may require explaining to the search engine the tactic you employed, why you employed it, and how you fixed it. Google, for instance, allows you to send in an explanation by going to the

Google Webmaster Tools (https://www.google.com/webmasters/tools) and clicking on the "Site Reconsideration" link on the left-hand side. This will take you to the web page which outlines written and video instructions to resubmit your website.

It could take a couple of months to a year to be reindexed into the search engine. In some cases it is quicker and easier to ditch the old URL and start a brand new one. Then you have to work your way back to the top of the rankings again. Just make sure that you have fixed or stopped doing whatever was done to get your URL banned in the first place.

Chapter 13 – Marketing Principles

Throughout my career I have been thought of by many as being one of the best sales persons both online and in real life. There are many things that help me make sales. In this chapter, I will outline the little things that add up one by one to help you make sales. Although the focus here is on online sales, these are sales principles that you should use every day both online and in real life to help you sell.

Sales Principles You Should Adopt

These are my top 12 direct marketing principles you can use to make sure your internet marketing really works for you:

Stability

People want to know you are not going to disappear overnight so if you've been in business for any length of time, this will add credibility to you and your offers.

Statistics

Use genuine statistics to give you more credibility when listing the number of customers served, money saved, profits made, true results, and so on.

Testimonials

I can't overestimate the importance of getting relevant and credible reviews from your customers and clients, saying how you and your products or services have helped them.

Self Credibility

If you can, establish yourself as an expert in your field. Not everyone can write numerous books or be on TV. However, you can write articles and have them published on your product, service, or industry. You can run workshops that are designed to demonstrate or train how to use your products or how effective your services are.

Reprints of articles about you in the press or having your articles published in the media lend weight to your credibility as the expert or authority in your market and are highly valuable to you. Show your market that you are in demand, and have status as an expert.

You can also show you're an expert with industry certifications, awards, memberships, and accomplishments that are relevant to your market.

Demonstrations

It's a lot cheaper to sell online with the use of online videos or 'how to' DVDs to sell your product. If you hire a sales person he can only be one place at a time. The internet can be the equivalent of hundreds of sales people. A website that is properly designed can make it very easy to show a demonstration of your product or services, both on and offline.

You can also create and distribute a demonstration eBook by printing it out and talking through what it contains live on screen. Camtasia is free software that lets you make a screen capture video where you can demonstrate your website talking though the sales letter or giving a demo of how easy it is to download your eBook.

> **NOTE:** *You can also print eBooks cost effectively at Lulu.com and CreateSpace.com.*

Guarantee

If you can't guarantee the product or service you're selling, then find something else to sell that you can guarantee. To really make your potential customers feel safe buying from you, have an ironclad guarantee.

Accessibility

On your website, having your full contact detail information is a big boost to your potential customer confidence. Using just an email contact or a form shows you are hiding. Put your email, phone, and address that shows that you are in the U.S. and are credible.

> **NOTE:** *Never give a P.O. Box as your address as it immediately makes people suspicious.*

The Personal Touch

Be visible in the business you're in and make sure you have a live voice answer your phone if possible. In my SEO business, if I let voicemail pickup for one day I never get a sale. If I answer the phone, I usually always make a sale. Also, tell your customers about yourself. Make it personal to them and show them you are a real individual.

Admit Imperfections Upfront

No matter how good your product or service is, it will most likely have a disadvantage somewhere. Admit it up front and honestly comment on this fact.

Answer questions and objections in a timely manner when a potential customer asks them via email or the phone. Buyers buy more often when they can call an office throughout the week and email at any time with questions and get a human response.

People Will Buy to Save Money

People who are interested in your product or service will usually do nothing unless you ask for the sale and give them incentive. People are just bombarded by too many sales pitches and try to choose the best one.

The best pitch is to create urgency to buy now, such as informing them that the price is going up next week. But you have plenty of options here: you can offer a reduced price, a bundled special deal on your products or services, or a smaller free item for buying an larger item now.

Special Tactic for Creating Urgency

A special tactic to create urgency is to put an end date on your promotions and discounts – buy it now before the price goes up next week, next month, tomorrow. Even if your regular price is your promotional price, do a monthly campaign. When they look online they see a higher price if you don't buy by the end of the month.

If your business looks like it is always in permanent sale mode, there's no urgency for the customer to buy. Customers are not stupid; they see the advertising and know that this company ALWAYS has a sale on.

That's why it's important you create a deadline for your promotion. By having a defined end date showing in bold letters, it creates urgency and a reason for your potential customer to act now or lose out on saving money.

Tell People the Value They Are Getting

The discounts and value to the customer are not always obvious. So make it clear. If you put a value next to the items you are selling, don't assume your prospect or customer has worked it out for themselves. If the total value is $250, tell them it is $250 because if you leave them to add it up for themselves they generally won't do it.

Research

Research is an essential aspect of marketing. Inadequate research of your products and target market is one of the biggest pitfalls that can affect a marketing strategy. Research provides a wealth of information that is vital to your sales.

Determine what market is going to most likely benefit from the product or service you provide. This is the group of individuals you will want to target – in some areas, there may be multiple groups. While it may be possible to market to all these groups, in most situations it is better to market to a single group which contain a large percentage of similar traits. This makes it easier to consolidate a marketing plan as well as eliminate a significant amount of research, time, and effort.

The second aspect which needs to be researched for a marketing plan to be successful is your competition. It is also one of the reasons why marketing fails to produce appropriate results. Researching your competition is not just about researching the prices of a competitor. It includes noting things such as their sales techniques, finding out what marketing tools and resources they use, and how often those tools.

Many business owners and beginning internet marketers fail to note anything more than price and perhaps general layout of their competitors website and end their research there. They miss vital information that can save time, money, and effort when it comes to setting up their own marketing strategy. If you are not the most successfully-marketed business on the internet promoting your product or service, find out who is. Find out how they market and what makes them successful.

Collect information on the types of deals, offers, discounts and promotions that your competition uses and offer something different to help your business stand out. Many people simply do what their competition does. In doing so, they often lower their marketability and their marketing plan can ultimately fail in this area. You might pick up more market share by doing what the completion doesn't.

Marketing Tools

Having enough research to create your marketing plan is only the first step in solving the problems that often cause marketing plans to fail. The next step is take the time to pick out the right tools. Having the right tools for the job is essential to ensuring you get the most out of your marketing strategies.

Marketing tools have diversified over the years. Tools are not limited strictly to email and promotional options. Video, social networking, SMS texting, Blogs, Twitter, Facebook, PPC, and many more are available to you. You just have to pick the tools that are going to be easy for you to learn, use, and require minimal maintenance with maximum potential results.

Don't Just Dream It, Do It!

One of the biggest reasons I am so successful is that if I get an idea, I do it. Nothing stands in my way. Hence you are reading this book because I came up with an idea for it while taking a shower. Don't picture that, by the way. In John Pinette's words, "You'll have nightmares!"

One of the biggest reasons why marketing strategies and businesss end up failing is lack of action and giving up. Marketing is an active part of your business, it is not a "set it in motion and let it run on its own" component of a website. In order to ensure that a marketing strategy succeeds you must be actively engaged in working that plan and revisit it and make the strategy better based on experience. This means that email marketing messages should be updated and redesigned regularly.

SMS, Facebook, and Twitter messages should be rewritten after every send. These messages should be short, contain only the minimum necessary information, and focus on one item at a time. It is important to remember that this type of marketing is relatively new and involves sending messages to Wiki's, blogs, members, and mobile devices that often indicate repeat messages.

Videos should be produced, edited, and updated to as high a level as possible. Computers and technology can turn just about any computer into a production studio with the right software. Keep videos interesting, engaging, and relevant. The videos should be related to the company, the products, or the services offered.

It is important to set up a marketing schedule and find out how much time, generally through trial and error, that you need each day, week or month to handle all your marketing tasks and keep everything up to date.

The reasons why a marketing plan might fail are numerous. I hate to outline some of them here, but you need to know so you can take steps avoid them. Some of these reasons include the following: failing to do the proper research into the market, not doing proper SEO, not having the right tools available, not researching cheaper delivery methods, having too many tools or not using the tools you have effectively, and not having inventory on hand that you are selling.

Taking the time to make sure that you have the information you need as well as putting in the effort to ensure your success can go a long way to eliminating these reasons.

When you develop a marketing message, you have to hit many levels of desire. Good marketing happens when you give logical reasons for your prospect's emotional-buying decisions. Some good marketing messages include:

- Save time
- Save money
- Make money
- Try for free
- Avoid effort
- Increase happiness
- Find success
- Be pain-free
- Get better health
- Have fun
- Enjoy your life
- Gain praise
- Feel safe and secure
- Feel liked or loved
- Be popular

Your task is to find a message which matches to your product or service and start promoting your marketing message in your marketing strategy.

See What Your Potential Clients Desire and Play on That

You should develop the ability to see what others want, need, and desire through your own research. You will be successful if you are always satisfying your customer's needs. Sometimes you have to look for the gap and create a new product or service or develop an improvement of an existing product or service.

You should always focus on service and deliver what you promise on time. My general rule is to always under promise and over deliver. Tell a customer that he/she won't have it until Friday even though it arrives on Wednesday. If something is delayed, the customer is not upset and when you deliver it early you look like the hero.

The internet allows you to start small and grow to any size business that you want to. Following the advice and principles I have laid out in this chapter will help your customer numbers grow and your profits grow with them.

Dealing With Adversity

My last words of advice are always maintain honesty and integrity in your dealings and stay true to your values even when dealing with stressful situations. Every business owner is going to have to deal with anxiety, frustration and problems, so cope with them by developing tenacity and perseverance.

If sales don't happen the first time you talk to a potential client, look at these statistics from the National Sales Executive Association:

- 2% of sales are made on the 1st contact;
- 3% of sales are made on the 2nd contact;
- 5% of sales are made on the 3rd contact;
- 10% of sales are made on the 4th contact (and)
- 80% of sales are made on the 5th – 12th contact.

For most businesses, if you don't offer an opt-in contact, like a regular email newsletter or blog postings, you're missing out on most of your potential sales.

When setting up an opt-in internet marketing campaign, you should offer incentives to subscribe. To entice people to opt-in, you can offer:

- Special pricing for email list members
- A first look at new products
- Ability for customer to select subjects and emails they receive
- Promise not to share email or other personal info with other companies

Using opt-in contact allows you to significantly increase conversions by introducing yourself over time to your potential customers, in a soft-sell manner

Website optimization is important; the goal is increased internet traffic, sales and sales leads. But whether you've hired an online SEO consultant or you're doing the process yourself, affordable search engine optimization by itself doesn't accomplish those last points which increase sales and sales leads. It just drives the potential customers to your website. You still have to close the deal.

Chapter 14 – Targeting Many Keywords

Most web sites selling anything need to target more than three keywords. Even if you just sell a single product or service. So what do you do to promote your web site and focus on many keywords since many of the major search engines only allow a web page to be relevant for three keywords.

The answer is a simple one but the execution is about the most complex of any part of your web site's code. The answer is that you need to create a perfectly optimized landing page for every three keywords you want to focus on. You then have to have the search engines index all those additional pages separately as separate landing pages.

Now, here is the hard part. Google and the other major search engines require a site map to tell them the landing pages you want to index. Not just any, there is a standard called Sitemap protocol 0.90.

> **WARNINGS:** *There are so many web sites and web developers on the Internet that claim they can create a sitemap. Many just create pages with links and call them a sitemap. Also, there has been many updates to the Sitemap Protocol and many web sites still push older versions. I highly recommend that if you are not a professional developer you go to a trusted source such as SMMaker.com or SMCreator.com and have them professionally create and install a Sitemap for your web site.*

In this chapter I am going to tell you how to make a Sitemap specially formulated to Google and Bing. And then how to tell Google and Bing where to look for your site map. As you saw from the warning above, it is a lot of work to create a site map and test it to see if it is working. It is so much easier to just visit either one of these sites and pay less than $15.00 to have it created for you at either of these web sites:

> **http://www.SMMaker.com**
> **http://www.SMCreator.com**

So let's take a look at how to create a site map.

Sitemaps XML format

Informing search engine crawlers This document describes the XML schema for the Sitemap protocol. The Sitemap protocol format consists of XML tags. All data values in a Sitemap must be entity-escaped. The file itself must be UTF-8 encoded.

The Sitemap must include the following:

- Begin with an opening <urlset> tag and end with a closing </urlset> tag.
- Specify the namespace (protocol standard) within the <urlset> tag.
- Include a <url> entry for each URL, as a parent XML tag.
- Include a <loc> child entry for each <url> parent tag.

All of the other tags are optional. Support for these optional tags may vary among search engines. Refer to each search engine's documentation for details.   For Google you must include this tag:

```
<urlset xmlns="http://www.sitemaps.org/schemas/sitemap/0.9">
```

Let's look at an example which shows a Sitemap that contains just a single URL:

```
<?xml version="1.0" encoding="UTF-8"?>
<urlset xmlns="http://www.sitemaps.org/schemas/sitemap/0.9">
  <url>
    <loc>http://www.SEOTechMasters.com/</loc>
    <lastmod>2005-01-01</lastmod>
    <changefreq>monthly</changefreq>
    <priority>0.8</priority>
  </url>
</urlset>
```

All XML Tags

Here are all the tags that can be used in your site map and their syntaxes and descriptions.

<urlset> (required)

Encapsulates the file and references the current protocol standard.

<url> (required)

Parent tag for each URL entry. The remaining tags are children of this tag.

<loc> (required)

URL of the page. This URL must begin with the protocol (such as http) and end with a trailing slash, if your web server requires it. This value must be less than 2,048 characters.

<lastmod> (optional)

The date of last modification of the file. This date should be in W3C Date/time format. This format allows you to omit the time portion, if desired, and use YYYY-MM-DD.

<changefreq> (optional)

How frequently the page is likely to change. This value provides general information to search engines and may not correlate exactly to how often they crawl the page. Valid syntaxes are:

- always
- hourly
- daily
- weekly
- monthly
- yearly
- never

<priority> (optional)

The priority of this URL relative to other URLs on your site. Valid values range from 0.0 to 1.0. This value does not affect how your pages are compared to pages on other sites—it only lets the search engines know which pages you deem most important for the crawlers.

NOTE: *The default priority of a page is 0.5.*

The priority you assign to a page is not likely to influence the position of your URLs in a search engine's result pages. Search engines may use this information when selecting between URLs on the same site, so you can use this tag to increase the likelihood that your most important pages are present in a search index.

> **WARNING:** *Assigning a high priority to all of the URLs on your site is not likely to help you. Since the priority is relative, it is only used to select between URLs on your site.*

Here is an example using the different tags:

```
<?xml version="1.0" encoding="UTF-8"?>
<urlset xmlns="http://www.sitemaps.org/schemas/sitemap/0.9">
<url>
<loc>http://www.seotechmasters.com</loc>
<lastmod>2010-05-20</lastmod>
<priority>0.5</priority>
</url>
<url>
<loc>http://www.seotechmasters.com/TA.php</loc>
<lastmod>2010-05-20</lastmod>
<priority>0.5</priority>
</url>
<url>
<loc>http://www.seotechmasters.com/SEO.php</loc>
<lastmod>2010-05-20</lastmod>
<priority>0.5</priority>
</url>
<url>
<loc>http://www.seotechmasters.com/SEM.php</loc>
<lastmod>2010-05-20</lastmod>
<priority>0.5</priority>
</url>
</urlset>
```

Saving your Site Map

Search engines know to look for a plain text site map at the root directory of your website where your Index page resides. It should be named "Sitemap.xml"

For instance it should be accessible using your site URL. If the Sitemap is located at http://www.SEOTechMasters.com/sitemap.xml and it can't include URLs from http://subdomain.SEOTechMasters.com.

You can submit a sitemap using a port. If you submit a Sitemap using a path with a port number, you must include that port number as part of the path in each URL listed in the Sitemap file. For instance, if your

Sitemap is located at:

http://www.SEOTechMasters.com:100/sitemap.xml

Then each URL listed in the Sitemap must begin with:

http://www.SEOTechMasters.com:100

Submit Your Site Map To Google And Bing

You can submit your website's site map URL to both Google and Bing. To do this go to the following websites and login with the Google and Bing ID's you used in Chapter 3. For Google go to:

https://www.google.com/webmasters/tools/

(Go to **Site configuration**, click **Sitemaps**)

For Bing.com go to:

http://www.bing.com/webmaster

Where to go for more information

For more information on how to configure a site map visit:

http://www.sitemaps.org/schemas/sitemap/0.9/siteindex.xsd

There are a number of tools available to help you validate the structure of your Sitemap based on this schema. You can find a list of XML-related tools at the following websites:

http://www.w3.org/XML/Schema#Tools
http://www.xml.com/pub/a/2000/12/13/schematools.html

Chapter 15 – Professional SEO Services

After reading this book you may have come to the conclusion that you don't want to or have the time to invest on optimizing your website. Or maybe you have investigated the competition and found that the amount of competition is too much for you to handle on your own. Whatever the reason, you may come to a point where you feel that hiring a professional is what you need to do.

I could just stop the chapter right here and say hey, e-mail me at:

Sean@SEOTechMasters.com

We will take care of you. If that is not what you want to do, let me give you some pointers to help you out. There are a lot of scam artists, cons, and the like which want to separate you from the money in your bank account. In fact I think it is easier to find the scam artists peddling SEO than the real thing.

If I were to guess on a ratio. There is probably 100 scammers for every one SEO consultant that knows enough to get you listed at the top of the search engines. The information in this chapter is crucial to learn to keep you from falling victim to scams.

Hiring the Right Professionals

In this business cutting corners is not an option, because the wrong SEO practices can be far more detrimental to your website than doing nothing at all. Virtually everyone of my major clients was first scammed by an SEO scammer before coming to me. In fact, it is not at all unusual to hear about a company or website owner that's been scammed by a supposed SEO consultant who guaranteed them top placement in hundreds of search engines in just days and they actually sent the fraudulent company money.

One of the first clues is the absolute guarantee part. It's just not possible for anyone, even an SEO expert, to guarantee that your site will appear at number one of search engine rankings all the time. Nonetheless, many people claiming to be SEO experts will tell you they can do just that and in just days. Don't believe them. Good organic rankings for keywords worth using takes months to achieve.

In most cases, what happens is this: A website designer or owner who has had to create a website for SEO decides he or she can implement SEO for others to make a profit. However, just because these people have done SEO on their own sites doesn't mean they can plan SEO and implement optimization techniques on your website in the most effective manner possible. Every site, company and industry have different optimization needs.

In most cases, it takes a team of people to perform proper SEO techniques for a business website. That team might include someone to submit your website to different directories and search engines, someone to create and submit articles to online resources, someone to design and implement SEO elements, someone else to code the website to make it attractive to search engines, and a project manager to manage the whole SEO program from beginning to end.

Recognizing SEO Scammers

There are certain things you should check or look for when choosing an SEO company. These are the following:

- Get references from them. See where their customers rank. Go one step further, though. If at the bottom of the referral website's homepage it does not show that the SEO company you are checking out does their web design or SEO work, call or email the company and verify that their SEO work is handled by them.

  It is not uncommon for scammers to find a highly-ranked site and claim it is their work. In SEOTechMaster's case, many of our customers allow us to keep a link at the bottom of their homepage that states, "SEO Services Provided By: SEOTechMasters.com" and a link to our page. It makes it easy for our customers to see we really do the work we say we do.

- Be wary if the prospective company says that they guarantee that your site will show up in the first page of results or even as the number one result every time! Time for a reality check: the algorithms that the search engines use are closely guarded trade secrets meaning that no one outside of a few people at the search engine companies knows exactly how it all works. Guaranteeing a certain page ranking is a sign of inexperience at best – and much more likely, indicates a scam.

- If you hear an obviously busy call center in the background, run. If their sales department is a room crowded with telemarketers trolling for business around the clock, it's a big red flag that you are being scammed.

- They promise to secure you top rankings for long-tail keywords which strikes you as unlikely to be used by anyone. For starters, they're trying to sell you a guaranteed page ranking (but we know better, don't we?). If the keyword they're offering you a top ranking for sounds a little fishy to you, look up its popularity with the free Google Keyword Tool we discussed in Chapter 1. See what its popularity is. Keywords that no one ever searches for are easy to main on page one of a Google search.

- If their services are offered at unrealistically low prices be weary. There are some SEO scammers who lure victims by offering to optimize your site and run promotional campaigns for prices that sound entirely too good to be true. Usually they want the amount upfront and from a checking account rather than a credit card.

- RED FLAG: "We can give your website and SEO tune up for $499.00."

- RED FLAG: "Results in 48 hours (or less). " If this could be done it would save everyone a lot of money and time. Everyone would be number one. Oh wait. They can't be.

Again, do your due diligence. Look at their credentials, find out who's used their services in the past and what they have to say about the company. You should expect regular weekly reports on how your keywords are performing and you should be able to easily get in touch by phone and speak to one of the SEO consultants to get their advice and input as needed. It needs to be an interactive process. If the reports are only monthly or quarterly that is not enough time to get notified when a keyword drops and take immediate action to correct the issue.

The best SEO companies have years of expertise in the field and know the most effective SEO methodologies inside and out. When algorithms change they also know how to determine the changes and react and have a process in place to notify their customers. Your placements on the major search engines may change from month to month but will return to normal as your professional SEO company does what is necessary to get you back to the top.

What to Expect From A Professional SEO Company

When you find an SEO firm that offers the services that you need, you can expect to receive certain specific services from them. The services vary from firm to firm, but here's a list that you can use as a good rule of thumb:

- You should be provided with an initial professional SEO audit. The audit should thoroughly examine your sites URL properties, current SEO elements, problems with the current design and structure of your existing website, provide keyword and competitor research, and look at the mechanics of a website as a whole and include recommendations.

- If you are trying to employ an SEO company that is a one man show who does the auditing, the optimization, the linking, the articles, the research, the social media, the web changes, monitors the analytics, does the billing, and everything else, you will soon learn that no one can be an expert at everything and you will soon be lost amongst his many clients.

  At SEOTechMasters.com everyone wears their own hat and focuses on just one part. That means there is a team assigned to every client.

- The company you hire should employ a project manager who tracks all the needs of your companies website(s) and follows the reports. This person needs to be able to bring in the experts needed at a given time they are needed and always be available by phone. If your SEO expert says he is only available by e-mail that is a red flag!

- You should be provided with recommendations for keywords and a plan to optimize your website. This report should indicate how each page of your web site is optimized including what on-page SEO elements such as HTML tags, keywords, and content needs to be changed on your website on an ongoing basis.

- You should be provided with information on how the SEO company plans to perform the optimization of the internal site navigation. Your internal navigation can have a serious effect on how your site performs in search results, so a good SEO will examine and optimize that navigation structure.

- Your SEO company should be able to scan the Internet weekly for mentions of your domain name in Blogs and other social

222

media and provide this in a weekly report. This is now known as "Reputation Management" and is a critical piece of any online presence. And should be part of your weekly SEO Report.

- The SEO company should be able to scan your website weekly for design changes made that inadvertently broke links or strayed from the SEO goals set in place. These warnings should also be in your weekly SEO Report.

- A plan on how the SEO company intends to perform link building for your domain and verify they are only white hat techniques to sites relevant to your industry or follow guidelines set at http://angelasandpaulsbacklinks.com/.

- The company you choose should have procedures and the ability to test the different search engine algorithms to detect changes. They should be able to immediately make changes to your website to combat those changes.

- A plan on how the SEO company will show their progress and the monitoring of your SEO efforts and keyword statistics. They should also be able to give you statistics on your major competitors as well. If the SEO company cannot provide you this information on a weekly basis, especially in the beginning, find another company.

- SEO requires ongoing efforts. The SEO company must be able to train your staff with the most successful methods for maintaining optimization and providing news articles and suggestions.

Professional SEO firms can offer a lot of benefits to your website. After all, your core business is not likely SEO, but an SEO firm's is. The good ones can properly optimize your site, and your services, in less time than you can. For that reason alone, it should be enough to make you consider hiring an SEO firm, whether or not you end up doing so.

Appendix A – SEO Resources

There are many free resources for SEO on the Internet. Here is a few of them that I find most valuable, productive, or unique.

Best SEO Blogs

The world of SEO is constantly changing because search engines constantly change their algorithms. These blogs help you to keep up on the latest news, information, and tips about SEO.

1. Search Engine Land (SearchEngineLand.com) – One of the most well respected search engine and SEO news website.

2. Search Engine Guide (SearchEngineGuide.com) – A blog with a heavy focus on SEO for small businesses.

3. Search Engine Watch (SearchEngineWatch.com) – One of the oldest blogs out there.

4. Online Marketing Blog (TopRankBlog.com) – A great mix of SEO, PR, and social media articles.

5. Matt Cutts (MattCutts.com) – This is a blog by the head of Google's Web Engineering team. When he talks, you better listen.

6. Search Engine Journal (SearchEngineJournal.com) – This is one that I personally follow.

7. Google Blog (GoogleBlog.BlogSpot.com) - Google's official blog however they only discuss everything related to Google.

8. Traffick (Traffick.com) – A blog with a strong focus on PPC.

9. Google Blogoscoped\ (Blog.Outer-Court.com) – This blog is also all about Google. But the difference is, this one is written by a third party.

SEO Information Resources

Blogs can be your main source of information, however they don't cover everything. Usually the latest changes. If you are going to start from the beginning of SEO, here are some good resources as well as some unique resources.

1. Marketing Terms (MarketingTerms.com) – This site has a dictionary which will help you understand all of the marketing terms you run into.

2. Google's SEO Guidelines (google.com/webmasters/seo) – Google's take on SEO as well as their rules and a starter guide.

3. SEO Chat (SEOChat.com) – Here you can find a weekly SEO video and more information.

4. Search Engine Colossus (SearchEngineColossus.com) – Here you can learn that there is a lot more search engines than you may know of. This is a place where you can find them all.

5. Web Pro News (WebProNews.com) – Information and video interviews from SEO expert.

6. SEO FAQ (HighRankings.com) –This resource answers the majority of newbie questions.

SEO Tools

If you aren't cheating and doing SEO right it is a very time consuming process. These tools will not only make your life easier, but they'll help you understand what you need to do and how to rank well on search engines.

1. SEOAudits (SEOAudits.com) – A tool to check your website for mechanics issues, browser compatibility, SEO issues and much more.

2. AccuQuality (AccuQuality.com) – Best website analysis tool I have ever used. They run 450 tests on every page which in include W3C compatibility, errors, code violations, browser compatibility, link problems, SEO, and they even spell check every page and provide a report.

3. Submission Complete (SubmissionComplete.com) – A very affordable tool to submit your website to all the major search engines and directories.

4. Website Submitter (WebsiteSubmitter.org) – Another affordable tool to submit your website to all the search engines and major directories.

5. SpyFu (SpyFu.com) – This site will help you understand what search terms your competition is using or is advertising with and how well they are doing.

6. Wordtracker (WordTracker.com) – You don't have to wonder how popular keywords and phrases are.

7. Google Toolbar (toolbar.google.com) – This toolbar will show you what your Google PageRank number is and much more. (See Chapter 1 for more information on to use this tool.)

8. Google Webmaster Tools (Google.com/webmasters/tools) – It seems this tool gets more and more important. You can now see the keywords people find your site with, errors on your website, submit an XML sitemap, and soon you will be able to see if your website has duplicate content somewhere on the Internet.

9. Digital Point SEO Tools (DigitalPoint/tools) – A collection of 17 different SEO tools.

10. AdWords Keyword Tool (adwords.google.com/select/KeywordToolExternal) – Although you might not be looking to pay for traffic, this tool will give you a good idea of how many clicks you can get from Google and help you with your keyword research.

11. DIYSEO (DIYSEO.com) – Tools to help you keep track of your SEO progress.

12. Backlink Checker (iwebtool.com) – See how many websites link to your website VS your competition.

SEO Forums

Sometimes you are going to be unsure of what to do. The best thing to do when this happens is to ask someone for advice. Through forums you can communicate with other SEOs or ask questions..

1. High Rankings Forum (HighRankings.com/forum) – A good community with a lot of friendly SEOs to help you.

2. Webmaster World (WebmasterWorld.com) – By far one of the oldest and well known SEO forums.

3. Digital Point Forum (forum.digitalpoint.com)– One of the larger forums in the SEO world.

4. Search Engine Watch (forums.SearchEngineWatch.com) – Almost 60,000 SEOs discuss search related stuff here. This is one that I use and highly recommend.

SEO Conferences

A good way to learn SEO is in person. Going to conferences won't just keep you up-to-date on the SEO world, but it will allow you to learn from some of the most successful SEOs.

1. Search Engine Strategies (SearchEngineStrategies.com– Many conferences all over the world throughout the year.

2. PubCon (PubCon.com) – This conference started from the Webmaster World forum. Not only will you learn about SEO. It is held in Las Vegas and Austin Texas once per year. Usually November in Las Vegas and in Austin in March.

3. SMX – This is by far the largest of the conferences and are held all over the world.

Appendcx B – Crawler, Bots, and Spider IPs

Sometimes you want to open your website login only areas to allow crawlers to access this but nothing else or you may want to know how often search engines come to visit your website. Here are the known crawler IP Addresses for the major search engines.

Google Bot	MSN/Bing!	Yahoo!
AdsBot-Google Googlebot-Image/x.x Googlebot/x.x Googlebot/Test Googlebot/Test Mediapartners- Google/x.x Mediapartners- Google/x.x Googlebot/x.x gsa- crawler 64.233.173.x 64.68.90.x 64.68.91.x 64.68.92.x 66.249.x 209.185.108 209.185.253 209.85.238 209.85.238.11 209.85.238.4 216.239.33.x 216.239.37.x 216.239.39.x 216.239.41.x 216.239.45.4 216.239.46.x 216.239.51.x 216.239.53.x 216.239.57.x 216.239.59.x 216.33.229.163	MSNBot MSNBot-Media MSNBot-NewsBlogs MSNBot-Products MSNBot-Academic 207.46.98.x	141.185.209 169.207.238 199.177.18.9 202.160.178.x 202.160.179.x 202.160.180.x 202.160.181.x 202.160.183.x 202.160.185.x 202.165.96.142 202.165.98.x 202.165.99.x 202.212.5.x 202.46.19.93 203.123.188.2 203.141.52.x 203.255.234.x 206.190.43.125 206.190.43.81 207.126.239.224 209.1.12.x 209.1.13.x 209.1.13.231 209.1.38.x 209.131.40.x 209.131.41.x 209.131.48.x 209.131.49.37 209.131.50.153 209.131.51.166 209.131.60.x 209.131.62.x 209.185.122.x 209.185.141.x 209.185.143.x 209.191.123.33 209.191.64.227 209.191.65.x 209.191.82.x 209.191.83.x 209.67.206.x 211.14.8.240.x 211.169.241.21 213.216.143.x 216.109.121.x 216.109.126.x 216.136.233.164 216.145.58.219 216.155.198.60 216.155.200 216.155.202.x 216.155.204.40 216.239.193.x 216.32.237.x 62.172.199.x 62.27.59.245 63.163.102.x 64.157.137.x 64.157.138.x 64.75.36.x 66.163.170.x 66.163.174.65

		66.196.101.x
		66.196.65.x
		66.196.67.x
		66.196.72.x
		66.196.73.x
		66.196.74.x
		66.196.77.x
		66.196.78.x
		66.196.80.x
		66.196.81.x
		66.196.90.x
		66.196.91.x
		66.196.92.x
		66.196.93.x
		66.196.97.x
		66.196.99.20
		66.218.65.52
		66.218.70.x
		66.228.164.x
		66.228.165.x
		66.228.166.x
		66.228.173.x
		66.228.182.x
		66.94.230.x
		66.94.232.x
		66.94.233.x
		66.94.238.51
		67.195.111
		67.195.34.x
		67.195.37.x
		67.195.44.x
		67.195.45.x
		67.195.50.87
		67.195.51.x
		67.195.52.x
		67.195.53.x
		67.195.54.x
		67.195.58.x
		67.195.98.x
		67.195.110.x
		67.195.111.x
		67.195.112.x
		67.195.113.x
		67.195.114.x
		68.142.195.x
		68.142.203.133
		68.142.211.69
		68.142.212.197
		68.142.230.x
		68.142.231.49
		68.142.240.106
		68.142.246.x
		68.142.249.x
		68.142.250.x
		68.142.251.x
		68.180.216.111
		68.180.250.x
		68.180.251.x
		69.147.79.x
		72.30.101.x
		72.30.102.x
		72.30.103.x
		72.30.104.x
		72.30.107.x
		72.30.110.x
		72.30.111.x
		72.30.124.x
		72.30.129.x
		72.30.131.x
		72.30.132.x
		72.30.133.x
		72.30.134.x
		72.30.135.x
		72.30.142.x
		72.30.161.x
		72.30.177.x
		72.30.179.x
		72.30.213.101
		72.30.214.x

		72.30.215.x
		72.30.216.x
		72.30.221.x
		72.30.226.x
		72.30.252.x
		72.30.54.x
		72.30.56.x
		72.30.60.x
		72.30.61.x
		72.30.65.x
		72.30.78.x
		72.30.79.x
		72.30.81.x
		72.30.87.x
		72.30.9.x
		72.30.97.x
		72.30.98.x
		72.30.99.x
		74.6.11.x
		74.6.12.x
		74.6.13.x
		74.6.131.x
		74.6.16.x
		74.6.17.x
		74.6.18.x
		74.6.19.x
		74.6.20.x
		74.6.21.x
		74.6.22.x
		74.6.23.x
		74.6.24.x
		74.6.240.x
		74.6.25.x
		74.6.26.x
		74.6.27.x
		74.6.28.x
		74.6.29.x
		74.6.30.x
		74.6.31.x
		74.6.65.x
		74.6.66.x
		74.6.67.x
		74.6.68.x
		74.6.69.x
		74.6.7.x
		74.6.70.x
		74.6.71.x
		74.6.72.x
		74.6.73.x
		74.6.74.x
		74.6.75.x
		74.6.76.x
		74.6.79.x
		74.6.8.x
		74.6.85.x
		74.6.86.x
		74.6.87.x
		74.6.9.x

Appendix C – Top Social Media Websites

Website	Page Rank	Category
9rules.com	6	Internet
a1-webmarks.com	5	General
autospies.com	5	Cars
backflip.com	6	General
ballhype.com	6	Sports
bibsonomy.org	7	Publications
blinklist.com	7	Internet
blogcatalog.com	7	Internet / Blogs
Blogger.com	9	Blogging
Bloglines.com	9	RSS Feed Reader
blogmarks.net	4	Internet
Blogspot.com	9	Blogging
bmaccess.net	4	Web Design and Graphics
bookmark-manager.com	4	Web Design & Development
buddymarks.com	5	General
buzzflash.com	7	News
care2.com	7	Social Action
caringbridge.org	7	Health
citeulike.org	8	Academic
clipclip.org	5	Internet
clipmarks.com	6	News
connectedy.com	4	General
connotea.org	8	General
corank.com	5	News
dealigg.com	4	Deals

del.icio.us	8	Bookmarks
designfloat.com	5	Web Design & Development
digg.com	8	Articles
diigo.com	6	Internet
dnhour.com	4	News
dzone.com	6	Web Development
easybm.com	5	Health & Medicine
Facebook.com	10	General
fark.com	7	Entertainment
faves.com	5	Internet
favoor.com	4	General
feedmarker.com	4	General
flashperfection.com	5	Flash Design
flickr.com	9	Images
folkd.com	7	General
fuzzfizz.com	0	Music
gather.com	6	Articles
givealink.org	4	General
good-tutorials.com	6	Web Design
Google Buzz	10	Message
i89.us	4	General
i-am-bored.com	6	Entertainment
iGoogle.com	9	General
kaboodle.com	6	Shopping
leenks.com	5	Vulgar
linkagogo.com	5	Internet
Linkedin.com	9	General
linkroll.com	5	General
ma.gnolia.com	6	Internet

megite.com	0	General
metacafe.com	7	Videos
Mister-Wong.com	8	General
mister-wong.de	9	General
mixx.com	8	General
mybloglog.com	7	Blogging
netvouz.com	6	Internet
newsvine.com	7	News
ning.com	8	General
nowpublic.com	7	News
oldrec.com	4	General
photoshop-pack.co	4	Graphics and Web Design
PerezHilton.com	7	Entertainment
pixel2life.com	5	Web Design & Development
plime.com	5	News Culture
plugim.com	5	Internet Marketing
propeller.com	8	News
reddit.com	8	General
rnel.net	2	Graphics and Web Design
rojo.com	7	General
saveyourlinks.com	4	General
scribd.com	8	Articles
searchles.com	5	World
shoutwire.com	5	General
showhype.com	5	Web Design
showhype.com	5	Web Design
simpy.com	6	General
sitejot.com	5	General
slashdot.org	8	Tech

sphinn.com	6	Internet Marketing
spurl.net	0	Internet
startaid.com	5	Internet
stumbleupon.com	8	Content Grader
stylehive.com	6	Fashion
swik.net	5	Open Source news
sync2it.com	4	General
technorati.com	8	Blogging
tweako.com	5	General
tweetphoto.com	6	Photo Tweets
twitter.com	9	Message
ustream.com	8	Videos
uvouch.com	4	Videos
webride.org	4	General
wirefan.com	3	Internet
work.com	6	Business & Work
Yahoo! Buzz	4	Message
youtube.com	9	Videos

Index

CPSIA information can be obtained at www.ICGtesting.com

235218LV00006B/87/P